WHAT ABOUT MEN?

Also by the author

Non-fiction

How to Be a Woman
Moranthology
Moranifesto
More Than a Woman

Fiction

How to Build a Girl
How to Be Famous

WHAT ABOUT MEN?

BY

CAITLIN MORAN

EBURY
PRESS

1

Ebury Press, an imprint of Ebury Publishing
20 Vauxhall Bridge Road
London SW1V 2SA

Ebury Press is part of the Penguin Random House group of companies
whose addresses can be found at global.penguinrandomhouse.com

Penguin
Random House
UK

A CIP catalogue record for this book is available from the British Library

ISBN 9781529149159

Printed and bound in Great Britain by Clays Ltd, Elcograf S.p.A.

The authorised representative in the EEA is Penguin Random House Ireland,
Morrison Chambers, 32 Nassau Street, Dublin D02 YH68

Penguin Random House is committed to a sustainable future for
our business, our readers and our planet. This book is made from
Forest Stewardship Council® certified paper.

To my husband, Pete, who let me rinse all his boyhood experiences for this book, despite the fact he'd written about them with far more elan in his memoir, Broken Greek: *£9.99, Quercus, Radio 4's Book of the Week, 'Lip-lickingly, dance-around-the-living-room good',* Observer.

Contents

CONTENTS

Prologue:
What About Men?

'Errrr . . .'

It's July 2014, and I've just been asked a question I can't answer.

Normally, I would like to think there are no questions I cannot answer. I am on a speaking tour for *How to Be a Woman*, and all the questions the audience ask are about women, and girls.

As someone with, at the time, 38 years of experience of being either a woman, or a girl, I've some chat about pretty much All The Women Things: bloodied pants; comfort-eating; the pay gap; abortion; Beyoncé. When it comes to the vag-based problems, I have the bantz.

Right now, however, I'm onstage in front of 1,198 people, and the silence after the question is getting longer, and more uncomfortable. Because while the first two questions were

'Can feminists wear pink?' ('Yes!') and 'What do you think of Paris trying to ban the burka?' ('Obviously, women should be allowed to wear whatever they *want* to wear. However, until there is a burka for *men*, we can see the *fundamental* idea is sexist bullshit'), the third question has stumped me.

The woman in the audience, holding the microphone, has just asked: 'So – do you have any advice for *men*?'

This is the first time I have ever been asked this question. I'll be honest: I feel a bit annoyed by it. Why *this* topic? I'm a feminist! My specialist subject is women! I don't do . . . the other guys. You might as well ask e.g. Sir David Attenborough a question about the Swindon gyratory system! That's not his patch! Men aren't mine!

I decide I'll make a joke about it. I'll play to the crowd. This room is dominated by women – earlier, I'd asked all the 'brave men' in the room to raise their hands, so we could see them; so I know there are 1,152 women here, and 46 men. I'll just play to a cheap yet effective stereotype, and move this question on.

'My advice to men? I guess, a) please, if you can possibly avoid it, don't rape us, and b) put the bowls in the dishwasher – rather than *next* to the dishwasher?'

It gets a laugh – the kind of bittersweet laugh you get from a room full of women who are familiar with the idea of spending 20 minutes discussing both the complete collapse in rape convictions in the UK, *and* housework.

I add a cheerful 'Hashtag #notallmen' – to let the men in the audience know this isn't an attack on them. Just the Bad Men out there. The small number of Bad Men. Then we move the conversation on.

I'm still a bit peeved. Men, though? Ugh. Why were we talking about men? I've spent the last ten years researching how shit things are for women around the world. Honestly, by comparison, the men are *fine*.

Two nights later, and I'm in a similar jam. I'm now in Edinburgh, still doing an hour of chat about women, and girls – but, yet again, when the audience start asking questions, the second question I get asked is: 'What advice would you give to the mothers of teenage boys?'

Urgh. Come now! I'm the Woman Woman! Why are you asking me this? Are people purposely trying to ask me difficult questions?

Now I know how Paul McCartney felt when I interviewed him, and asked him what he'd do if he were in a car crash that totally destroyed his face. 'So, Sir Paul – would you use plastic surgery to build back the face of Paul McCartney? Or would you choose *another* face? So you could live the rest of your life in pleasant anonymity?'

I thought I was honouring him with a tricky, yet clever, inquiry. Instead, he treated it like a joke – 'I'd get the face of David Cameron, instead' – indicated that this had been my final question, and terminated the interview.

Unfortunately, this is not my final question.

'It's just, I have a teenage girl, and there seems to be loads of advice for mothering a girl,' the woman in the audience continues. 'That's why I read your book. But I also have a son, and for him – I can find nothing. I just wondered if you had any advice for women trying to raise . . .' and here her voice falters for a minute, '. . . *good*, happy boys, and men?'

'Well, obviously, I have no experience of raising boys – I have two girls,' I start. 'But I guess my question – and it's to all of us here – is: why should this be the women's problem? Interestingly, this is the second time this week I've been asked about men – and both times, it was a *woman* asking me. But why is this a question for feminism? Feminism is the only socio-political invention dedicated solely to helping women. It would be ironic, would it not, if women – having spent the last hundred years knackering themselves trying to solve the problems of women – now had to go and solve all the problems of men, as well?'

It's getting some laughs, so I keep going: 'They need to solve their own problems! They're the best-qualified people to do so! Why are men not asking other *men* this question? Your husband should be asking, I don't know, *Gary Lineker* this. Not me!'

For the rest of the tour, whenever I get asked about men – which I am, almost every night – this is basically the reply I give. It always gets a laugh. And I believe it. It wouldn't be *fair* to make women solve the problems of men. Particularly *this* woman. I believe most men are good, lovely, kind, fun, decent, awesome human beings. I'm violently opposed to the branches of feminism that are permanently angry with men, or who just hate men on principle, or think men can't be feminists. Of course they can! There are as many decent men as there are decent women! Men are awesome! I married one! All four Beatles were men! Men invented John Frieda Frizz Ease Serum! I am an absolute fan of men!

But, ultimately, if forced to pick a team, I'm Team Tits. Up the women! God bless them – but let the men sort *themselves* out.

For the next three years or so, this very much continues to be my stance. Indeed, in this, I am bolstered by being on Twitter, every March, on International Women's Day.

For, regular as clockwork, as soon as thousands of women start excitedly Tweeting about events, feminist heroes, feminist initiatives, charities and arts events, they are met by thousands of men Tweeting in return, peevishly, 'But when is International *Men's* Day? Huh? What about the *men*? No one cares about *men*. This is *sexist*.'

Year after year, in vain, the comedian Richard Herring would spend International Women's Day replying to each of these Tweets, patiently, with a simple fact: 'International Men's Day is 19 November. Maybe put on an event? Tweet about it then?'

But the effect is always the same: I become massively irritated about men stomping all over a women's thing, shouting, 'WHAT ABOUT US?'

What about you? Honestly? I don't *care*. Make your own things – don't piggyback on ours.

It's 2019 and I have changed. I am starting to care very much. Because now, it's not me that's being asked these questions about men.

It's my teenage daughters.

I am currently on a Zoom call with one of my daughters, two of her girlfriends, and four of their male classmates. International Women's Day has rolled round, and we're supposed to be having a conversation about feminism – this is what I have been drafted in to chat about. My presumption was that Gen Z boys were the most liberal and feminist generation so far. I thought ideas about equality, and feminism, were so accepted among their teenage friends as to be almost passé. I thought this was going to be a straightforward bit of 'Up the women!'

That's not what I'm hearing on this Zoom call.

'It's harder to be a boy than a girl now,' Milo says, right at the beginning, blinking. 'Everything is stacked against boys.'

While the girls look outraged, all the boys nod.

'Feminism has gone too far,' George says. His certainty in saying this is . . . unexpected. This is a sentence I expect to hear from some angry, 50-something hard-right Republican on the campaign trail in the Midwest – not a middle-class 18-year-old boy at an arts college, wearing a Sonic Youth T-shirt.

I've told everyone that for the first half of this Zoom call, I only want the boys to speak. I want the boys to tell me what *their* problems are – what *they're* scared of. Before we start a conversation about feminism – the problems of girls – I wanted to let the boys talk first; so that they would be more prepared to listen. I wanted to engineer a friendly communal chat! Bring the sexes together! However, it is *not* going the way I thought it would.

'The girls talk about how scared they are of sexual

violence – but boys are *much* more likely to be attacked,' Milo says. 'That's just a fact. Every day, I'm scared I'm going to be stabbed.'

'Me too!'

'Constantly.'

'Like, we just expect it's going to happen.'

'Girls don't have to worry about being stabbed, or getting into a fight,' George says.

'So you're worried about violence from other boys, or men,' I say, trying to find some common ground. 'Well, you have that in common with the girls. They fear violent boys, and men, too.'

'Yeah – but then we *also* have to be scared of the girls,' Milo says.

The girls look outraged, but I gesture for them to just listen, for now.

'Why are you scared of *girls*?' I ask.

'Well, there's a *lot* of "he said, she said" stuff,' George says, looking uncomfortable. 'Rumours and gossip going around schools that such-and-such a boy has raped a girl – then it turns out they did have sex, but she just changed her mind, after, or wanted to get back at him. It gets nasty. Boys' lives get ruined by it. A lot of boys are too scared to even talk to girls now – you don't know how it's going to be portrayed later. That's what I mean when I say feminism has gone too far.'

'Men are just seen as bad, or toxic. It's always like, "What have the boys done now?" We're blamed for everything. People just automatically presume we're all rapists.'

'We're always the *wrong* ones.'

'And we're told to talk about our problems or feelings, but when we do it's like, "You're whining," or "You're mansplaining, shut up," or "Men don't have problems, they're *fine*. They're always the winners" – but we're not. It *is* easier to be a woman than a man now.'

'That's what Jordan B. Peterson says – that we talk about men like just actually being a man, just actually existing as a man, is wrong. That straight white men get blamed for everything. And then you look at how many young men are killing themselves, and you think: this is all fucked up. Who cares about the men?'

By this point in the conversation, I was starting to feel very uneasy. I could see how angry and misunderstood these boys felt – how much pent-up emotion they had.

I thanked everyone for being so honest. The boys seemed startled: 'It's been *amazing* to talk about this stuff. I haven't really done it before.'

'I've literally never had someone say, "What are the problems that boys have?" You only ever hear that asked about girls.'

They all, very politely but genuinely, thanked me, and said they really looked forward to the next chat.

After I stopped the Zoom, the girls immediately started texting me.

'They were just being *polite* with you.'

'On WhatsApp, they call feminism a "cancer", and feminists "Feminazis".'

'They make rape jokes – they say it's all banter, but it's clearly never occurred to them that we know women who *have* been raped.'

'Why didn't you talk to them about all that? You don't *know* how boys talk when you're not around. *Why aren't the mums talking about that?*'

After the Zoom call, I go outside for a ciggie, feeling very unhappy.

Why aren't the mums talking about that?

This last, anguished question has reminded me of something I've been noticing for a while, but hadn't joined the dots on until today. For, in my social circle, I have started to notice a big divide – a divide between those women who are Mothers of Sons, and those women who are Mothers of Daughters.

The Mothers of Daughters report that their teenage girls are coming home and bursting into huge, long, impassioned speeches about what's been happening at school: febrile relationships, complex friendship circles and power dynamics. The info-download is vast, and almost daily.

But the most recurrent and important information they download is on what that Zoom call just touched on – which boys are becoming 'problematic'.

'Joshua slept over at a girl's house after a party – and she woke up with him on top of her.'

'Charlie broke up with a girl – then showed all his friends her nudes.'

'Piotr tried strangle-sex with his girlfriend – and she passed out. Now she just keeps crying in class.'

To be a mother of a teenage daughter is to engage in frequent anxious phone calls with other mothers, discussing these kinds of incidents. Mothers of Daughters talk to each other *endlessly* about what's going on with their children: half the wine I've drunk in the last four years has been with other Mothers of Daughters, sharing our war stories, and various incidents and outrages that have occurred. Giving advice. Counselling the girls. Mothering feminism is all about these mini-conferences, late into the night.

But my conversations with the Mothers of Sons are very, very different.

'How's your boy doing?' you'll ask – a leading question, for which you are braced, as you would be with the Mother of Daughters, for an hour of hair-raising tales of horror, anxiety and repelling unwelcome sexual attention.

'He's . . . fine?' the Mothers of Sons will say, shrugging. 'Seems pretty happy. Exams are a bugger, right – I think they get him down – but he doesn't say much, to be honest. Just comes back, kicks a football around, then goes to his room.'

'He doesn't talk to you about friends, or . . . girls?' you ask, trying to see if the boys are conveying anything of the constant ticker tape and headlines of the frequent, ruinous incidents that consume the World of Girls.

'Nah – you know what boys are like. They're private. They don't really talk about that stuff.'

Or:

'I don't think boys get embroiled in all those complex situations girls do. You know? Boys are quite simple, aren't they? They're like dogs. They live in the moment. So long as they've got their mates, and their PlayStation, they're fine.'

Or:

'Yeah – he seems a bit down, to be honest. I try to talk, but he just shuts it down. Being a teenager is shit, right? I can't wait until this phase ends.'

There are exceptions, of course – I've had deep conversations with Mothers of Sons about their neurodiversity, OCD or, in the case of Noah, his worry that his bum is 'too small'. But, by and large, the gulf between the Mothers of Daughters and the Mothers of Sons is so large as to make it seem like they inhabit two different worlds – and this reaches its apogee in the fact that there are two teenage boys I know who have *terrible* reputations among the girls, to the point of borderline criminal behaviour, and yet their mothers *seem not to know*.

Worse than that: I *know* these mothers – and I literally do not know how to tell them. Even more basic than that: I don't even know if I'm *allowed*. Can you ring a fellow mother and say, 'Are you going to yoga on Tuesday? Also, quick sidebar, there are very strong rumours going around school that your son sexually assaulted a girl when she was passed out from drinking too much'?

What *is* the etiquette, in these matters? What are the *rules*? When they were six, and poking a cat with a stick, in the playground, I knew it was the Mother's Code to report on them, with a conspiratorial, 'Coh, kids!' look. But now? With this? When the 18-year-old girls – technically adults, now – concerned *beg* you not to get involved? 'It will cause a whole incident! You can't report on him to *his mum*!'

I like to think I'm not a bad communicator. I like to think I am good at talking about things that are difficult, awkward or taboo. But when it comes to this – to honestly discussing the trouble that boys and men are both causing, and are in? I don't know any template for it. I don't know what tone I would use. I have never seen women talk about boys, or men, like this with each other. I don't know how to do it. And one final, further point: I don't know any *fathers* who have ever even raised the question. The fathers don't seem to feature in these problems at all.

And, as I smoked that miserable cigarette, I started to realise something very uncomfortable about myself.

I had, let's face it, spent the last five years humorously refusing to even countenance the problems of boys, and men. I had told the mothers of teenage boys that women shouldn't engage with the unhappinesses, and fears, of boys. That boys, and men, should simply talk to other men about their problems, instead. I'd kind of . . . *teased* men for saying they were troubled. For wanting the same kind of space for their conversations about themselves that women have. For being hurt that International Women's Day is such a big deal – but no one even knew when International Men's Day is. I think I might even have used the word 'butt-hurt'.

'Let the men sort themselves out!'

Well – they *had*. Clearly. In the absence of appealing, relatable, sound advice coming from the good liberal progressive men of my generation, boys had found the only men who *were* talking about it: men in chatrooms, influencers on YouTube and TikTok. Places where phrases like 'feminism has gone too far', and 'Feminazi', and 'feminism is a cancer' are just day-to-day chat. A world of 'ironic' sexism, the 'Manosphere', Jordan B. Peterson, Men's Rights Activists and Incels.

But that advice doesn't seem to be making boys, or men, happier. Instead, it seems to be stoking their anger. It seems to be stopping them from having conversations with their parents. It seems to be sending them to their rooms to spend hours, alone. It seems to be connecting them with a worldwide group of similarly unhappy, angry, paranoid young men. And it all seems to make them feel like there was only one ultimate cause of their unhappiness – girls.

'Tell the boys what they *should* be reading,' one of the girls had pleaded, earlier. 'Tell them some websites, or facts, or a TV show or . . . *something*. Something that is about the problems of boys and men – but that's positive, and, like, good, and which will make them understand it's not all *our* fault.'

And I couldn't think of anything.

I couldn't think of any book, play, TV show or movie that basically tells the story of how boy-children become men. What 'being a man' is, in its ostensibly mundane but actually momentous detail: how to shed your child-body and become an adult; how to negotiate the white-water rapids of sexual desire; how to self-soothe your sadness and anger; how to cope with defeat and loss; how to be a father; how to love; how to age. How to understand how and why the world responds to you, simply because you are a boy, or a man. How to gain the kind of confidence and happiness that not only make *you* confident and happy, but everyone that you love, too. In short, how to be a well-adjusted, average, content boy, who grows up into a well-adjusted, content man – able to talk about his problems without shame or fear. Or, indeed, able to even know what his problems *are*. Or, as those mums put it, when asking for parenting advice: how to end up a good, happy man.

Women's stories – from *Jane Eyre* and *Little Women* to *Broad City* and *Bridgerton* – are all about this. Women and girls are bombarded with information and advice, from day one, on how to grow up, be themselves, be happy, be excellent. Be *proud*. And, obviously, there are dozens and dozens of non-fiction, self-help books about women adulting. I know – I've written two of them myself. So: why isn't there anything like this for men?

And so now, at the age of 48, I have, finally, taken absolutely seriously something that some boys, and men, have been saying for a while now – the biggest complaint of Men's Rights Activists and the Manosphere. Which is, in our culture, 'It's easier to be a woman than a man, now.'

If boys, and men, really feel this – if they observe that there is more discussion, support, cheerleading and belief in girls, and women – then *I believe them.* You have to believe people when they keep saying the same thing, over and over, more despairingly each time. Surely that is one thing social progress has taught us.

And what's more: *I think it's true.* Straight white men are not encouraged to celebrate what they are. There *are* no big events on International Men's Day. 'This is all the problem of straight white men' has become a default statement on social media – applied to absolutely everything, despite the fact that 'straight white men' also includes utterly powerless, depressed 13-year-old boys, sitting in their beds, starting to wonder if there's any point in getting up in the morning.

If I were to Tweet 'I am proud to be a woman', I'd probably get a bunch of 'YAYS!' and 'ME TOO – and in the good way, not the rapey way!' and a half-dozen hand-claps and dancing-girl emojis in reply.

If a man typed 'I'm proud to be a man', however, the reaction would be more . . . suspicious? I mean, even *I* would be suspicious. I don't think there'd be any dancing-girl emojis there. I mean, is there even a male equivalent of the dancing-girl emoji? That 'women having good times – rejoice!' symbol? I don't think there is. And all of this is not a good sign. If there is no acknowledgement of the group you are in, if you cannot be proud of how you are born, then I would suggest – to wheel out one of the lines from *How to Be a Woman* in a new, unexpected role – that there might be some sexist bullshit afoot.

So this book is me leaving the World of Girls and Women – where I have spent my whole life, sharing tights'n'giggles – and traversing over to the unfamiliar World of Boys and Men, to ask: 'Hey, literal dudes – what's going on here? What are you anxious about? What are you angry about? What aren't you talking about? And, while I'm here, could you open this jar of pickles for me – my hands are too small and ladylike?'

There are some things I've observed about men I want to share with them. There are some aspects of men I want to find out about. And there's also a lot of jokes about dicks and balls because, let's face it, they are funny. Just as funny as vaginas – and I don't say that lightly.

But mainly, I just want to try to start talking about boys and men, as we have recently come to about girls and women: talking about the minutiae of their lives. Taking their concerns seriously. Trying to unpick just how ideas of what a boy, or man, 'should' be like came about, and whether it's time to change them. And talking – a lot – about the funny, ridiculous stuff. I often think it's the funny, ridiculous stuff that's the most important. That's usually where everything – good and bad – starts.

And so it is, primarily, a book about straight white men.

It's not *not* about all men – but it's *mainly* about straight white men.

Partly about the kind of men who will say, in their angry moments, 'No one's talking about *us*.'

But mainly about the kind of straight white man who would murmur, mortified, 'Well, there's nothing really to talk about. I mean, I don't want to make a *fuss*. I'll just crack on. There's nothing really to *say* about us.'

As it turned out, I found a *lot* to say about straight white men in the twenty-first century. There is *plenty* to make a fuss about. Or joke about – as it pleases you.

And, finally, I'd like to say, to all those women, at all those events: I'm sorry. I'm sorry that I tried to deflect your questions, or make a joke out of it. You were right to say, 'Is there any advice for the mothers of boys?'

You were right to think there is a problem. You were right to say, 'What about men?'

Chapter One

How to Be a Boy

Of course, I am not a man. I do not know what it's like to be a man, or a boy. Not a clue.

When I was young, the gender segregation at school was pretty rigid. At playtime, the girls plaited each other's hair, played skipping or clapping games, and casually psychologically manipulated, and occasionally destroyed, each other, via sly comments about hair, pencils or socks.

The boys, meanwhile, sporadically had fights – 'BUNDLE! BUNDLE!' – and once, there was a fairly hearty attempt by one boy to stab another boy in the eye with an icicle. But although this boys' world seemed more brutal – 'BUNDLE! BUNDLE!' 'MY EYE!' – it also seemed much simpler, emotionally.

Towards the end of my last year at junior school, I was temporarily rejected by my female peer group, for reasons I cannot now remember – probably 'lesbian' socks – and the boys wordlessly but cheerfully beckoned me over, to play football with them. Even though I was terrible at it.

'Just stand by the goal, and the balls will bounce off you,' Simon Rowley said, wholly without malice.

When a tennis ball hit my left breast, and I doubled over in pain, Philip Bostock said – with touching thoughtfulness – 'Are girls' tits like balls for men?', and gave me a sympathetic arm-punch.

After a week of football, the girls let me back into their gang – again, I cannot remember why: presumably my new socks were more 'hetero' – and I returned to the World of Girls, accompanied by another cheerful, no-hard-feelings shrug from the boys.

While I would talk to boys during class, or in the corridor, we never *did* anything together again. When I wrote a (terrible) play and put it on, no boys turned up to the casting – all the male roles had to be played by girls. Eager girls. Because rehearsals happened in breaktime. And breaktime was for football. Hence Emily Perry heroically playing a now-problematic young Chinese fisherboy called 'Han'.

At the time, it was so obvious that boys and girls lived in totally different worlds that it wasn't really noticed. It's only now, as a middle-aged woman – starting to ask the question 'What about men?' – that I realise: this means that 90 per cent of all my information on what it's like to be a normal, average boy actually comes from *The Secret Diary of Adrian Mole, Aged 13¾.* Which was written by a middle-aged woman. Whenever my male friends mention their childhoods, I basically imagine they lived in Leicester, anxiously measured their willies with a ruler, and admired Nigel's better, cooler racing bike.

I realise I have never asked any man, ever: what is it actually *like*, being a boy? What was happening, over there, on the other side of the playground? What is your species like? I know every single thing about being a girl. I know *nothing* about being a boy.

And so I set out to remedy this and began asking men, essentially, just one question, over and over again: what's it like, in the World of Boys?

'Before we were old enough to go to school?' Stephen considers. 'Before school, it's not a World of Boys. All the kids would play together. Boys and girls.'

'I had an older sister, so I'd tag along with her – play with her friends,' says James.

'I had sisters, who had Sindys – the off-brand Barbie – and I had Action Men,' says Alex. 'And we would just have parties in the Sindy house, where Action Man would turn up – in uniform, obviously – and just, like, have a little dance, and help himself to the hostess trolley.'

'Female cousins, the girls in the street – you just play with whoever's *around*,' says Pete, my husband, nodding. 'When you're a very young kid, your whole world is just what's near, right? You never really make any choices. You don't even know you can *make* choices.'

All of them, between the ages of 40 and 55 now, had the same story – before Proper School began, it was generally a carefree, proto-Elysian, multi-gender world of worm-collecting, mud-poking, trike-riding and blithe socialisation with whoever was around, and vaguely nice. Or simply related to you, and therefore unable to avoid.

Once proper school began, however, the World of Boys and the World of Girls started, slowly but inexorably, to come into being. Why? When I asked, the men replied with the same word – and the one thing I did already know about boys:

'Football.'

For my generation – despite *Gregory's Girl* – football was for Boys Only. We were 40 years away from the Lionesses. No girls played football. Or if they did, like me, it was only for a week. And badly. For the boys, however: it was simply what boys *did*.

However, the way the men said 'football' greatly varied – which surprised me. My impression had been that *all* boys loved football with a passion that was equalled only by their love of their own legs, and *Star Wars*. This, however, turns out to not universally be the case.

'Even if you weren't into it, you just had to *pretend*,' James says, sighing. 'I mean, I could get into it in a spectator way, when everyone else was – because it's the culture. But I just wasn't physically very good at it, and I didn't really *care*, to be honest. But I *pretended*.'

'I wasn't any good at any sports – or anything that involved hand–eye co-ordination,' Alex says, still wincing. 'I was not sporty. And PE lessons seemed to be different to all other lessons – if you weren't any good in history, or maths, and got a question wrong, you wouldn't have the whole room turn around and go "Oh! You idiot! You messed up!" And yet in PE, and in sport – that was totally the thing. You were encouraged to be furious at the person who'd fumbled the pass or catch. Which was often me. And it was horrible.'

'The only currency was football,' Stephen agrees. 'My father never supported a team. He just liked watching it. But in Ayrshire in the 1970s, if you got stopped by big boys in the playground, the first thing they would ask you is, "Are you Celtic or Rangers, wee man?" And I would have to reply, truthfully, like a ponce, "Neither." And then you'd get the shit beaten out of you, for being a ponce.'

For others, football – playing it, talking about it – provided their first rung into finding friends and settling into school. Happiness.

David: 'When I started playing football, there's a thing that happens that has never happened in any other part of my life – apart from, later, in sex – which is: I forget myself. My body leads the way. I don't think about what I'm doing – my body takes over. And there's a joy in finding your body can do that – because in all other aspects of my life, my mind leads the way. It's a . . . release. It's like dancing. Except I'm shit at dancing.'

'Even though I was rubbish at football, you needed kids like me to make up the numbers,' Pete says. 'And I wanted to play so much that, even though I was so bad at it my nickname was "Peter Pathetic", I could still spend every playtime "in defence", passing to the good players. Which was a definite improvement on my previous playtime tactic of dealing with having no friends – running backwards and forwards in the playground, really fast, pretending I was playing Chase with someone. Even though I was absolutely alone.'

David, again: 'However much I loved football, I did have one problem, which is very specific: I didn't learn how to tie my shoelaces until I was 13. And in the only game I ever played for the school team, my shoelaces kept coming undone, and I had to keep asking the ref – who was also a rabbi – to tie them for me. The third time I asked him, he told me to go away, which meant I did not play very well for the rest of that match.'

Has that left emotional scars?

'Well, I learned how to tie my shoelaces.'

Who Are the Alphas?

So, if you weren't good at sport, what were the other ways to get status, and friends? Who were the alpha boys?

'Not the clever ones. Not in Ayrshire,' Stephen says. 'Being clever was a mocking offence. I know some guys would deliberately dumb-down on purpose, and pretend not to know anything, so they wouldn't look like . . . a nerd. If you used a long word, you'd get called "Dictionary Cornflakes".'

'Dictionary Cornflakes?'

'Yeah. Like, in the morning, you ate a bowl of words, instead of cornflakes. Big insult in Scotland in the 1970s. And Wales, I believe,' he adds, anthropologically.

'At my school, it was kind of irrelevant to be clever,' says James, who is also Scottish, disagreeing slightly. 'I was always towards the top of my class, but there was no status in that – in either direction. You didn't get bullied for it. But it just wasn't interesting.'

So what *did* give you status?

'The kind of shit my brother did,' Stephen says. 'Fear-lessness, cheek, not caring about the consequences. Mild vandalism. The kind of analogue in movies would be like Kenickie in *Grease* – the kind of guy who gets busted and goes, "Fuck, *whatever*." James Dean. Steve McQueen in *The Great Escape*, getting sentenced to the cooler, or the belt, and not caring.'

And who *didn't* have status? Who would get bullied, or teased?

James: 'Weird, geeky kids. Kids with funny faces, kids who were physically awkward. Quiet kids. Nerdy kids. Although I should point out a lot of kids did get bullied because they were genuinely annoying – to the point where you look back and go, "How come he got all that shit, and *still* didn't learn how not to be a prick?" I think boys are very conservative, and they don't like people who stand out for the wrong reasons, and they try . . . it's like an organ-ism, repelling an invader. That's what a lot of bullying is, at that age.'

Trying to establish 'the right kind of boy to be'?

'Yeah.'

This is very different from the World of Girls. When girls are rejected by other girls, or fall out with them, the remedy is almost always the same: you basically have to go around kissing their arses, sharing crisps, complimenting their hair-slides and agreeing to play the games *they* want.

You make yourself more agreeable. You make up, as fast as possible – even if you are seething inside. In the World of Boys, meanwhile, it seems quite different.

At Some Point, You Have to Hit Someone

'Oh, there's a lot of fighting,' Stephen says. 'Violence was weekly, if not daily.'

'I used to get into lots of fights,' James concurs.

For context, I should mention that James and Stephen are both now middle-aged, middle-class dads who know about wine, recycle, have views on thoughtful novels – and, I'm pretty sure, would both cry if they saw a dog struggling with a slight limp. I am surprised by how casually they refer to fighting, when they clearly haven't thrown a punch this century.

'With boys, in reference to other boys, often fighting is something you have to . . . just get out of the way,' James explained. 'It's kind of . . . fine? I guess, in a very animal way, you need to clash, in order to figure out how your relationship is going to work. Then, after the fight, you move on.'

'At our school, it was less physical fighting, and more with words,' Julian muses. 'I mean, there *was* one guy who stabbed someone, and I did have a fight with my best friend – but it was a stupid fight. Which I won, because I had longer arms, and I just held his throat, while his shorter arms flailed around, and failed to connect with me.'

'You definitely don't go through your life not expecting

violence,' James says. 'You spend a lot of time thinking about how you'd win a fight. Or if you could. If you're clashing with someone, it's important, in your mind, to understand what will happen in a fight, and what you would do if it happens.'

This suddenly makes sense of something that had long puzzled me about boys, and men – how much time they spend in the playground, on social media, or in the pub, talking about what could beat what in a fight. 'Could a shark beat a gorilla in a fight?' 'Could Sean Connery's James Bond beat Daniel Craig's James Bond in a fight?' 'Could Inspector Gadget beat Judge Dredd in a fight?'

I have heard this debated by both a pair of six-year-old boys, on a beach, while building a sandcastle – and two slightly gone-to-seed hip-hop dads, at a wake. It all makes sense now. I just thought they were being . . . ironically whimsical.

Without wanting to be Dolly Dolorous, I tell the men that this constant awareness that there might be a fight just around the corner – this constant calculating and mental rehearsal, in case of emergency – is how women are, but with regards to rape. We always presume it might be soon, and that we should be prepared for it.

All the men nod.

'But I guess men don't need to have ironically whimsical conversations about that – as a man can always beat a woman in a fight,' I add, as is my duty as a feminist.

'Sorry about the rapists,' Stephen says. 'Can't lie – they really do sound like a bummer.'

How to Fight Like a Man

'What are the rules of fighting?' I ask. 'I mean, I've literally never been in a fight. Most women haven't. This is totally alien to us. What are the different kind of fights?'

'Well, first, there's just your random violence – stuff that's not really a fight at all,' Stephen says, like a connoisseur. 'Getting your balls kicked, getting your face spat in, a dead-leg. A big guy just running up to you in the playground and smashing his fist into your thighs, or arm.'

'That would not be considered "correct fighting" at my school,' James quibbles. 'In a *proper* fight, there's no biting, spitting, scratching or open-handed slapping. Slapping's very bad. It's seen as insulting.'

'How about kicking someone up the bum?' I ask. 'That was very common in Wolvo. And then, when we discovered the word "coccyx", it allowed boys to scream "He kicked me in the coccyx!", which *sounded* like a rude word, but wasn't.'

'It would be humiliating to be kicked up the bum, I guess,' James nods.

'Could you twist a nipple?'

'No – no nipples.'

'Kick in the balls?'

'It does happen. I kicked a kid in the balls at Sunday school, and got into a lot of trouble for it. But, as you get older, it would be frowned upon. It would be a bit gay, I think. But then, I went to a boys' school – so talking to girls was seen as gay.'

And what fights did you get into?

'When I was 11, my parents bought me a new duffle coat,' Stephen says, 'and this kid, Dale, comes up to me in the playground and rips the toggles off. I had a red mist of disbelief that this new coat my mum had bought me had been destroyed. I didn't punch him – I still didn't even know how to, or head-butt – so I just literally picked him up, and threw him around three feet in the air, into a puddle. And he never fucked with me again.'

'Yeah – Hulk-throwing is proper fighting.' James nods.

Clowns Do Not Bleed, Or: The Beginning of Bantz

There is, of course, another way to become powerful and make people too scared to fight you. A third way to become 'alpha', after being good at sport, and being fearless, and it is the most important one: humour. Every man I talked to remembers the first time they made other children laugh.

'I ripped off a Robin Williams routine – about how men would only know what it was like to give birth if they passed a bowling bowl through their anus – and the whole room creased,' Alex says, still looking bucked at the memory. 'Although, maybe I didn't say "anus". But the whole room stopped to laugh. The whole room.'

Stephen: 'They'd asked me to MC the annual school show. I introduced all the acts – and one of them was this girl called Angela, Angela Packham, and she was singing some kind of opera-ish number. And I got a pair of ear-defenders, and came back on stage after she'd finished, ear-muffs clamped over my ears, saying, "Thank you, thank you, Angela!" and wincing.'

What happened?

'Obviously I got fired from the gig – quite rightly – but it *killed* in the room. The kids loved it. I suddenly realised I had an arrow in my otherwise empty quiver: humour.'

'There is definitely a thing to do with maleness – certainly back then – which is the relationship between maleness and being funny, and social ranking,' David agrees. 'People think "alpha-ness" is about money, and cars, and having women – that Andrew Tate view of alpha-ness – but in real life, social ranking is almost entirely humour. How do you choose your friends? You choose the ones you think are funny. Who do you fancy? Someone who makes you laugh. Who has all the power in the room? The funniest person. You can control a situation by being funny. Humour is both a currency and a power.'

And it's one that works in quite complex ways. James noted that, often, if humour was used *against* you by other boys, it didn't necessarily mean you lost your power.

'I got off with a girl everyone hated – or *pretended* to hate; she was really hot – at a school disco. And then the next day, at breakfast, nine or ten of my friends converged on me in the school dining room, basically dragged me into the middle of the floor, and removed not all, but *most* of my clothes, in a "This is your punishment beating" kind of way.'

Oh my God – naked at breakfast? Were you emotionally devastated? I think most girls would still be in therapy for this punishment for overt sexuality.

'No – I was laughing, and quite proud, because it made you the centre of attention. People were asking why I was naked next to some All-Bran, and the reply was, of course, "He pulled this girl". It was a double-edged humilation, where it's intended to humiliate, but you're still glad to be the centre of attention. For pulling.'

This, of course, leads us into:

Banter

Alex: 'There is definitely a kind of male conversation/ humour which isn't really conversation/humour, which a group of men or boys will be laughing at, hysterically, and which is definitely a bonding exercise, but which isn't *actually* funny. It's . . .'

The *shape* of being funny, but without funny *in* it?

'Yes. Exactly. It's a kind of . . . performative jollity. Within a gang. Where men are abusing each other – not in a nasty way – but in a way that just seems . . . quite pointless. Like that football thing, where you say, "I support Arsenal," and another man will say, "Oh, you cunt, they're useless. They're going to get smashed. Chelsea!" And you can't really imagine it in a different social setting. Like, if a woman said, "I like Arctic Monkeys," another woman wouldn't go, "Oh, you cunt – they're useless! Their next EP will be shit. COLDPLAY!" That just doesn't happen. As far as I know.'

'I think [banter] is generally quite benign,' James muses, 'in that it fills up some conversational space that might otherwise be silent, and awkward. Where it becomes more, as the young people say, "problematic", is when it's become such a default way for men to talk to each other that it becomes too much of a dizzying tone-shift to be able to say, "Dave, I heard your mum's got cancer, I'm so sorry." When it's there because no one knows how to say a more . . . emotionally engaged thing. When it's filling up space because everyone's too . . . panicked to have a proper conversation.'

'Banter is often a proxy for actually talking to someone,' Pete says. 'I mean, no one ever asks someone else a question about themselves in banter, do they? Unless they're setting up some kind of trap. You don't get much *information* out of banter.'

David: 'I definitely had to learn how to have more emotional conversations from girls, and woman. Definitely.'

'When I was about 15, I began to vastly prefer the company of girls to boys, because you would have very different conversations with girls,' James says. 'You would, like, learn things about them. And they would ask you questions about yourself, which I found quite startling, at first.'

Would you ever have had an emotional conversation with another boy? Could you have come into school crying, and talking about a problem you had, with a male friend?

James: 'No.'

Alex: 'No.'

David: 'No.'

Stephen: 'No.'

Pete: 'No.'

Can you remember *any* boy crying, or showing vulnerability, or asking for help?

'Literally never.'

'Never happened.'

'No.'

'I cannot remember a single instance of that.'

James: 'It just didn't happen.' He pauses, for a moment, and then says, wistfully: 'But I hear younger people do it, now. Boys hug, and stuff. Apparently they've invented that, now.'

Perhaps not surprisingly, this unspoken ban on being sad, emotional, and vulnerable had a knock-on effect, as evidenced by:

Dark Times

'You have a lot of violent thoughts, as a boy,' James says. 'A lot of thoughts informed by shooting and blowing up and hitting and that kind of stuff.'

'I was angry a lot of the time. I was full of anger, but I didn't realise it then,' Pete says. 'I could actually be quite cruel to other people, but I was so miserable and furious I didn't realise it.'

'Around about 12, I just sort of stopped eating,' James says. 'Not in any traumatic way – I just wasn't very interested in it. And I became very depressed. You couldn't cry at school, but you could be *depressed* – like, all dark, and mysterious, and sad, like Kurt Cobain.'

'I had a minor breakdown at my secondary school,'

David says. 'I didn't recognise it at the time, and neither did anyone else – but I pretended to be ill for three months, and ended up in hospital. I was so miserable at school, but I couldn't get away from it – in my family, you could only avoid going to school if you had a temperature. So every morning, I'd put the thermometer on the radiator, to get out of going to school – and eventually they put me in an observation ward at hospital, where the doctors said, obviously, "There's nothing wrong with him." But it was just because I hated school, and it was the only way to escape it.'

'I was abused as a kid, and I got really, really depressed, and didn't know how to talk to people,' Alex says. 'And I'd get drunk and become super-extrovert, and crazy. A group of us would go off and do vandalism in the neighbourhood – a competition for the most creative vandalism. You'd tear up "For Sale" signs and use them to knock someone's satellite dish out of alignment; take big flower pots and dump them on top of people's cars. Really fucking out of order. I gatecrashed one guy's birthday party, and we started a fire in his back garden, using bits of his fence. We took his birthday cake out of the fridge, ate the cake and threw the plate on the fire. Then his mates found out and chased us down the street. I'm quite ashamed, now – but there was this definite "ARGH!" feeling. That kind of destructiveness young men have. I understand that feeling of riot coming from young men who want to fuck shit up. But I never felt it towards people,' Alex is at pains to point out. 'Just violence towards *stuff*.'

For those who went through periods of depression, anger and isolation – not really knowing who they were, or what to do to relieve it – most seemed to outgrow it aged around 16 to 18, through the presumably medically inadvisable yet traditional route of finding a new peer group, and getting quite pissed/stoned/high.

'Drunk boys can talk about things that sober boys can't.'

'When I got to 15, 16, and found a new peer group, who were into music, and movies – and who I could get drunk with, which I think was key – we would start to have those kinds of conversations.'

'Talking about your emotions? That only really happened when I got to 15, and joined a band, and started taking acid, which was useful. We had a bedrock of common humour, and jokes, and TV shows, which allowed us to communicate more. Also, being in a band is great, because you can spend hours together not really talking much. You're just . . . *together*.'

'Finding some new people, and smoking a bit of weed. That changed everything quite quickly. I suddenly realised it wasn't that mysterious a process, after all – making friends, and being happy. But those [earlier] years – they really are the tricky bit. It's where a lot of boys fall down a deep, dark hole – because life does seem very difficult and disappointing, and therefore you often need a culprit. If someone had said to me, at my lowest point, "You feel terrible and lonely and awkward because wokeness is making you ashamed to be yourself", or, "This is all because women are awful, and hate men, and have destroyed the concept of masculinity" – I mean, I can see why being given a very simple answer would be very appealing. Thankfully, I was much, much too stoned to be radicalised.'

Girls. What Did You Know of Girls?

Alex: 'Our school only became co-ed in sixth form, and there was a girls-only common-room, and there was always a sense of powders and potions; this whole thing of perfume and make-up. It seemed like this tribe of exotic creatures had arrived. Almost like it was a Frontier town full of prospectors, and suddenly all the ladies in petticoats had turned up, and it was like, "This is *wild*!"'

'They seemed to have much more poise, and, like, nice pencils and things,' James says, wonderingly. 'I could never sustain the nice pencil thing. They seemed much more . . . in control of stuff. And by the time I was 15, they seemed much more sophisticated than the boys – they'd know, like nice cafés you could sit in, and they were much better at buying booze, as well. They were just more grown up. Around them, you felt like a little boy.'

'Their side of the fence looked more peaceful. It looked lower stakes, in an enviable way,' Stephen agrees. 'Also, it seemed easier for girls to be swottier than it was for boys. You could be funny and cute *and* clever. You couldn't be a clever, cool boy.'

Alex, again: 'And it seemed like they had more power than the boys – that they could have their pick of the men. It's only later you realise many of them were probably as panicked and insecure and anxious as the boys. At the time, they seemed like powerful, magical creatures. We were totally bewitched and befuddled by them.'

Stephen, again: 'Also, girls could *blossom*. A girl who was average at school would suddenly turn up at the school disco in hot-pants and hair and make-up, and you'd be like, "Oh my God, that's Alison McGovern!" There's no equivalent for boys. That sudden makeover, like Sandy from *Grease*. So in that way, it looked *easier* to be a girl.'

But did you want to *be* a girl?

'No. I definitely thought boys were . . . better. It was old-skool times. You knew, ultimately, that men had the power. We were the stronger sex. It might be an easier life to be a girl, at that age – but you definitely didn't *want* it.'

As an initial experiment into understanding where and how boys of my generation were raised, I was astonished to see – even though the men had grown up in different parts of Britain, in different socio-economic classes, with different religions, and very different parents – how many similarities there were in not only their stories, but the stories of a huge number of boys, of whatever generation.

I found this commonality of experience striking – because, two nights before, I'd started to prepare for my journey into the World of Men by embarking upon former SAS man Ant Middleton's book *Zero Negativity*, and Carol Gilligan and Naomi Snider's *Why Does Patriarchy Persist?*

Although Ant's was definitely higher in stories about shooting things and pissing in his boots, Gilligan and Snider's book had, in the first ten pages, outlined what happens to young boys when they begin to socialise in the wider world, and start learning what our idea of 'masculinity' means.

'Masculinity . . . is a pseudo-independence, [appearing "masculine" by] hiding relational desires and sensitivities,' they summarise.

Boys being put in a 'masculine' environment – say, a school with hundreds of other boys, many of them older – quickly learn they must hide 'their tenderness, their empathy, their vulnerability', as it will not be responded to positively. Or at all. No hugging, no crying, no fear.

There then follows a fairly common template of eventually being so cut off from your emotions that you struggle to know who you are – a real wilderness phase – allied with anxiety, anger and depression, which commonly resolves by finding some new friends, getting a bit pissed, and finally beginning the *actual* work of your teenage years: figuring out what kind of man you actually want to become. What will make *you* happy.

And it's this last part that leads to my final question, which is: were you ever, at any point, given any advice on how to be a boy, or a man? On how to find happiness?

No One Tells You How to Be a Man

'No.'

'No.'

'Nuh-huh.'

'No.'

Huge pause, then: 'No. Not at all. Nothing in that regard.'

Women, I tell them all, are absolutely bombarded with

advice from day one. Relatives, problem pages, magazines, self-help books, endless movies, TV shows and books about being a teenage girl.

Are boys getting *none* of that?

'Nah,' James says, breezily.

'Did you never even read a *problem page*?' I ask, astonished.

'I mean, the one on Ceefax. Mainly voyeuristically. Not really for advice. More shits'n'giggles.'

Stephen: 'The only advice I *ever* got given was the pure, standard west coast of Scotland one: "You néver hit a woman, you never cross a picket line." I've kept pretty firmly to that.'

'If it wasn't *direct* advice, then what about in, say, art?' I ask. 'What films were you watching, what books were you reading, about being a teenage boy?'

'Comic books.'

'Comic books.'

'Superhero movies.'

'Superhero stuff.'

'Mainly sci-fi, and comic books. *New Gods*. Things about other worlds. Battling evil. James Bond.'

'I read a lot of S. E. Hinton. American teens in the fifties in leather jackets who stabbed each other a lot. And Stephen King.'

So all the movies and books that you were reading that featured teenage boys – they were never normal teenage boys, in the normal world? They were people with super-powers, and dark secrets, engaged in life-or-death battles?

'Yeah.'

'Yes.'

'Yes.'

What about, say, Adrian Mole? Just a normal working-class boy in Leicester, dealing with being a teenager, falling in love, worrying about exams, trying to improve himself, dealing with his parents' divorce? That's gotta be a classic for teenage boys, surely? That's your *Little Women*.

James spoke for everyone when he summarised it thus: 'I love Adrian Mole, but . . . but that's a woman's vision of a young boy, isn't it?'

So did you read *nothing* about an actual, normal, Earth Boy that chimed with you?

James pauses. 'It's not interesting,' he says finally, and flatly. 'I'm not sure I would ever have wanted to read something like that. Now? Now I'm in my forties? I really like books about teenage boys. I want to write one! But even then, it tends to be about boys who are incredibly fucked up in some way. There are no normal boys in movies, or fiction.'

Because?

'Because . . . because it would be boring.'

And there it was. Despite the fact I had found talking to the men about their boyhood absolutely fascinating – honestly, I recommend to every woman that you do it to the men in your life: societally, we tend not to talk about the experience of 'being a boy' in the way we do about the experience of 'being a girl' – there was an odd sense of disconnect, and even puzzlement, from the men, as I asked for their stories.

These stories – about anger, and fighting, and abuse,

and finding women utterly mysterious, and setting fire to fences, and never being given any kind of help – were, to the men who told me them, not *real* stories. *Real* stories about young men involved quests, and intergalactic battles, and super-powers, and adventures, and mysteries. Real stories were *big*. Normal boys' lives were . . . little. No matter what actually happened in them.

Or, as one man put it, about his teenage years, 'It's not exactly Luke Skywalker, is it?' – despite the fact he'd just shown me the three facial scars he had received from three brutal beatings, which he seemed to shrug off as just . . . normal. Dull. Not to be made a fuss of.

And *this* is the first, and primary, problem of men, I thought, as I turned off my tape recorder in half a dozen pubs, cafés and kitchens. The primary problem of straight white men and boys. Because in our culture, they are seen as the 'default human being' – the 'normal' that the 'otherness' of women, people of colour and the queer community are defined against – it's almost as if the actual details of their lives have become see-through. Invisible.

Never being able to cry or admit vulnerability; the bubbling anger; the shrugging acceptance of violence; the memory of hitting friends; the prizing of recklessness; the need for alcohol or drugs; the total lack of advice, or guidance? As a woman, these all seemed so wildly different from my childhood, and adolescence, as to have happened to another species. I felt like I'd just interviewed a bunch of centaurs about their centaur lives, while they smoked cigarettes with their centaur hooves and shrugged, 'Yeah, I've got the torso of a man and the body of a horse. No biggie.'

There seemed to be this – to me – heartbreaking stoicism, and acceptance, among men. That there was nothing exceptional, questionable or changeable about the fundamental elements of being a young man. That it was all okay in the end, really. That it was boring to talk about it. And, therefore, it shouldn't be talked about.

And yet: now, so many mothers of young men, and young men themselves, kept asking, 'What about men?'

All their fathers seemed to have experienced the same set of problems.

And yet: none of the fathers seemed to discuss this among themselves, or with their sons.

As I put all the transcriptions of the interviews away in a big folder I had started, with 'MEN' written on it, I wondered: is the reason *women* keep being asked 'What about men?' because we're traditionally the gender that's . . . intimate about stuff? Men might be good at making plans – like how to blow up a Death Star – but women are good at talking about *people*. Emotions. Personal events. Is the current crisis in young masculinity the biggest-ever case of, 'Er, you'd better talk to your mum about stuff like that'?

The first, and most fundamental problem, it seemed, was the way men talk to each other. Or are *taught* to talk to each other. Or: aren't taught at all.

The first problem was chat.

Chapter Two

The Conversations of Men

My husband, Pete, is my primary spy in the world of men. He is a man, but he read *Just Seventeen* magazine as a teenager – which means he is, essentially, gender-bilingual.

It is he who tells me how men talk when there are no women around. In this case, in the locker room of the local YMCA gym, on the day war breaks out in Ukraine.

It was 8am, and he and one other man were in the changing room when a third entered, and the following exchange occurred:

Scenario 1

'All right mate? Where you been?'

'What do you mean, where have I been?'

'I haven't seen you for a while.'

'Yeah – I've been here. Just later – nine o'clock, usually.'

'You all right?'

'Yeah, I'm okay. You?'

'Yeah – can't complain.'

'What do you think about all this, then, what's going on?'

'About what?'

'You know. What's going on. All this . . . *nonsense*.'

'Terrible. What do you think?'

'Well, what can you say? They done what they done. And now it's all messed up.'

At this point, my husband went to the shower. When he returned, five minutes later, they were still talking. Things had clearly taken a deeply philosophical turn.

'Well – it is what it is, isn't it?' the first finally sighed, darkly, pulling on his shorts.

The other guy shook his head. 'I don't see any way back though, mate, do you?'

'Nah, mate. But – there's still the Champions League.'

Or let's look at a second scenario – this one witnessed by my friend Jojo, on a train, when two cyclists boarded, with their bikes, having just taken part in a race.

Scenario 2

The two men are mud-splattered, and breathing heavily. They do not know each other, but – in acknowledgement they have just shared quite an extreme experience – sit next to each other. It's clearly been a very strenuous, and possibly emotional, day. It's pissing down with rain outside.

Cyclist 1, mopping his face with a towel: 'Huh. That reminded me of the Great Sussex Cycle Track. Did that last year. Great surface.'

Cyclist 2, tending a nasty-looking graze on his leg: 'Yeah – they've put a substrate down on the disused railway sections. Superlative drainage.'

Cyclist 1: 'Great Sussex was the first time I used one of those Mondraker Carbon jobs. I tell you what – they *smash* the inclines.'

Cyclist 2: 'Huh. Cesar Rojo worked on the Mondraker.'

Cyclist 1: 'It's funny, because Rojo himself rides an Unno Ever.'

Cyclist 2: 'They only make 50 of those a year.'

Cyclist 1: 'I saw one at Pumptrack. Sexy beast. But parking there is a *nightmare*.'

And so on, for the next 70 miles. Jojo marvelled, 'It was just a constant back and forth of bits of information – deployed like bullets. No questions of each other, no real curiosity. It was like an anthropological exercise in how to spend an hour trading *only* in bike-based facts. Quite amazing, really – especially as one was bleeding quite heavily.'

In this scenario, we can see – unlike Scenario 1 – there *is* information: but nothing emotional or personal. These are informations that have been lovingly collated from biking magazines, biking YouTube channels and fellow biking enthusiasts. These are Official, External Informations: proveable, real, non-personal. They feel like possessions that can be racked up, memorised, and then traded with each other, in a turn-taking duet, like a card game. Top Trumps.

We can also note that not one of these informations was prompted by a question, or inquiry. This isn't a *conversation*, as such – but a long-established socialising framework, in which it is understood that the rules are to take it in turns to produce a fact about a subject to each other, and to never veer towards anything intimate, or emotional.

In a situation where two women had just taken part in an exhausting cycle race, and were now sitting together – one bleeding – I can absolutely guarantee you that before ten minutes had passed, they would have discussed why they got into cycle-racing ('My dad was into it – it was the only way to spend time with him. He was later diagnosed as bipolar II,'), mutual people they knew in racing ('You know Kelle Casaubon? She's a fucking bitch, isn't she?'), and – thanks to the prompt of the bleeding – vivid descriptions of both participants' experiences of childbirth.

Quick fact about women: 90 per cent of women who have had children in the last 20 years will invariably start describing their births to each other within seven minutes or less of meeting each other. If you ever get into a lift that has already got two women in it, just as you hear the words '. . . like a *bucket* full of entrails. It was my worst New Year's Eve ever', then that is what has been happening.

By the time those two women got to Euston, they would probably be able to write a 5,000-word essay on each other's lives.

In the case of the male cyclists, however, they could

easily leave the train without even knowing each other's names. And who knows what would have happened if they ran out of biking facts before Watford? I presume they would have lapsed into silence. Or turned to the Champions League.

The thing is, all the talk about there being massive differences between male and female brains – or the amount that women talk, compared to men – is bollocks. Men and women say roughly the same amount every day – around 16,000 words – and all the latest metadata is that there is a negligible amount of difference between our actual brains. In terms of straightforward biology, and wiring, we are very similar.

Culturally, however, the way boys and girls learn to communicate is observably different. In order to discuss it, we must, as is traditional, 'go on a journey': we must, now, climb onto the Banterbus, and take a journey to Banterbury, where I, the Archbishop of Banterbury, will take you through the Bible of Banter – *The Banterbury Tales*, if you will – and chronicle the most formative moments of a newborn boy's life: the Road to Banter.

The Road to Banter

I would now like to list the stages of verbal development in a boy-child. Obviously, none of this is 'proven' by 'scientists' or 'facts' – this is merely stuff I have observed, and now relay here, so that we might investigate that most pivotal of all male skills: banter. With my own banter. I am going to banter about banter!

STAGE ONE: Be born. There is a 70 per cent chance the first words the newborn baby boy will hear, as he is pulled from his mother's womb – covered in oomska, and wailing – are, 'Well, *he's* got nothing to be ashamed of there. He takes after his dad! Blimey! Go *on*, my son! He'll have to coil that around his leg, like a hose! That's gonna pose storage issues! What a *whopper*!'

Awkward pause. Nurse: 'That's the umbilical cord, Dad.'

Dad: 'I know. It's just banter.'

STAGE TWO: Latching on to the breast. Ninety-nine per cent chance the first words he will hear, while doing this: 'Ooooh – he's a tit man, like his dad! He *loves* your knockers, babe! Look at him gnawing on your jubblies! *He's in heaven!* Get *in* there, dude!'

Mum: 'Stephen, you didn't say this when Daisy started breastfeeding. You didn't say she was . . . a voracious little lesbian.'

STAGE THREE: Learning to walk. The toddler-boy waddles over to something, and tentatively pokes it. It's probably the dog, or the cat.

Visitor to the house: 'Oooooh! He's gonna be trouble! Look at little Hulk! What a bruiser! Don't want to run into *him* at closing time at the pub! You wouldn't like him when he's angry! Smash smash, mate! SMASH SMASH!'

The wobbly child sits down. He has smashed nothing at all. But, nonetheless, his actions have provoked *banter*.

STAGE FOUR: Toilet-training. 'Imagine your winkie is like a little gun, mate – and the potty's full of naughty monkeys. Pow! Pow! That's it! That's your lightsaber! The force is strong with this one! Guys – he's C3 PEE oh! C3 PEE OH!'

The *real* lesson here: not potty-training, but *banter* training.

STAGE FIVE: Learning to talk himself, or: THE BEGIN-NING OF BANTZ.

When a man-child is born, so too is a whole new BAN-TER MACHINE, which will produce THOUSANDS OF HOURS OF BANTER, right up until that man is on his deathbed, whispering, 'I know what I want written on my gravestone: "I told you I was ill"' – then dying: banter-ing until the last.

From a very young age, we teach boys to be as amusing and banterous as possible. It is, admittedly, a slow start – while they are toddlers, or at nursery, the banter levels remain relatively low. At that age, boys are still generally allowed to be serious, or sad, or whimsical, as their mood sees fit. A very small boy can still talk about elves and fairies he's 'seen'; talk about 'snuggling' with his dog; be sincere about how much he loves people.

While banter will happen *around* him, in a way that does not happen with very young girls – girls are *not* potty-trained with cries of 'Use your urethra like a gun!' – he is not yet expected to contribute to the banter *himself*.

But, around the age of seven or eight, playgrounds across the world start to ring with the sound of a million little Chandler Bings, or Jason Stathams, starting to communicate only in quips, bantz, lols, gags or shouts of 'OI OI!' – even as the girl-children peel off into female-only groups, and have in-depth discussions about their feelings, hair, pets, favourite pencil cases, colouring-in abilities, and ambitions to, one day, run for Parliament.

Although there have, surprisingly, been no in-depth studies about how and why the Beginning of Banter occurs, a couple of years ago, I came across a research paper that, to be honest, broke my heart when I read it.

It noted that while, as mentioned before, there are no major differences in the *language* skills of boys and girls, girls develop their *fine motor skills* earlier than boys.

This means, crucially, that girls *master handwriting* far earlier than boys – something that can be confirmed by anyone who's looked at the stories, or poems, pinned to a mixed-sex schoolroom wall. The girls' writing is usually neat, precise and orderly. The boys', meanwhile, often looks like a pencil and a piece of A4 had a major fist-fight, in which both were losers.

Essentially, the schooling system means that boys are forced to start writing *before they can actually, physically manage it* – and this is bad news in two respects. The first is that learning to write kick-starts massive neural development – in being able to order your thoughts, reason things out, develop an idea, and describe your own emotions.

While girls are able to race ahead in doing this, boys are

hampered by still physically struggling with the actual use of a pencil – and so don't get to enjoy this sudden rocket-boost of synaptic connection, as they are weighed down by a physical world of hand-cramp, breaking pencils and frustration.

James*: 'I could never sustain the nice pencil thing. They seemed much more . . . in control of stuff.'*

And the second is that – obviously and heartbreakingly – every day, boys are made to feel that writing, and therefore, by extension, thinking, and language, are things that they are . . . just a bit shit at. That they will fail at. Every day, they turn up to school knowing that, however hard they try, their work is going to make them look messy, incapable and, to be frank, stupider than the girls. Their communication abilities *on paper* are inferior – which means they are failing at 'official' language, and the system is already punishing them with lower marks, or extra homework. So it's easy to see why they might disengage from it, in order to preserve their self-esteem.

James*: 'It was irrelevant to be clever.'*

As I say, there is no official research or data on the consequences of this – but my feeling is that these are the *exact* conditions in which boys' verbal communication would start to become very different from the girls'. When you feel like you're struggling in a system; when you need to find a different way to assert yourself; when you need to put on a bit of a front – a bit of *swagger* – to deal with failure; when communicating in the 'proper', official way is something you feel you are being excluded from: well, *obviously* you're going to jump on the Banter Bus – next stop,

LOLZtown. Of *course* you're going to want to look up from your messy, frustrating essay and shout out a joke to the class that makes everyone laugh.

David: *'Who has all the power in the room? The funniest person. You can control a situation by being funny.'*

Of *course* you're going to burst out into the playground – hot with pent-up energy, sore with your 'faultiness' – and cosplay at being The Rock in *The Fast and the Furious*. The Rock doesn't need to dot his 'i's, or remember to end every sentence with a full stop. He just coolly negs-off Vin Diesel, shouts *'THIS* IS A CAR!', and blows up Tokyo. If you're getting 2/10 for your spelling, it's very reassuring to know you can still get 10/10 for your bantz in the playground, later.

The knock-on effects of making young boys feel that writing is 'not for them' continue in other, pro-bantz ways. There is an obvious link between writing and reading – and all the statistics show that boys, the poor fuckers, constantly score lower than girls in reading skills, too. Boys are 20 per cent less likely to read for pleasure than girls – and when they do read for pleasure, their tastes have two notable traits: they prefer graphic novels, with far less text than the books read by girls, and they prefer books by male authors.

What did you read?

Comic books.

Comic books.

Sci-fi, and comic books. Stephen King.

Although this is a wild generalisation – there are, obviously, thousands of different kinds of graphic novels, and male authors – this does tend to mean boys' reading matter skews away from the kind of smaller, more intimate, more emotionally literate stuff girls are reading.

While girls are absorbing the full, detailed social implications of Jo March only having one clean glove at a ball, or Anne of Green Gables being teased for having red hair, boys are more likely to be reading punchy stuff about alien invasions, soldiers, spies, quests and superheroes: all characters likely to be popping the verbalisation of complex and delicate inner quandaries on the back-burner in favour of explaining a heist, or a raid, or technical details on how the hyper-drive on a spaceship works. And, of course, bantering.

Fast-forward 20 years, and any research you want to pick will outline the now-embedded difference between adult male and female communication. Remember – there is no notable physical difference between male and female brains. Any difference we're seeing is cultural. Simply google 'difference between male and female chit chat give me facts please', and you will see thousands of pieces like one from the London Image Institute, describing the difference between male and female conversations, which can be summarised as: men like very direct conversation; they like plans; they like very technical details; they like to work within a hierarchy; they don't want to ask questions or betray ignorance; they dislike apologising; and they love 'playful antagonising' – or, bantz.

Women, on the other hand, are more relationship-oriented; they will admit problems or dilemmas; they ask questions; they share experiences; they will not disagree in public; they nod and encourage. Their humour is more self-deprecating.

And as you can see, we've just sketched out the exact conditions in which that male conversational style develops.

Of course, no one way of talking is innately superior to the other. As a younger woman, I used to actively avoid conversations with women: they'd all be discussing their problems – and asking you about yours! They're so *emotional*! They'd agree with you to your face – and then you'd later find out they disagreed with you, or were bitching behind your back! I preferred conversations with the men: they were busy being funny, arguing to your face and planning to take over the world.

And, as Pete says, general male conversation – Banter Lite, or BlokeChat – is, in many ways, a very sophisticated invention. After he'd recounted that conversation in the men's changing rooms about the Russian invasion of Ukraine, he mused: 'As I've got older, I've really grown to love BlokeChat. It's their equivalent of birdsong. There's a sort of art to it. Never too specific. Never too emotional. Never too weird. Those two men knew they had five minutes of potentially awkward time being naked together, and they needed some chat that filled that time which kept everyone feeling safe, comfortable, and able to wrap up the conversation as soon as they'd tied their shoelaces. In that respect, it gets the job done.'

Instead, BlokeChat and Banter Lite remain – beautifully

and elegantly – a way for any man to talk to any other man, happily and harmoniously, for as long as men need to be with each other. A simple set of conversational tools that become as well-worn, and remain as useful, as the shears, spade and saw – carefully cleaned, oiled and hung up in the shed.

Of course, the problem comes with the fact that no tool does *every* job. You can't use shears, a spade or a saw for open-heart surgery – or around children. And none of those tools, as we can see, are the ones that could start the conversation, 'What about men? What are our problems? How can we change them?'

Really, it was a piece of piss for women to invent feminism: we spend all our time sharing awful experiences, admitting we don't know how to change things, and asking people who *do* know endless questions – until we feel like we have the answer. If there's one thing the female conversational style is absolutely perfect for, it's talking about all the reasons it's shit to be a woman, and working together to change it.

If there's one thing the male conversational style is patently unable to do, it's the same, about men.

But we'll come back to that later. Now we've covered the basics of how young men start to think, and talk, let's have a look at the other, key element of being a man . . .

Chapter Three

The Bodies of Men

I was born in 1975. When the eighties started, the hero of the biggest action film of that time – *Raiders of the Lost Ark* – was an archaeologist who was definitely fit *for an archeologist*, but was in no way ripped, and spent the movie in a comfortable pair of slacks, and a nice shirt.

It's notable that in Harrison Ford's other big movie franchise – *Star Wars* – both he and Mark Hamill, as Luke Skywalker, had similarly average bodies, kept their trousers on, and often looked, while running down spaceship corridors, like they could probably be outpaced by a reasonably fit 12-year-old; or R2-D2, if he took the brakes off.

Ford, in particular, always looks 30 seconds away from leaning against a cardboard space-wall, lighting a fag, and sighing, 'I am *knackered.*'

By the end of the eighties, however, things were utterly

different: by then, the *literally* big action-movie heroes were Sylvester Stallone and Arnold Schwarzenegger. The body-inflation was vast: Stallone and Schwarzenegger both had biceps that look like the torso of a small piglet. Let's be honest – Schwarzenegger's physique exists on the very outer limits of a recognisably 'body-shaped' body: it looked, in the words of Clive James, 'like a condom full of walnuts'.

Go into any modern toyshop, and you will see that the action figures five-year-old boys are playing with, right now, look like a cadre of Balkan warlords, preparing to raid a neighbouring city. It's pretty alarming. The Luke Skywalker doll is a case in point: in the 1980s iteration, he looks like the kind of callow youth who might have the odd 'dizzy spell', or regularly peruse a slim volume of poetry. In the most recent version, however, his top is slashed halfway down his torso, revealing pecs so big they look, frankly, like a nice pair of tits.

Everywhere you look, where once we had 'normal' bodies, and role models, they have gradually been replaced by super-ripped men.

Billionaires used to be portly, cigar-smoking grandpas: now we have Jeff Bezos, the on/off richest man in the world, in his super-tight T-shirts.

Demented, Dr Evil-type world leaders would sit in a lea-ther armchair, stroking a cat: now Putin releases PR shots of himself, stripped to the waist, on horseback, doing judo, or wrestling a bear – although I might have got that last one confused with publicity stills from *The Revenant*.

The physical standards of alpha-ness have definitely been

raised, over the last two generations. When I was a child, you could definitely be a 'good enough' richest man in the world, or the planet's best-known and most successful psychopath.

Now, it seems, you also have to have a possible side hustle – if your whole evil empire suffers cash-flow problems – as a ripped underwear model, as well.

When women became alarmed about young girls being exposed to unrealistic role models of physical perfection, they started the Body Positivity Movement: flooding Instagram with pictures of themselves with rolls, stretch marks, lavish thighs and triumphant wibbly-wobbly bums. As a woman, it is your duty to respond to any picture like this with a string of fire emojis, and to tell every woman you know 'YOU LOOK AMAZING, BABE!' – thus slowly fostering a world where all kinds of bum are accepted.

So far, sadly, there has been no Body Positivity Movement for young straight young men. There is no culture of boys, or men, posting either 'fat', 'weedy' or 'non-muscular' pictures of themselves – and all their male friends going 'YOU LOOK AMAZING, BABE!' and posting aubergine emojis. In the World of Boys, hyping up your friends for exposing their physical vulnerabilities has not yet been invented. Why? Let me introduce you to Moran's Rule Number One, invented from decades of observation of men:

Fifty per cent of young men's problems occur because of a fear of being called 'girly', 'soft' or, primarily, 'gay'.

Even though each generation's opinion polls show homophobia on a steep and continuing decline, it would still be unthinkable for a skinny 14-year-old boy to Insta himself in his swimming trunks, looking soulfully at the camera, in the way 14-year-old girls seem contractually obliged to. Every ten minutes. To hundreds of positive replies from their friends.

Why? Well, I think we all know what the comments below a *boy's* picture would be. They would range from Banter Lite ('Still can't believe you went to Tesco like that') to Banter Heavy Artillery ('Dude, you look like Stick Man'). And if someone – even this boy's best, ride-or-die friend – said, 'You look fucking hot, mate!'? As every girl says, every day, hundreds of times to her friends? Then, obviously, would be the beginning of the 'Bender!'-pocalypse.

We can see it's a fear of being called 'gay' that stops straight boys being positive about their bodies, and supporting others – because Gay Instagram is far further ahead in Body Positivity. Although any gay man will tell you just *how* judgemental and perfection-oriented the gay community can be about each other's bodies, googling 'gay body positivity Instagram' *will* give you some uplifting returns: stretch marks, big thighs, scrawny darlings and a *lot* of Bear-Spo. If you want to see a gloriously round, furry tum framed by boxers and a silk kimono, every day is your lucky day, on the Gay Internet. And the comments underneath are just a joy.

Compare this, then, to straight men, who might well go through their whole lives without ever being able to tell a friend/son/brother/dad, 'You look really hot today' – unthinkable! – and yet will happily call a car, bassline or watch 'sexy'. I don't understand. No one thinks you're going to bang your watch. Surely they've worked out you're not going to bang Simon, either. Of course, they *have*. But the Rules of Bantz means that comment *must* be made. It is the custom. When you are a young man, banter is a shrine onto which *all* the possible jokes about being gay must be laid, regularly – or the crops will fail.

While straight men flounder in the emotional desert of never being able to appreciate or support each other – up to the point of living wildly miserable and insecure lives, until their deaths – for fear of being called 'gay', here's Mark Wahlberg's Daily Fitness Regime:

2.30am wake up

2.45am prayer time

3.15am breakfast #1: steel-cut oats, peanut butter, blueberries and eggs

3.40–5.15am workout #1

5.30am breakfast #2: protein shake, three turkey burgers, five pieces of sweet potato

6am shower

7.30am golf

8am snack: ten turkey meatballs

9.30am cryo chamber recovery

10.30am breakfast #3: grilled chicken salad with two hard-boiled eggs, olives, avocado, cucumber, tomato and lettuce

11am family time/meetings/work calls
1pm lunch: New York steak with green peppers
2pm meetings/work calls
3pm pick up kids from school
3.30pm snack: grilled chicken with bok choy
4pm workout #2
5pm shower
5.30pm dinner/family time: fish (halibut or cod or
    sea bass) with veggies (such as sautéed spinach
    and bok choy)
7.30pm bedtime

And he's not even the most ripped man in Hollywood.

Around 2014, I went for a long, drunken dinner with the writer/director of a massive superhero franchise. By the time we got to the second bottle, he started to talk about the regime his current leading man was going through – in order to get ripped enough for the role.

At the time, the shoot was still three months away.

'He's having to go to the gym *four* times a day; the amount of protein he's eating has made him really constipated, and I'm pretty sure his trainer is secretly giving him steroids, to get him where he needs to be, because his *moods* . . .' And here the director rolled his eyes.

He looked down at his dinner – steak and fries. We had now moved on to our third bottle of wine. Neither of us had been to the gym in many moons. We were very comfortable on our chairs.

'I've worked on all-female vehicles where they're all competitively starving, to be the thinnest girl on set, and that's brutal,' he continued. 'But I can tell you now, hand on heart, physically, it's *way* harder to be a male actor on an action movie than for a woman to "get into shape" for the average female role. These guys are in so much pain at the end of every day, they have to sit in ice-baths. They're necking painkillers. They don't go anywhere, or see anyone. They're having to put on muscle density at a rate any medical professional would tell you is incredibly stressful for the body. And on the days we shoot them topless, they have to be massively dehydrated, too – to get the best muscle definition. They're living the lives of the most elite, driven Olympic athletes – but then we ask them to deliver really emotional dialogue to a ping-pong ball against a green screen, and then cry on cue. It's fucking *batshit*.'

Of course, as mentioned above, female body ideals are just as nuts as male ones. Neither Hollywood nor the catwalk are exactly bursting with cheerfully realistic female bodies – casually swinging a saggy tit around the neck, like a scarf, or howling 'MY THIGHS ARE CHAFING! I NEED TO STOP AND PUT MY CHUB-RUB SHORTS ON!' during a chase scene.

But at least women have started an honest-to-goodness bitching club about the whole thing: TikTok bursts with sassy young teenage girls talking about diet culture, and singing songs about Victoria's Secret models ('*I know Victoria's secret/Selling skin and bones with big boobs/She was made up by a dude*'). Every other female stand-up has a routine about it. Actresses take their uncomfortable heels off on the red carpet, and admit they can't walk in them; or throw them into the audience. Tina Fey hosts the Golden Globes and admits that awards season, for actresses, means not eating for months: 'Or, as I call it, *The Hunger Games*.'

By way of contrast, we have not *ever* seen a male stand-up talk about the literal Arms Race – in that the arms are getting bigger – between Hollywood's A-list actors. We've never seen a young man accept an Oscar, hold it in the air and shout, 'I humbly pray one day the Marvel movie franchise will invent a superhero called Dad-Bod Man, and I can start eating carbs again!'

It's harder for boys, and men, because while women can always address their complaints to 'the patriarchy' – 'They're male designers making clothes for anorexic girls!' 'All casting directors are perverts!' – *men* blaming 'the patriarchy' for stuff isn't yet a thing. Sadly, the Patriarchy Complaints Department has yet to receive a single letter from a high-profile straight white man. All change begins with the delicious moment when you work out who is to blame for your problems – but how can men blame 'the patriarchy' when, as a straight white man, you *look like* the patriarchy? Then you're just in a *Fight Club* situation, where you're hitting yourself in the face.

This, of course, is what wizened old feminists have been trying to explain for years: all men *aren't* the patriarchy. Only a few select old bastards are making up these rules. Everyone else – men *and* women – are simply being told to follow them. One of the things I've found myself most repeatedly explaining is Moran's Rule Number Two:

> *The patriarchy is screwing men as hard as it's screwing women.*

Men are being told what 'a real man' looks like, and does – and women are being told what 'a real woman' looks like, and does. And it's making us *all* unhappy.

Once you know patriarchy is a belief system we're all having to operate in, you can either continue to play by the rules – or start questioning it, and fight against it. Women, notably, have. That's the whole point of feminism. Men, as yet, have not. Perhaps it's harder for men to rebel against other men – their father figures? But then, 90 per cent of movies seem to be about men rebelling against their dads: Luke Skywalker fighting Darth Vader is possibly *the* iconic pop-culture moment of the last 50 years. Darth Vader is *absolutely* the patriarchy, and Luke chooses not to play along with him. So the template is there.

Maybe, if there is to be some kind of feminism for men, it needs to start with some Ben Kenobi-like grandpa – telling younger men to rebel against gender stereotyping. After all, Ben Kenobi *was* wearing a dress. As bell hooks says, 'Males cannot love themselves in patriarchal culture if their very self-definition relies on submission to patriarchal rules.'

But impossible body ideals, and Ben Kenobi's maxi-dress, all lead us into the next subject.

Chapter Four

The Clothes of Men

I am standing in the main shopping centre of Solihull, in the West Midlands, watching people doing their Saturday shopping and latte-buying.

More specifically, I am watching the young men doing their shopping and latte-buying.

Ultra-specifically, I am looking at the young men's trousers. Hopefully, not in an alarming or inappropriate way. More like that of David Attenborough – collecting visual information about an intriguing species.

As anyone who has looked at the bottom half of young men in recent years can testify, currently, they are in the grip of a fad for ultra-tight, high-Lycra-content jeans. Jeans so tight that a good proportion of twenty-first-century male youth is walking around in what look like women's black 100-denier tights; or medieval hose. These are jeans so tight that they looked sprayed-on – but sprayed onto the *inside* of the skin. *That* tight. Jeans so tight that the genitals are crushed against the crotch seam, in vivid detail: looking like Han Solo's unhappy face, frozen in carbonite. It cannot be fun, down there. I'm sure the kind of people who claim they can hear plants screaming, when they are pulled up, can also hear the nation's male genitalia wailing, 'Help me! I have done nothing wrong! Call Amnesty International!'

For years, women have complained that there is no male equivalent of the Pill; that it is women who must bear the burden of preventing conception.

Looking at the bollock-torture happening inside these trousers, I feel I can conclude: well, fashion has done that for you now. No sperm can flourish in what is basically the trash-compactor in the Death Star. This is the end of accidental pregnancies.

Of course, I will be the first to defend young people's desire to wear absolutely batshit fashions. What is youth, if not the time when you are so boundlessly glowing, young and beautiful that you can wear something absolutely ridiculous – and *still* look hot?

However, as a woman, I know what the side effects are of wearing fashions that are mercilessly tight and body-revealing. Particularly when there is a pressure to have an unrealistically fit body. These jeans are basically the equivalent of the body-con dress for women. There is nowhere to run, and nowhere to hide, in clothes like these – unless you have an absolutely perfect body. There are, in the end, only two types of clothes:

ONE: Clothes that do *you* a favour, when you put them on: clothes that are cleverly cut, and will make your body – whatever it looks like – look better.

TWO: Clothes that *you* do a favour: clothes that *you* have to make look amazing, by dint of having a super-ripped, super-hot body.

These jeans – with their absolutely brutal revelation of every inch, pound, lump and testicle of the male body – are clothes which are *not* doing a favour to a lot of the young men who are wearing them. You can see every perfectly average calf; every acceptably un-worked-out quad; every adorably wobbly glute.

As a woman, I know what happens to young women when fashion becomes brutally revealing: how eating dis-order services brace themselves when hipster jeans – which need prominent hip bones! – and crop-tops – which need washboard abs! – come back into style.

And my concern with observing all the tight jeans around me is compounded, because I have spent the last week reading reports on the growing unhappiness that young men feel about their bodies.

Almost half of all men under the age of 40 said that poor body-image was affecting their mental health. Only 26 per cent were 'happy' with how they looked. One in ten said they were so depressed by their bodies that they had experienced suicidal thoughts. It was the third-biggest con-cern of men under 25 – just behind lack of job opportunities and worrying about failure at school. I had also been reading reports about 'Bigorexia' – the ridiculously titled disorder, wherein one in ten gym-going men and boys look in the mirror, and feel that, no matter how they actually look, that they are not big, or muscular, *enough*.

And I can't help but think: although the reasons for all these mental disorders are, of course, complex and many, if you weren't wearing trousers that were actively betraying you, a lot of these problems might disappear. Literally. Under another five inches or so of fabric, around the leg. If clothes are, in many ways, your armour, sometimes, the things they are protecting you from are your own bad thoughts.

The Twenty-First-Century Tight Jeans are a dolorous and unusual turn of events – because, by and large, boys, and men, have avoided making 'what you wear' as obsessive an occupation as many women have. Indeed, I would say one of the great triumphs of the male sex is that they have dealt, practically and sensibly, with the whole business of not being naked in public: i.e. clothing.

Let us, for a moment, rejoice in the full spectrum of male clothing – the half of the fashion world that is usually ignored, by comparison to the mad season-by-season, trend-by-trend whirlwind women live in, but which is generally 'not mad', and which should be celebrated as such.

Athleisure

Tracksuits, hoodies, joggers, trainers, gilets, tight sports-fabric T-shirts, one of those super-thin cagoules that suggest you do a weekly 10k in all-weathers, but actually wear to get a coffee from round the corner when it's too sweaty to wear a 'full fat' cagoule: athleisure has taken over from the 'jeans and a top' weekend outfit that has reigned supreme for most men since the mid-seventies.

Many older commentators have been scathing about the rise of athleisure – I think it was Clive James who decried the trend for soft, stretchy jogging bottoms and tops, saying, 'It makes men look like big babies, in expensive babygros.' I can only imagine how disgusted James must have been when fashion apparently heard him, went, 'Actually, that's a great idea!', flipped it, and then started making those 'cute' babygros that look like tracksuits.

Personally, I think it's always a good thing when fashion prioritises comfort. I congratulate men on this being the worst accusation that they can have thrown at them – 'looking too comfortable'. And I have no problem with adults looking like big babies, either. That sounds *lovely*. It's far better than looking like a 'sinister undertaker' (black suit), or 'off-duty murderer/assassin' (long black leather coat, sunglasses).

When I think of how uncomfortable our dads must have been in their stiff, ironed market jeans and lace-up leather shoes – with every 1980s leather shoe requiring a *minimum* of six crippling, skin-shredding months to finally be 'broken in' – the common trope of all our dads being permanently quite tetchy, quick to anger and apt to explosive fits of rage – 'I've been running around all day like a blue-arsed fly!' – starts to make a lot more sense. When they stood up, their feet hurt, and when they sat down, their balls would be crushed by the unforgiving seam in their non-Lycra jeans. No wonder they did things like 'kick the dog' and 'spend all day in the pub, then drive home drunk'. So hurrah! for athleisure. The infinitely preferable leg-option to the Ultra-Tight Jean. The Beatles to their Stones. The Blur to their Oasis.

The Suit

The Suit is one of the greatest technologies men have ever invented for themselves – up there with guns and vibrating robotic vaginas. If all clothing contains in it some kind of message, then The Suit is an all-time classic speech to humanity – an 'I have a dream', or the bit in *Ghostbusters* where Venkman convinces Ray to get a third mortgage on his house to pay for the Ectomobile. The Suit says, 'I am a man, I know what I'm doing – now leave me alone.'

Whether at work, attending a meeting, getting married, attending court, going to a party or getting buried, there is just one simple answer to the question 'What shall I wear?' and it is: 'The Suit, obviously. Don't be silly. I mean, there are no other options.'

Although fashion bloggers and magazines like *GQ* have invented whole industries from pretending there are constant new inventions in The Suit, these differences are, in reality, merely over a slight alternation in lapel size, or which new fabric they're being made of this year. The simple truth about suits is that they are an amazing invention, as they are seen as totally Fashion-, Class-, Size-, Race- and Sexuality-Neutral: a suit is a piece of clothing that can be worn, over and over, by any man, while never once involving any thought, 'fashion crisis' or genuine worries that you might not be dressed 'appropriately'.

Men in suits are never asked 'who they're channelling' today. Men's suits prompt no comments or questions at all. With the exception of a) the beach and b) ski slopes, a suit can be worn anywhere, at any time of day or night, in the knowledge it is totally appropriate. A suit can be worn at a breakfast meeting, at work, for lunch with friends, at a party, and then – if needed – on to a strip club, to discuss 'business matters' with out-of-town clients. There is no single item of female clothing that allows this – hence women talking about things like 'day-to-night' outfits, whereby 'merely' stuffing your handbag with two different pairs of shoes, a sheer pair of tights, some jazzy jewellery and an overflowing make-up bag, complete with hair-tongs, she might be able to go from work to a party in the 'same' dress.

The essential, useful invisibleness of a suit was brought home in 2014, when Australian TV host Karl Stefanovic wore the same suit, every day, for a year, to present his show – and no one noticed. 'No one has noticed, no one has given a fuck,' he told *The Age*, a year later.

Stefanovic told the newspaper that women are judged

'more harshly and keenly for what they do, what they say and what they wear. I'm judged on my interviews, my appalling sense of humour – on how I do my job, basically,' he said – explaining that he was prompted into his secret experiment after his female co-host, Lisa Wilkinson, gave a speech about sexism, and how often her choice of wardrobe while presenting attracted comment, or criticism.

Men – I congratulate you on The Suit. I genuinely think it's one of the reasons why you continue to enjoy, as a species, continued economic, business and political world domination: the thousands of hours you have spent *not* worrying about 'what to wear' has allowed you to found whole businesses, and run whole empires. Its absolute neutrality allows groups of you to bond, instantly – free of the disruptive 'Oh! That's a *sexy* dress!' pass-agg comments from a bunch of women who are all otherwise dressed in pantsuits. If you doubt me, simply start noticing what everyone is wearing in photographs of key UN meetings, diplomatic meetings, conferences and summits. It's just wall-to-wall suits – with the odd woman, in a red dress or blue skirt-suit, sticking out like a sore, uniform-less thumb.

The Suit says, 'We don't need to talk about what I'm wearing.' The Suit says, 'Listen to what I'm saying, instead.' The Suit says, 'Despite women being the gender that's "into clothes", men have won this particular category, outright.'

T-Shirts

Fairly observably, men tend not to wear bright colours. The colours for Man Clothes are black, brown, navy, blue and grey. Man Colours are essentially the same range you see in concrete, or aggregates. It is a bold and confident man who sports something in an acid-yellow, or adorable rose. 'Keep it simple, and muted' is the general vibe. I have gone on holidays with teenage boys, to the Mediterranean, where their sisters have lugged two huge suitcases full of all the colours of the rainbow, and in every style, cut, vibe and era. By way of contrast, the boys bought tiny carry-on cases, in which every item was purchased, the night before, from JD Sports, and everything – save a single white T-shirt – was made of black polyester sports-fabric.

The T-shirt, then, is the one area men are allowed to be creative. Particularly as that man gets older. By the time you're 40, your T-shirt collection is, to you, as your wife's lovingly collated wardrobe of second-hand Chanel, designer jeans and Zara brogues is to her.

Band T-shirts, slogan T-shirts, colourful T-shirts, T-shirts with swearing on, T-shirts that you can only buy from the back pages of *Viz*, like 'Breast Inspector', or 'Fart Loading – Please Wait' – the T-shirt is the one place where men who have otherwise given up or never engaged in fashion are allowed to express themselves.

Whether it's a band T-shirt so old it proves, without a shadow of a doubt, you really *were* into the Pixies before they started being used on mobile phone adverts; or a new

T-shirt that shows e.g. The Velvet Underground drawn as characters from *Scooby Doo* – thus showing you are 'playful' about popular culture, and also *exactly* between the ages of 35 and 55, for men, the T-shirt works by way of *both* a nipple-coverer, *and* a neat Tinder bio of your interests.

It is also, as we know, the one item of clothing that is in danger of provoking an aggressive reaction from other men. If you're wearing a Ramones T-shirt, you'd really better know your Ramones back catalogue – as you will almost certainly get some other dude coming up to you, at some point, and going, 'What's your favourite B-side, then?' If you don't want your T-shirt to write a cheque your mouth can't cash, *think* – before you press 'Buy' – 'Could I, in a crowded pub, during a quiz night, give a potted biography of the cultural phenomenon represented on this item?' Because unfortunately there will always be some ass-hat who will call you on it, and will not accept your *real* reason for wearing it: 'To be honest, this shade of blue really makes my eyes pop.'

Note: as is so often the case, a teenage girl has come up with the perfect response to this kind of man. My daughter's friend, Monica, was 15, and walking around Brent Cross in a Nirvana T-shirt – the classic one, with the picture of Kurt wearing eyeliner. Unfortunately yet inevitably, the T-shirt caught the eye of an on-duty member of the Culture Police – in this instance, a 21-year-old dude, hanging out with a couple of mates.

'Do you even know who Kurt Cobain *was*?' he asked her, sneeringly.

She just stared at him with the icy disdain that is the

greatest weapon of the teenage girl, and replied, 'I don't care. He's *fit*.'

There is, of course, no comeback from this. Cobain is fit. Whatever you *think* a T-shirt of Kurt Cobain from Nirvana is 'saying', ultimately, it's a T-shirt of someone who was really fit, and that's why so many people buy it. You'll note there are no T-shirts adorned with the face of Jeff Lynne from ELO – despite the fact he wrote *far* more bangers than Cobain.

While on the subject of older men, there is one area of clothing in which they are deemed, by women, to fail quite badly:

Disgusting Gym Gear

I'm not talking about *proper* gym gear: the sweat-wicking fabrics and Lycra shorts; the slightly weird-looking leggings; the mad cycling shorts with, seemingly, a cushion sewn into the bum.

No – I'm talking about the sizeable portion of the male population who 'don't believe' in buying 'fancy' gym gear, and 'make do' with a 'perfectly reasonable' outfit consisting of 'a pair of old shorts whose pocket lining has disintegrated, meaning your locker-key constantly falls out of them onto the running machine', and 'a T-shirt so ancient that ten years ago, it was demoted to "the T-shirt you wear while decorating the house", and which now leads an unearthly third existence as the emulsion-splattered T-shirt you wear to the gym'.

My husband has one of these – a T-shirt that might well have been orange in 1997, but which is now more of a 'consumptive peach' after multiple washings. It's so stretched and shapeless it resembles the tunic worn by the cartoon character Bod, from *Bod*, and there are six moth holes around the nipple area.

'It makes me run faster,' he insists, putting it on in the morning.

'Is it because "terrible social shame" makes you run faster?' I ask.

'No!' he replies, blithely ignoring me. 'I figured that it's the ventilation – from all the holes! I've got a through-breeze! All the air is keeping me *cool*. It's a waste of money to buy anything *fancy*, when this does the job *perfectly well.*'

If you also own just such an item, because of just such beliefs, you will probably be constantly surprised by how distressed it makes your girlfriend, or wife. You might even be annoyed when she keeps buying you 'proper, nice' gym gear for Christmas, or your birthday, when you've made it perfectly clear you really *like* this knackered old T-shirt, and want her to 'stop fussing'.

As part of my eternal duty in healing any and all rifts opened up by the Gender War, I'd like to explain to you why your woman keeps nagging on about this thing that really doesn't concern her at all. It's because it *does* concern her. Or, at least, she has been raised to think it does.

When 'your' man appears in public in something so 'vest of Shrek', it sends out a message to all the other women at the gym: 'This man is not being taken care of by his wife. She neglects him. Therefore, if you are single, and in the market for a new man, *this* dude is clearly six months away from a divorce. If you want to call dibs on him by the weights rack – go for it!'

It doesn't matter that this *isn't* what's happening in your marriage: to women, your horrible T-shirt is claiming that it *is*. Women are ever alert to what clothes *mean*. Your skronky, 'up for an affair' T-shirt will legit have been discussed by the woman on reception, *and* that female trainer with the nose-piercing. If the thought of being flirtatiously engaged by the water-bubble makes you anxious, I suggest you change your outfit, fast.

Just here to help.

Note: my husband read this entry just before going to the gym. Chastened, he silently changed out of the tattered, pale orange 'vest of Shrek' – and then put on his extremely worn, faded Harry Nilsson T-shirt, instead. I can't even begin to analyse how he receives information, and then actions it.

At first glance, then, it seems like – disgusting gym gear to one side – men have totally *aced* the whole 'wearing clothes' thing. Compared to women, they have generally avoided the whole 'fashion crisis', 'I have nothing to wear!', 'Don't look at those bags from Zara in the bottom of the wardrobe! I know now that the polka-dot romper suit was an error!' madness.

However, there is one area of clothing that I would suggest could do with a little more examination. For while huge amounts of men reap, with perfect contentment, the factual harvest that is 'the clothes of men' being quite straightforward, limited and practical, if slightly boring – there are, observably, those for whom this chafes.

Hallowe'en

Not just Hallowe'en, of course: but also stag nights, 'themed' events, trips to *The Rocky Horror Picture Show*, festivals and fancy-dress events in general.

The glee with which a huge number of straight men enjoy dressing up as vampires, ghosts, members of the Spice Girls, elves, pirates, vicars and/or Margaret Thatcher suggests one thing, very clearly: some men really do like to dress up in something weird, colourful, exciting, revealing, sexy, 'female', outright silly, or otherwise comment worthy. It's just that they live in a society where it's only 'safe' to do so on very certain, limited days, when it's guaranteed all the other men will be doing it as well.

I live near Alexandra Palace – where, during the winter of 2022/23, the Cazoo World Darts Championship was held. I've no exact idea how long the tournament lasted, but it seemed like, for a solid month, the W3 and W7 buses were *filled* with men dressed as penguins, traffic cones, naughty Santas, Teletubbies, 'Scousers' (black curly perm wig and moustache), sharks, lobsters, toreadors, Smurfs, Mario Brothers, hot-dogs and nannas.

Likewise, at Glastonbury, there is always a solid contingent of men dressed as fairies, lions, wizards, babies, characters from *Game of Thrones* and showgirls. Notably, more men than women. Notably.

Straight men, it seems, need a couple of day-release passes from their otherwise crushingly boring, normal, restrictive world of clothing. They can only tolerate being confined to suits, joggers and T-shirts if, a couple of times a year, they get to put on pink flares and stack-heeled gold boots to a 'Last Days of Disco'-themed party, and dress like, well, Harry Styles or Prince do when they put out the bins.

Interestingly, this 'straight men can only break the fashion rules when in a like-minded gang, three times a year, max' guideline seems to be heavily dictated by age and location. Gen Z and Gen A boys – and those in big cities – seem increasingly happy to wear a pearl earring; their girlfriends' trousers; a fake-fur coat or blouse. I live in London – so it's not that surprising that, during the 2022 summer heatwave, I saw dozens and dozens of young men wearing skirts, or dresses, when the weather became intolerably hot.

But then, in Solihull, I saw a young man walking around dressed exactly like the Joker in *Batman*. He wasn't on his way to a fancy-dress party – it was 2pm and he was feeding the ducks in Tudor Grange Park.

Younger men are starting, cautiously, to wear whatever they like – whether it's from the 'women's' section of a vintage shop, or the 'men's'. However, it's notable that, when I asked older men if they ever longed to try something new – wearing a kaftan on a hot summer's day, say; or lovely silver space-boots in the snow – they ummed and ahh-ed for ten minutes or so, before basically revealing that the idea scares them. They fear ridicule. They fear being different from the other men – or being presumed to be in the throes of a nervous breakdown.

And I thought how odd it is that men, who are so physically and socially dominant, could be 'scared' to try something new, and that gave them joy. As any woman will tell you, she has to carefully assess any and every outfit she wears, in case it attracts the kind of unwelcome attention that manifests in 'Oi! Tits McGee! Sit on my face!' being shouted out of a passing van; and then possibly having to run away from the Horrible Man in a pair of kitten heels that keep falling off. By way of contrast, men can wear eye-catching outfits without risking anything more than teasing from their mates. Half of whom might secretly be thinking, 'That off-the-shoulder buccaneer's blouse would *really* showcase my novel pec-tat of *The Goonies*.'

Men, you have a freedom that *you don't even know you aren't using*. If you are wearing tight, black, painful jeans, because 'That's what everyone is wearing' – even though, when you look in the mirror, they make you unhappy; *and* they are destroying your testicles – just remember how happy you were when you were dressed as a panda, watching the darts. And remember: *no* clothing should mash your bollocks up. Protecting your nads is a bare minimum. And talking of genitals . . .

Chapter Five

The Cocks and Balls of Men

Part One: Cocks

The first time I ever touched a penis was New Year's Eve, 1992. At 11.55pm, it became clear the boy I was getting off with next to the cigarette machine at the Silver Web nightclub, Wolverhampton, had got an erection. I suddenly realised, with a thrill, that if I put my hand in his trousers, and started wanking him off, *fast*, I could write 'First hand-job' in my diary, under 'List of Achievements in 1992' – a major entry to tick off with just five minutes of the year left to go.

I'll be honest – it wasn't one of history's finest sexual encounters. Unfortunately for Jeremy – that was his name – he was a fan of The Jam, which meant his jeans were very tight, so there wasn't much room for manoeuvre inside them. In this respect, Paul Weller has done a lot of young men a massive disservice, sexually. As we can see, this inability to be wanked off in a nightclub is yet another disadvantage of the overly tight jean.

The denim had clamped his cock tight to his right thigh – and with limited space, all I could really do was kind of 'make a fuss' with my hand until he came in his boxers. As it was my first wanking of a boy, I didn't know that, immediately after orgasm, the cock becomes incredibly sensitive, and basically wants to be left alone, to think about what it's done – and so I carried on cheerfully knob-wobbling away until he said, in an agonised voice, 'ARGH!', just as everyone started singing 'Auld Lang Syne' over The Wonder Stuff's 'Size of a Cow', which was the unexpected tune the DJ had chosen to ring in the new year.

As a modern gentleman, Jeremy then attempted to return the favour by putting his hand into my knickers – but, as I explained to him, I 'couldn't be arsed' to 'hang around' for the five minutes it would take me to come, so he stopped. We had a quick chat to see if there was any future for our relationship, before he revealed that he lived in Wightwick – which wasn't on a direct bus route from my house, and therefore made any potential partnership, sadly, unviable. He then also mentioned he had a girlfriend. Sarah. Oh, well. *She* didn't know about the unfaithfulness; *he'd* just come in his pants; and *I'd* achieved my Girl Guiding 'Wank' badge – so we were all, in a way, winners that night.

Despite the fact it had been a pretty patchy experience, I was still, nonetheless, elated by my first Penile Contact. A girl never forgets her first erection. There's something quite

magical about, essentially, a whole new body part manifest-
ing in a man's trousers, simply because he's looking at you,
and likes you. Even 'just' in the hand, I found it a very
pleasing thing: that night, as I'd always suspected I would
be, I became an instant fan of cocks. There's something
very *cheerful* about a stiffie: it has the positive, can-do, 'I
want to play' energy of a puppy; the contrast of soft skin
and rock-hard erection makes it one of the world's great
sensory playthings; and ejaculation is Nature's splendid
custard-y firework display. My ultimate review of cocks,
after my first experience? 'They're *fun.*'

As 1993 started, I remember lighting a cigarette, wiping
a stray bit of jizz off my hand onto my dress, and thinking,
with gleeful anticipation, 'So, cocks, then. That will be *the
first of many.*'

In the end, it turned out to be the first of 14. I have
touched 14 penises in my life. And this, weirdly, makes me
more of an expert on penises than most men – as most
straight men will only have ever touched one penis: their
own. Despite the fact that men are the guys who have the
penises, women often know far, far more about them than
men do. We're professional cock-wranglers. We are, over-
whelmingly, the people who first notice if men are having
medical problems with their genitalia, and who urge – or
nag – them into seeing a doctor. We are both far fonder of,
and more scared of, penises than you would ever know.

And we are now, thanks to feminism, so accustomed to
talking about our own genitalia – the vadge-chat never ends
at the Germaine Greer Community Hall for Wimmin! –
that it seems mysterious, and puzzling, to us that men don't

ever really talk about their cocks. Not *real* conversations – like what they're scared of; what they like about them; what they've vaguely repulsed by; what's happened to them; how to take care of them. 'Do you talk to your male friends about your cock?' I asked my male friends. Every single one said, immediately, and in tones of great horror, 'NO. NEVER. JESUS CHRIST. THAT WOULD BE UNTHINKABLE.'

By way of contrast, I think I know every single thing that has happened to the vaginas of my girlfriends, daughters and sisters. I could write you their biographies. I have helped get stuck tampons out of them; I have talked them through cystitis; I know exactly how many stitches they have in them; and I know which men make them wet, and which ones 'make them sandy, and close up like a clam'.

I'm always astonished by how little men know about their most iconic body parts. I once fucked a man and, the next day, casually mentioned the difference between circumcised and non-circumcised penises, 'because you're circumcised'.

'*Am* I?' he asked, wonderingly.

'Er, *yes*,' I said.

'*Huh*,' he said, thoughtfully – before recalling that his mother had said something 'vague' and mysterious about his penis 'needing an operation' when he was younger, and that he would 'find out about it' when he was older.

'I guess that day has come,' he said, musingly. 'So – what do cocks *usually* look like?' he then asked, looking down at his own. I ended up drawing him a picture of someone wearing a polo-neck jumper.

He was 27.

Perhaps it's the lack of cock merch that left him so in the dark. In the twenty-first century, women can buy beautifully embroidered vulvas to sew onto their clothes; wear T-shirts with artful, feminist depictions of the fanny; hang Georgia O'Keeffe's fleshy, folded flower prints on their walls. We tell each other, constantly, to rejoice in our minges – we tell our daughters to be proud of how beautiful they are. But imagining an equivalent for men, or teenage boys, seems – demented? Threatening? Obscene? That has to do something strange to the male psyche – to regard the penis as some mad Trouser Voldemort, which must never be mentioned, or seen, let alone loved. Something which must always be kept hidden away, even if you are with other penis-owners. *Especially* if you are with other penis-owners.

I often wonder how I would have coped having teenage sons, instead of teenage daughters. Together, my girls and I have made endless jokes about our vulvas – while also taking care of them, learning about them and feeling proud of them. Would my imaginary son and his father have done the same with their dicks? Even though we are in the chatty, over-sharing twenty-first century, I'm not sure the vocabulary is there yet. I don't think they would have known how to begin to address the physical and cultural aspects of being born with a penis. Yeah, sure – *rich* guys get to pay homage to their dicks by building massive, penis-shaped skyscrapers, or rockets that look like penises, or buying penis-extension cars – and we all take the piss out of them for it. But what about most normal, non-millionaire guys, and their normal relationships with their normal willies? There is no low-cost, lovely way to ponder upon and represent *their* cocks, such as e.g. holistic, woo-woo 'make your own macrame genitalia' evening classes.

Of course, I know there are *lots* of men who are now going, 'Er, Caitlin, it's nice you're trying – but I don't really feel the need to talk about my willy, or write a song about it, or wear a badge with an Impressionistic portrait of it on, thanks. I don't want to make a fuss about it, or even particularly think about it. If I started talking about my penis in the way women talk about their vaginas – even on chat shows, now! And in Parliament! – all my friends would think I had lost my goddamn *mind*.'

But there's a cost to this, of course. Only 25 per cent of men with erectile dysfunction seek medical treatment. Four in ten cases of prostate cancer are only detected when they reach stage three or four. Thirty per cent of men are unhappy about the size of their penises. Dr Alicia Walker, who attempted a study of links between mental health and penis size, told *Vice*: 'I've talked to men who haven't been to the doctor for a physical in over a decade, because they don't want to be naked in front of their doctor. I've talked to men who have never even approached anyone for a romantic relationship, because they don't believe anyone would be interested in them because of their penis size. I've talked to men who have attempted suicide because of their penis size.'

As anyone in the feminist movement could tell you, there is never anything to be gained by being too embarrassed to talk about your body. Wherever there is a silence or taboo, there will, *always*, be people – young and old – enduring fear, or misery, or 'just' a lifetime of feeling sub-optimal, or 'not normal'.

There must be a saner halfway house between boys and men either never talking about their winkies – or else, the flipside: being part of that small, dark cohort that flashes women in the park, or sends endless dick-pics. Cocks are simultaneously the most secret, and least secret, thing about men. So, oh my God, *why* aren't you talking about them? Women are talking about them *all the time*. Honestly, you wouldn't believe how much we discuss your penises. Here's Everything We Know About Cocks, and Have Always Wanted to Discuss With Men.

First of all, let's start with the biggie: bigness. One of the eternal facts about men seems to be that, when it comes to penises, it's presumed the more, the merrier.

Not in *number*, I hasten to clarify – very few men feel insecure about having fewer than two penises. But in volume – both length, and 'girth', which is a word only ever used when referring to a) penises and b) the belly of a horse – the general rule of thumb seems to be 'to infinity and beyond'. You just can't have *too much* cock. A man with a big wanger has just crossed one 'reason to feel sad' off his list; and a man with a small penis must do everything in his power to conceal the smallness of his penis, lest public knowledge of it become a (small) stick with which to beat him.

In this respect, cocks are like houses – most people

presume you could never have one that's 'too big'. Big = winner. You want a mansion in your pants. A castle in your long johns. And this is because, somehow, penis size has become inextricably caught up with the perception of how successful, noble, smart and sexy a man is – we are a society that still thinks a man's cock is, somehow, part of a man's *character*. Remember how, when Stormy Daniels infamously alleged that Donald Trump's penis is 'smaller than average – a dick like the mushroom character in *Mario Kart*', the world went, 'Yes – it makes sense the horrible man has a small, weird, mushroom penis,' and Trump immediately had to open a Republican live debate in Detroit by saying, 'I *guarantee* you – *there's no problem.*' But everyone was still like, 'Trump has a terrible, tiny penis. We knew it. Of course he does. That's *justice.*'

Logically, of course, these prejudices and beliefs are both awful, and make no sense. Assuming that only a bad, or weak, person would be born with a small or ingloriously average penis has its roots in medieval thinking, where it was presumed that you would only be born with e.g. cerebral palsy if God was punishing you, or your parents, for sinfulness. We talk about small cocks as if every baby boy was visited, in the cradle, by an unpleasant Tiny Cocks Witch, who *cursed* him.

This belief persists despite the fact that, statistically, 68 per cent of men's cocks are not very big: between three and four inches, on the flop – meaning that approximately two-thirds of *Ocean's 11* have lovely, yet modest, wangers; at least two of The Beatles were packing mere hand-luggage; and seven out of ten male comedians you see on *Live at the*

Apollo have ample material to do a routine about not having ample material. And yet they prefer to just do 'observational' comedy about supermarket-checkout queues, or not being allowed to say the 'n' word, instead. Comedians, musicians and actors are ignoring a *massive* market of men with similarly sized penises, crying out for someone to represent them. Who will be the Average-Sized-Penis Jesus who first speaks out on this taboo? I'd like to think that future glory and worship awaits that bold pioneer.

And there will be one – I don't doubt that. For the female comedians, actresses, writers and pop stars who have recently mined all the equally taboo stuff on female genitalia have, with their jokes and candour, allowed these subjects to become part of perfectly normal, if amusing, conversations for millions of women across the world. When, in 2013, Lily Allen opened the big-vagina floodgates by performing 'Hard Out Here' under balloons that spelled out 'LILY ALLEN HAS A BAGGY PUSSY', it was something *just as unthinkable* for women to admit to as a man admitting he has a non-epic penis. And the two issues are kind of related. Let's face it – the reason Lily Allen was the first, to my knowledge, to admit she had a 'baggy' vagina, is the presumption that the bigger the fanny, the shitter the shag. Women want to say it's *tight* down there – that you have a tiny, dainty fairy's fanny; like a mouse's ear. No one wants to hear that sex with *their* vagina is 'like chucking a sausage up Oxford Street'. We fear being dubbed with the Order of the Wizard's Sleeve.

Men's fear of having a small willy comes from the same fear – *you* don't want to be the sausage being chucked up

Oxford Street. If you're banging Oxford Street, you want to be the Megabus, right? Or one of those big carnival floats, with a steel band on it.

So much straight male and female fear, and sadness, about their genitals comes from it being presumed that every fanny should be tiny, and every wanger should be huge – despite the achingly obvious fact that both sets of sex-kit come in every shape and size, *and there's nothing you can do about it*.

This belief is a recent, Western problem. In the *Kama Sutra* – infamous as the oldest Rude Book in the world – the authors are very matter-of-fact about genitals coming in a Variety Pack. The whole text is informed by the chapter which lays out, with perfect obviousness, the varying sizes of wangers and noonies: women are categorised as either 'doe' (small fanny), 'cow' (medium fanny) or 'elephant' (large fanny); while men are either 'hare', 'bull' or 'horse'.

Of course, when I first read the *Kama Sutra* at the age of 16, I was *horrified* by the idea I might have an elephant fanny – so indoctrinated as I was into the Western denial of fannies being any larger than, ideally, a tear duct. Similarly, I couldn't imagine ever meeting a man who admitted to having a rabbit cock. In 1991, I was dumber and less sexually enlightened than the authors who were writing in 400 BCE.

And I wasn't the only one – it took until the release of *Magic Mike XXL*, in 2015, for there to be a mainstream movie in which the wisdom of the *Kama Sutra* made it to the screen, with the character of Big Dick Richie (a 'horse', I think we can safely presume – maybe even a 'whale'), despairing over all the women he's tried to sleep with being either does or cows. To be brisk – it doesn't fit. No woman is willing to take on the health and safety risk of trying to back Big Dick Richie into *her* space, and Big Dick Richie is in despair.

'Maybe it's like Cinderella, and the glass slipper,' Mike suggests, romantically, as Big Dick looks utterly woebegone. 'You just need to find *the right one*.'

Three-quarters of the way through the film, Big Dick meets Andie MacDowell – an actress who deserves a Lifetime Pioneering Achievement Award, purely and simply for being the first A-list actress to play a character openly in possession of an elephant fanny.

'You found your glass slipper!' Big Dick Richie's friends rejoice, the morning after he and MacDowell get it on. Well, *in*.

However bold *Magic Mike XXL* is, however, we note that it was only bold enough to address elephant fannies. Not even funny, handsome, confident Channing Tatum had the literal balls to give one of his male heroes a hare penis. And yet, billions of them exist, *right now*, being perfectly normal and lovely, having amazing sex, being loved by both their owners and all who encounter them. When, I wonder, will the first King of the Hare Penises announce himself, and lead his people to freedom?

I hate to admit this, but one of the stumbling blocks to this happy day is: women. We like to come across all genitally liberated, and kind to men – 'It's not what you've got, it's what you do with it!' we say, and we mean it: it is true. A big penis is in *no way* a guarantee of a good shag.

But then, catch us on a bad day, where we're being really unpleasant, heartbroken bitches, and we are absolutely part of the problem. For one of the Big, Eternal Gender Crimes committed by women is the Post Break-Up Penis Trashing.

'. . . And I'm *glad* he dumped me, because he'd keep cancelling dates to watch football with all the curtains drawn; and he'd always put the Big Light on in the front room, instead of turning all the lovely little lamps on; and he was drunk on my mother's birthday – AND HE HAD AN ABSOLUTELY TINY COCK!'

In the weeks, and sometimes months, after a break-up, women will almost always accuse their ex of having a tiny penis. Sometimes they just do it to their friends – 'It was *microscopic*, and also really thin? Like a witch's finger?' – and sometimes, they involve their ex.

'YOU HAD THE TINIEST COCK I'VE EVER FUCKED,' she might text him, probably a bit drunk, as the couple wrangle over who gets to keep the IKEA foot-stool (joint purchase). Often, it sorrows me to say, women will screech it at ex-boyfriends *in public* – at parties, in front of friends. Sometimes, in front of his new girlfriend: 'And I hope *you* can find his penis, babe. I heard rumours it was buried *somewhere* in the folds near his balls – but I never made visual confirmation myself.'

If you have been on the receiving end of one of these Small Cock Accusations, first of all, I'm so sorry. My people – women – should not be saying this to your people – men. We would be full of righteous feminist outrage if ex-boyfriends regularly marched up to us at parties, bellowing 'YOUR FANNY WAS THE SIZE OF A BADGER HOLE – JUST SAYING', or texted us pictures of e.g. the Large Hadron Collider, captioned: 'Your minge'. By and large, thank God, men just don't do this.

If this *has* happened to you, it might have left you thinking, '*Do* I have a small penis? She never said it was while we were still going out? I *think* I'm perfectly normal. But oh God, now I'm worried. I mean, compared to the guys in pornos, obviously, it's microscopic. OH GOD NOW I'M WORRIED ABOUT MY PENIS.'

Men: please don't worry about your penis. First of all, as we've already discussed, if you do have a small penis, it really, really doesn't matter anyway. But, secondly, you must know this about ex-girlfriends: they tell *every* ex-boyfriend that they have a small penis. It's an unthinking part of modern break-up rituals – as standard as 'setting fire to all his possessions', 'getting drunk with girlfriends', 'eating ice cream while watching *Pretty Woman* and angry-crying' and 'getting a sassy new, slightly-too-short haircut.' Women do it *automatically*. They do it about *penises that were actually so big they gave them recurrent cystitis*. I can assure you, half the girlfriends I've heard tearfully screaming 'AND HIS COCK WAS TINY!' were telling me, four weeks earlier, that they could only get three-quarters of it in, 'because any further, and it feels like it's coming out of my eyes'.

Women just say this because it's the easiest way to hurt you or humiliate you publicly – and the quickest, too. If you're on a tight break-up schedule of 'smoking, drinking and crying', it's far easier to shout 'DWARF COCK!' in a Wetherspoon's than it is to list the complex reasons why you were both, in the end, fundamentally incompatible. It feels like a modern, edgy, liberated thing to do – like something one of the *Sex and the City* girls would shout – rather than what it is: a literal dick move.

But it does also give you an interesting insight into straight women's sexual psychology – a phenomenon I call Schrödinger's Dick. When a woman loves you, her eyes, brain and fanny add *at least* two inches onto your cock. She is telling *everyone* you've got Moby-Dick in your pants.

But when a woman hates you, her eyes, brain and fanny take three inches, minimum, off your knob. In an on/off relationship, your penis will be, simultaneously, to a woman, absolutely massive, *and* pathetically tiny, depending on how she feels at the time, and what day it is.

I hope this information is useful to you – as I have just given away one of the Big Secrets of Being a Woman. You're welcome.

Part Two: Balls

When it comes to men ever starting to talk about their cocks, I feel like the gateway drug might be – balls?

Because they're the more accessible genital character, right? Like, they're *funny*. If the cock is the swaggering, slightly dumb action hero, balls are his nebbish, humorous sidekick. They are Baldrick to Blackadder; Penfold to Dangermouse; Harry and Ron to the main event that is Hermione.

In a movie called *Inside Men's Trousers: The Movie*, the

role of 'Balls' would definitely be played by Jonah Hill, or James Corden. Balls would be slightly cowardly ('Oh no! Danger! I'm *retracting*!') – they're the character who, as soon as they get hit in a fight, fall to the floor, and cry out, 'It's okay! Go on without me!' Balls turns up hungover at the wedding and loses the rings; Balls wakes up in Vegas not knowing what happened; Balls gets mistaken for an international crime lord – with *hilarious* results.

But you're always on Balls' side: everyone knows, underneath it all, Balls has a heart of gold. While Penis is feared by many, everyone's got a soft spot for good old Balls. If you were feeling sad, you'd be knocking on Balls' door for a hug.

Because balls are so harmless, non-controversial and funny, and men will talk about anything *so long as they know how to be funny about it* (see: 'Bantz'), the difference between 'conversations about penises' and 'conversations about balls' is like night and day.

When I started writing this chapter, I went into the Twenty-First-Century Saloon bar that is Twitter, and asked men how they feel about their balls. 'I get the feeling you find them funny?' I said. 'Tell me how you feel about your balls.'

Honestly, what followed was almost revelatory. It seems that if you ask modern men how they feel about their balls, they are able to describe them with astonishing flair: like a cross between James Joyce and Eddie Izzard. Turns out, men have been thinking about their balls *a lot*. They have pondered just what they are, their appearance, their significance, their function and their emotional role in the lives of men.

The most notable aspect is how men seem daily astonished by the impracticality of their testicles. They find them to be a . . . *backwards* technology.

@TheKevBrown: 'The ballsack is a catastrophic design flaw. The equivalent of hanging a car's battery under the front bumper – in a Tesco carrier bag. The slightest glancing blow and it's game over.'
@happygilmour71: 'They're essentially that wee hole in the back of a Sontaran head. They have an important purpose – but invariably they're "Achilles balls", and just render you unable to function if someone hits them with a ping pong ball.'
@JohnERhino: 'The prime tenet of evolution is surviving long enough to breed. Yet the essential elements needed are dangling in the wind ready to be cut, crushed or lost in a fight. It makes no sense.'
@NRoolz: 'The positioning is also at the top of an inverted V of the legs – so that any object moving upwards between the legs is guided towards them. THIS IS DANGEROUS. It would be better if they were on top of the head – so they could be covered with a sturdy hat.'

There were solid suggestions for a future upgrade. @Cknagg1: 'I have a female friend who feels that male genitalia should be hidden away, and winched down when required – allowing a more *streamlined* look to be achieved.'
However, despite their thunderous impracticality, when it comes to describing their testicles, men come across like

an awestruck, yet slightly repulsed David Attenborough, staring into their own pants.

@dvnam: 'Reclining in a hot bath after a cold walk, I'm always fascinated to find the skin on mine slowly morphing from "angry walnut", to "hippy pancake". It moves like a snail performing Tai Chi under a gastropod blanket.'

@royston_vassey: 'When they get hot and clammy, they stick to your legs, and resemble bat's wings.'

@FilthyJeesus: 'Mine look like an elderly naked mole rat reversing into a bush, carrying a bag of giblets.'

@TheHumbleEgg: 'Old bollocks are quite grotesque when they've greyed up, and withered in age. Like two little tribute turns: one to Don King, one to Freddie Boswell outta *Bread* . . .'

@mark_woodroffe had a more positive, sexy take: 'Their delicate form makes them erotic; like hanging hairy clits . . .'

But all the men were unanimous in how fond they were of their balls, and their unexpected extra utility, on top of carrying sperm:

@TonyWeb80791059: 'They are perfectly placed for having a quick scratch at when you are waiting for a thought to turn up.'

@sloughnan: 'All men love, and I mean REALLY love their balls. We cup them, squeeze, scratch, flick them – it's like smoking. We just cannot think of life without them – they are our tits. Hope this helps.'

And, as a casual observer of the opposite sex, I have noticed this to be absolutely true. Testicles seem to be the ultimate executive stress toy – to be manipulated whenever a man is caught deep in thought.

I once interviewed Robbie Williams in his penthouse suite in Chelsea, and he spent most of the interview with his hands down the front of his joggers, juggling his clackers throughout. It was absolutely non-sexual – he seemed to be doing it in the same way a toddler will play with a Duplo train set while cheerfully talking about their day at nursery.

I often wonder if the popularity of jogging bottoms is partly to do with the fact that their elasticated waist, and general roominess, allow for modern men to access their balls very easily, in those moments where they find them comforting to hold. Now we can't smoke in public places, they seem to be the substitute. On the top decks of buses, for instance, hordes of young men will shout at each other while unselfconsciously 'shuffling' their nads.

For anyone else using the bus, there is the unhappy knowledge that every rail you touch or pole you grip will also have been touched by these boys – and that a fine layer of what we might call 'bollock-mist' lies upon every sur-face. Is that better or worse than inhaling secondary smoke? I can't tell.

However, perhaps my favourite encomium on behalf of testicles came – unexpectedly – from a woman.

@rachael_k_owen: 'If you've ever changed a baby boy's nappy, you'll know that they serve as a beautiful little weather station! And then you can dress baby accordingly.'

The fact that Rachel sounded like Mary Poppins while saying this – 'Oh, baby's balls have gone in! Looks like snow! I'll pop a thermal nappy on – spit spot!' makes it all the more delightful.

Personally, I like how . . . *emotional* balls are. They're very *reactive*. I once spent a very idle – okay, stoned – afternoon, talking to my husband's testicles, and seeing how they reacted to my varying chats. When conversing with them in a relaxed and loving manner, they would almost *bloom* with joy – relaxing and spreading out, as if feeling very secure. When I shouted at them, however – 'You mad bags of jizz! What are you *playing* at?' – they rippled in horror, and then tried to withdraw from the conversation entirely. It reminded me of a documentary I once watched about cuttlefish, who kaleidoscope through different colours and textures, dependent on their mood. You know – if you went to the London Aquarium and saw a pair of nads floating around, or trying to hide from a tuna, under a rock, you wouldn't be at all surprised. I'd spend a long time standing outside that tank. If there were sessions where you could feed them, by hand – like rays – I'd be right in there with my bag of ball-food. I think they're adorable.

I think what I'm trying to say is, I'm glad men have such an honest and ribald relationship with their own testicles – 'They're like a brother to me,' as one man said – but, psychologically, I do feel that penises need now to be brought into the fold, and shown a bit of the banter and affection balls are. After all, as the ultimate emblem of manhood, it is a bit bizarre that women are the ones who see all the penises, discuss all the penises, make public pronouncements on which ones are 'good' and 'bad', and are the people who urge their owners to seek medical help, when they look a bit 'peaky'. My classic test for 'Is there some sexism afoot?' is always to imagine a situation with the genders flipped: and if we consider a world where women never talk about their vulvas, and it was *men* who discussed them with their friends, over-saw their medical treatment, and drunkenly screeched about how 'huge' and 'baggy' they were, women would be outraged. Reclaim your knobs, dudes! Otherwise, it seems you're a bit . . . scared, or ashamed of them, and that is neither physically nor mentally healthy.

One day, a man will come along who will start The Conversation About Normal Penises. And, hopefully, *he* will be the person who then gets sent all the dick-pics. For research purposes. For – finally – the *right* reason to send someone a picture of your dick.

Chapter Six

The Sex of Men

I would say that, for the first 25 years, minimum, of my life, I lied about sex, whenever I was talking to men about it.

What's more, I would say most young women do, too.

Why? Well, before I had sex, I never wanted to admit I was a virgin – so when I did 'dirty talk', it was always based on stuff I'd seen, or read, or heard about. I was basically bullshitting, in order to look more experienced. As everyone does.

And then, once I *had* started shagging around, I didn't want to . . . ruin the evening. If it looked like I was on for a shag, I didn't want to say anything that would put the situation into peril. A man indicated he was into anal sex, or spanking, or threesomes? Well, what a coincidence – that was what *I* was into, too! Let's go back to your place!

Of course, at the time, it wasn't *strictly* a lie: I had never tried those things before, so – maybe I *was* into them! This was my opportunity to find out! Let's go!

And then, when I tried them, if I *didn't* like them: well, maybe it would be different with someone else!

I rarely, if ever, said what *I* was actually into. Partly because I didn't know. I just hadn't tried that much stuff! And partly in case . . . they were the *wrong* things. Too much. Too dark. Or too needy.

Or just – which was usually the case – too boring, and normal. A young woman does not want to be known as 'sexually boring'.

Boys, and men, do this too, of course. At the beginning of our sexual adventures, *none* of us really know what we *actually* like: we have fantasies, and preferences, but it takes actually *doing* them to find out if they're as good in real life as they were in your head.

Some of the things work out best when they stay in your head.

Others are a total success.

Some work with some lovers, but not with others.

Some you feel too embarrassed, or too ashamed, or *too much*, to ever admit. Until you find someone into that, too. It's all an experiment.

But what I'm saying is, young, single, horny women – the ones, presumably, you are looking for, when you are a young, single, horny man – are *never* going to be honest to you about *everything* they think about sex, because: they want to have sex with you. And so they don't want to look weird, scare you, or make you so sad your erection dies. They're going to say what they think you want to hear.

They're going to say the lines they've heard countless Cool Girls – on *Love Island*, in clubs, in movies – say. *They're only going to tell a horny truth that there's a horny buyer for.*

Whereas I, on the other hand, am a 48-year-old married hag. And so although I probably *do* want to have sex with you, I've signed a legally binding contract with my husband promising I won't, and so I have nothing to lose by telling you all the *truly* honest stuff about sex that young women have been telling me for *decades*, often while drunk, or on MDMA, and definitely *not* wanting to have sex with me – and so which I know is the *actual* truth: the stuff women want men to know about sex, but are too scared to tell you. Let's go:

ONE. Women *are* as horny as men. Indeed, women are actually *hornier* than men: the 2009 book *What Do Women Want?* quoted research that found straight women became aroused not only when watching straight pornography – but also when watching footage of gay men having sex, lesbians having sex, and monkeys having sex. Monkey see, *lady* do.

Straight men, on the other hand, did *not* get aroused by the monkeys, or the gay men – although they loved the lesbians. Straight men's sexual menu is, then, smaller. By and large, as the research suggests, they just . . . want to fuck women. They *love* fucking women. They have a sexual shopping list with one item on it. Indeed, I remember, with fondness, a conversation I had with a man at the point it was obvious we were about to leave the party, and bang.

'So – what's going to happen next?' I asked. 'Sub? Dom? Rope-play? Golden showers? Naughty schoolboy and strict matron? Octopuses? Feathering? Muppets? What are you into?'

Only for him to reply, with a look of delirious, joyful simplicity: '*Fannies.* I'm into *fannies.*'

Collectively, women can get turned on by *anything* – a fact that is borne out by one friend who genuinely fancies St Paul's Cathedral ('Imagine bumping into it in a bar. You *know* it knows what to do'), and the more 'colourful' magazines are frequently filled with stories of women who have 'married', and claim to have had sex with, chandeliers, the Eiffel Tower, the Berlin Wall, a briefcase, teapots and ghosts.

The female sexual imagination is wild: a quick flick through Nancy Friday's *My Secret Garden*, a collection of women's sexual fantasies, sees women getting off on the idea of being robots, a cloud, or a giantess lying on her back, legs spread, with whole armies of tiny men marching into her vagina. Women are into a bunch of shit you'll never see on PornHub. Women are *freaky*. There aren't even names for a lot of the stuff they're into – they're just personal, weird dreams in their heads, which they often don't admit to *anyone*.

On top of this, let's admit a fact: women can fuck all night. After orgasm, we don't need to wait for our genitals to regenerate, like a penile Doctor Who. We can come, come again, and then come again. We are remorseless climax machines. The female world record for 'most orgasms in an hour' is 134. 134! For men? 16. And I think we're *all* surprised about that 16. I presume that dude had both Viagra and cock-splints. Literally fair fucks to him.

So women are both more sexually omnivorous than men, and physically capable of more sex. Why, then – despite all the progress and 'WAP' and 'ladettes' and work to destroy the concept of 'slut-shaming' – is there still a perception that it's men who are 'the sex people'?

After all, they're *presumed* to be the ones who want it more: they're the ones whose tastes define the pornography industry (every category is a kind of woman! MILF, Asian, Teen! It's presumed no *women* are looking for *men* on those websites – there is no 'Mark Ruffalo looking adorable' category!); the ones buying the realistic sex-dolls.

As a sex, men want sex so much *more* than women that there is a whole, multibillion-dollar worldwide industry, in order for them to pay for it when they want it. Again, using the broadest of brushstrokes, sex is a thing men have to *get* from women. They need to plan, and campaign, or use 'lines', or pursue. Or get their credit card out.

'No straight man could ever say, with 100 per cent certainty, that he is going to get laid tonight,' as my friend Toby used to say, ruefully. 'Whereas any woman – *any* woman – can get laid just like *that*. Demand outstrips supply.'

Why?

TWO. Here's the big, life-defining statistic every woman knows: in the UK, one in four women will be raped or sexually assaulted (in the US, the stats are one in five), and 90 per cent of those assaults are committed by a man she knows. A friend, someone she's just been on a date with, someone at work, someone at a party. By and large, your rapist is *not* waiting for you at the end of a dark alleyway at 2am. Instead, you have his number in your phone. Perhaps – and this is the bit that breaks my heart – you did, at some point, quite like him. Until he assaulted you.

If there was one – just one! – thing I could convey to men, above all else; if you take *nothing* else from this book, I beg that it is this: that you consider those statistics for just one minute, and then realise the biggest possible truth about women: we are so scared. *So* scared.

We are scared.

The toughest thing about being a heterosexual woman is that the thing that, very often, we love the most – that you are bigger than us; your beautiful strong hands; the solidity of your arms; the weight of your body on top of us; your cock; the fact you want, so badly, to fuck us – is also the thing we are most scared of. Terrified. As Louise Perry put it in her recent book, *The Case Against the Sexual Revolution*, 'Adult women are approximately half as strong as adult men in the upper body, and two thirds as strong in the lower body. In short – almost all men can kill almost all women with their bare hands – but not vice versa.'

Or, as a famous comedy routine had it: 'The courage it takes for a woman to say yes [to a date] is beyond anything I can imagine. How do women still go out with guys, when you consider that there is no greater threat to women – than *men*? Globally and historically, we're the *number one cause* of injury and mayhem to women. We're the worst thing that *ever* happens to them. Men, you know what *our* number one threat is? Heart disease. If you're a guy, just imagine – for a minute – if you could only date a gigantic half-bear, half-lion. "Oh, I hope this one is nice! I hope he doesn't do what he's statistically likely to do!"'

It's the perfect encapsulation of the risk straight women have to confront every time they are alone with men. Of course, *most* men aren't rapists! *Most* men are just nervous, or horny, or in love. The problem is – *there is absolutely no way of knowing which are the good ones, and which are the bad ones.* None at all. Which ones are going to be your future husband – and which ones are going to be your future court case. In the pub, at that wedding reception, in the night-club, at the after-work drinks: we cannot know if you're one of the the Good Ones – or one of the Bad Ones. There is such a thing as Female Intuition, but we're not actually magic. A history of heterosexual rape could be called, were the author the owner of a very dark yet realistic sense of humour, *Oh God – Not You?* As the Jimmy Carr joke about rape goes, rape is 'just' 'surprise sex'. The most painful, frightening, humiliating, disease-spreading, vagina-tearing, life-ruining surprise. Of course we did not *dream* you would ever rape us. We did not have 'Rape?' written on our calendar for this day. We thought we were safe with you. We thought you were . . . something else.

As a case in point, the comedian who came up with that classic riff about mayhem, and bears – a guy who was, for years, hailed as 'the most feminist man in comedy' – was Louis C.K., who was later revealed to be a serial abuser of women: trapping them in their dressing rooms and wanking himself off in front of them. The feminist guy who pointed out that men are a threat? He was a threat, too.

Margaret Atwood: 'Men are afraid that women will laugh at them. Women are afraid that men will kill them.'

Oh, men – women want to be as sexually open and free and spontaneous and hungry as you. There are hot summer nights where we want to run down the street screaming, 'I AM A LADY SEX-PIRATE! I WANT TO DO ALL THE THINGS!' But the one thing bigger than our libidos is our fear. Do you know how *brave* girls have to be to go back to the house of a new lover – when she has almost certainly had to counsel a weeping friend who was assaulted after doing *that very thing*? One in 16 American women's first ever sexual encounter is rape. Half of the women who *have* been raped have been raped more than once.

I hope some of the behaviour you might have observed in women that – at the time – mystified you, now makes a little more sense. Why that woman rebuffed your stuttering chat-up line in the pub; why she refused your offer of a drink; why she 'prick-teased' you with a kiss – then suddenly 'went cold'. If the *tiniest* thing scares us; jars; alarms; seems weird – we will back away, from self-preservation. The only thing we want more – on a hot summer night – than to have sex, is to feel safe.

I think it would astonish you to know how much women talk about rape, and fear, when they are alone together. How *many* of the women you know have awful stories. One in four women being raped or sexually assaulted: that's your mothers, your sisters, your nans. Your teachers and your neighbours and the women you see on TV. Your pop-heroes and your favourite celebrities.

Actually, I *know* how astonished you would be to hear

these stories, because when #metoo and, in the UK, the Sarah Everard case, hit social media, and women – in their millions – started posting their stories, the response from the Good Men was the same: 'Oh God, I didn't *know*. Why didn't you tell me? I had no idea.'

And the women were equally astonished because we realised, oh, yes. You're right. We *didn't* tell you. We *have* never talked about this in front of men before. We thought it was just something women discussed, between them-selves. It never occurred to us to tell you. I guess we didn't want to make you sad? Or worried? Or . . . feel guilty? We don't want men to feel bad about men. Oh, men, we love you so much. We don't want to tell our 13-year-old sons that some of his friends will grow up to be rapists! But we do start warning our 13-year-old girls to . . . be *careful*.

And that is one huge difference between the World of Girls and the World of Boys, right there. Some of the first information we have to give our young girls – to let them know the statistics, and the truth, and so keep safe – will make them scared of boys.

But we do not tell our boys how scared girls are of them.

There's a weird sense of protecting boys' innocence – or not making them feel guilty on behalf of their gender? – that does us, ultimately, no good at all.

Because, as we're about to see, fear of rape goes both ways.

THREE. False rape allegations. If we do not tell our boys how scared girls are of them, then we do not tell our girls how scared boys are of *them*, either.

For, aside from a fear of violence – of being in a fight, or being stabbed – the thing that came up, over and over, from the young boys, and men, that I talked to, was this: the fear of having sex with a woman, *they* believed consensually – only for her to subsequently accuse them of assault, or rape.

This fear appears monstrous to young men. They clearly feel they, or their friends, are constantly at risk of being lied about by a woman – and seeing their social circle, reputation and life destroyed in an instant. And destroyed in a way that there is no defence against.

'I know a boy it happened to – now I'm terrified it will happen to me,' one said. 'He had to leave the school – he had a nervous breakdown. His life is ruined.'

'There's no way you can prove it didn't happen – and people are more likely to believe the woman than the man.'

'Even if they don't go to the police, if the rumour spreads around school, or the people you know, that's it: you'd always be known as a rapist.'

'I think about it all the time. Even when I'm talking to a girl, and I think she likes me, I'm thinking: "What will you say about this tomorrow? Do I need to get a witness?"'

I absolutely understand why young men – some of them still basically boys – are terrified of this. There are very few things it is worse to be accused of than being a rapist – a sexual criminal – and there *are* very few ways, ultimately, for you to prove your innocence. Which is an utterly petrifying thing to know – especially when you are very young, and inexperienced. Fancying people; talking to a girl; having sex – these are already things that make you feel vulnerable, and open to ridicule if it goes wrong. To additionally be panicked that the whole thing could result in being accused, put on trial and jailed, and/or put on a Sexual Offenders List – it's not the ideal mindset to be in as you get up the nerve to kiss someone for the first time. It's like living on the edge of a nightmare.

Although every boy I spoke to knew 'someone, who knew someone' who had been falsely accused of rape or sexual assault, all I can do is note a few facts. Firstly, the latest statistics suggest that only between 2 per cent and 4 per cent of rape cases that made it to court were found to have been false allegations. Or, as the Channel 4 'Fact Checking' service put it, bleakly, in 2018, 'Men are far more like to be raped, than to be falsely accused of rape.' Hardly an ultimately comforting thought, but one that does give some perspective. These are very small numbers.

However, the boys and men worried about false rape allegations weren't really worried about accusations that made it to the police – as they didn't know anyone who'd *actually* been reported to the police. Instead, all the lives they knew that had been ruined had been ruined, instead, by *gossip*. Stuff that never made it to the police. False allegations that had been spread – by whispers, and rumour – around their school, or social circle. It's easy for a girl to just say something to a friend. Out of anger, or spite. And then suddenly, *wham!* Everyone you know is talking about it. Everyone is taking sides. And there's literally nothing you can do to prove your innocence.

The awful truth is this: ultimately, there *is* no way to

stop a girl or woman just *lying* about you. In the same way there's no way you can stop *any* human lying about you. This is one of the dolorous facts of being human.

The only thing that gives us any sense of power and control over this is understanding *why* people might lie about us. Investigations into false rape allegations have shown several different motivations, which are: women who subsequently regret having sex; women who are *ashamed* of having had sex; women who fear being punished – by family, or their community – for having had consensual sex; women who are troubled, or mentally ill, and possibly believe what they are saying; and women who want revenge. Some women are motivated by several of these factors.

A wise, feminist overview would note that a lot of these reasons are caused by the fact that this is still a society which is judgemental about women being openly sexual, or wanting sex. Hopefully, if feminism succeeds, there eventually won't be any such concepts as 'sluts', or 'slags', or 'honour' that can be 'ruined'. Or female sexual shame so intense it intersects with mental illness. Or female shame so intense it goes on to ruin men's lives, too.

Until that happens, however, there are a few solid, practical things worried boys, and men, can do which will radically reduce their chances of being falsely accused of rape.

Obviously, make sure everything you do – *every time* – is consensual. It might feel awkward to ask, 'Is it okay if I put my fingers in you?', when you feel like you should be acting like a wordless, devil-may-care bang-machine – but it's considerably less awkward than finding out, later, she *didn't* like it, it hurt, and she's going round telling everyone you used her, or hurt her.

Also, there is a lot to be said for you both agreeing to keep your sexual relationship private. At least at the beginning. No posts on social media; no moments like the bit in *Grease* where Danny Zuko sings to the rest of the T-birds about getting Sandy 'down in the sand'. If no one knows you're fucking – if no one is commenting about it, or gossiping about it – then there is far less danger of your lover feeling, for whatever reason, she has to lie about how, and why, you had sex. If there is no judgemental public narrative she feels she has to change, she has less reason to chuck you under the bus. A good old secret hook-up will benefit you both.

But the main advice is nothing magic; no fix, no technique. It is, instead, an old, old wisdom. For if you really are terrified of being falsely accused of rape – if this is genuinely haunting you and affecting your day-to-day peace of mind, as so many young men said it was? Then the one thing you can practically do to reduce the chances is to only have sex in a situation where you both like, and trust, each other. When you know each other well enough for a discussion on what you want to do not to feel impossibly awkward. When you're both sober, and equally willing. And with, best-case scenario, a woman that you intend to know for more than just one night, or a couple of shags.

These kinds of sexual encounters are very unlikely to

result in a false accusation of rape. Yes, there are women who are so damaged and/or mentally ill that they still might do it: but all you can do is try not to have sex with incredibly damaged and/or mentally ill women.

I'm surprised this isn't more commonly promoted. Indeed, it seems to be the opposite. I'm amazed at how often you still hear men chuckling, 'Crazy chicks are best in bed!' as a recommendation/tip to other men. I think it's best to clarify that the kind of 'crazy' you're looking for is 'maybe wears a beret; has a small collection of porcelain frogs'. If she's actually regularly white-out drunk, dancing in traffic, prone to suddenly crying hysterically, and does that thing where you really quickly stab a knife in between your fingers, when your hand is on the table? She doesn't need a lover. She needs a therapist. She needs help. She – and the problems she might bring with her – is way beyond your sexual paygrade.

I know this seems like impossibly old-fashioned advice, from 1823 – but, as yet, there is still no piece of technology, or legal hack, as reliable as only ever making yourself sexually vulnerable with someone you absolutely trust. With someone you know well, and who isn't drunk, or much less experienced than you, or unstable, and likely to post about it on social media halfway through.

Women have spent *years* advising each other *not* to fancy Bad Boys – reckless, sexy, damaged men, possibly wearing leather, possibly into drugs, possibly in a terrible band, absolutely certain to treat you badly and leave you: possibly with chlamydia or herpes.

There needs to be similar advice handed out to boys: about the kind of girls who seem to be that most intoxicating thing – up for a fuck – but are also palpably reckless, unbound-aried, and very possibly heading towards some kind of life crisis in which your dick will be, at best, unhelpful.

The big, ultimate truth about sex is this: although it can be joyous, fun, meaningful, meaningless, ecstatic, average or just 'a thing you did while a train was delayed in a sid-ing', it is also, often, inherently risky. *For both men and women*. Women are scared of being raped; men are scared of being accused of rape. In a weird way, this unites us: in our vulnerability, and fear. In our worry it might end up being something we regret; or which haunts us.

If, as all the statistics and reports suggest, most young people get the majority of their actual nuts-and-bolts sexual education from pornography, it's worth remembering this: that however crazy, spontaneous or 'forceful' professional pornography *seems* to be, the people you're watching agreed *everything* in advance. There were *meetings* about it. There are *witnesses*. It can all stop *whenever an actor says so*. The people who are paid to fuck, regularly, have learned how to make sure it does *not* end up being a situation anyone regrets, afterwards.

The most useful thing anyone could really learn from watching pornography isn't really the fucking – but the rigorous application of constant consent. What industry-standard banging looks like. If that means both enjoyably and hornily drawing up a 'sex contract' beforehand, then it could be both the most enjoyable, and reassuring, paper-work of your life.

But one final thing to bear in mind: if 2–4 per cent of those rape allegations were false, the other 96–98 per cent were true. It might be your friend-of-a-friend is lying. False rape accusations might not be as prevalent as you fear they are.

After all: all humans lie.

FOUR. So look, that's all the heavy stuff out of the way. Apart from sexual strangulation, on which I have to say, 'THIS IS NOT A FUN AND REASSURING SEXUAL HOBBY TO HAVE. DO YOU KNOW HOW MANY PROFESSIONALLY TRAINED HORNY STRAN-GLERS THERE ARE? NONE. IN THE UK, 60 WOMEN HAVE DIED FROM STRANGULATORY SEX THAT HAS GONE WRONG. COMPARE THIS TO THE NUMBER OF WOMEN WHO HAVE DIED FROM "SOMEONE GOING DOWN ON THEM REALLY WELL FOR 20 MINUTES", ON WHICH THE STATS ARE: ZERO. YOU KNOW – THERE'S AN OBVIOUS CHOICE TO MAKE HERE, DUDE. YOU ARE MESSING WITH SOME HIGH-STAKES SHIT. IF YOUR PARTNER WANTS TO FEEL "A BIT DIZZY", JUST DO WHAT EVERY GENER-ATION BEFORE YOU HAS DONE – AND GIVE THEM SOME POPPERS, FOR CHRIST'S SAKE. OR SHE COULD JUST HOLD HER BREATH! NO RISK THERE! TRUST ME – THE LAST THING YOU WANT AT THE END OF THE NIGHT IS AN UNCONSCIOUS OR DEAD WOMAN. THAT IS REALLY NOT SEXY.'

This aside, it does feel like this Sex Chapter is overdue talking about actual sex. Good sex. Fun sex. Sex in which absolutely no one is traumatised, and everyone leaves happy. What is it that women would like men to know about sex? Know with the same certainty as you know the lyrics to 'Mr Brightside', or how to adjust your balls inside your trousers without anyone else seeing?

There's just a few things – the first of which is:

During anal sex, we're worried about the poo. However naughty and transgressive and pleasurable anal sex is, the ultimate truth of the matter is that it is 'sex in a poo-place', and we are spending a *lot* of the time you're up there wondering if your cock's going to come back out wearing a small brown bowler hat made of plop. If you found it difficult or distasteful to read that last sentence, I would humbly suggest you are *not* actually emotionally qualified to have anal sex. To paraphrase Jack Nicholson in *A Few Good Men*, 'You want the anal sex? You can't *handle* the anal sex.'

In case you were still wavering on this issue, I have a friend who has a terrible story about this very scenario that involves one, single grain of sweetcorn 'presented in the centre of the bell-end. Like a golden jewel, nestled on a pink cushion. We both stared at it for a while, utterly at a loss for how to acknowledge it in conversation, and then never mentioned it again. Because we never saw each other again.'

Anal sex in porn is, obviously, deeply unrepresentative – as professional porn actors will have either starved themselves, or applied enemas, or both, before banging. Their anal tunnels have been diligently pressure-washed before use – like a patio before a party. I'm sorry to say that the chances of the woman you're fucking having done this are pretty low – primarily because she's not being paid to have an empty sphincter – and so you both really need to be prepared for what I would politely call 'aftermath'.

Additionally – and call me 'political' – but I do believe that men should only have anal sex with women if they themselves have had a penis – or similarly dimensioned object – up their bum. Frankly it's *greedy* if you're running a 'two holes' system on women, but have 'ROAD CLOSED: NO ACCESS' on your own crevices. Knowing what it feels like to have something mahoosive up your kidneys means that, when *you* are the massive thing up someone *else's* kidneys, you will treat that area with the respect and care it deserves. Also: why live a life when you haven't tried putting something up your bum? If strangers are just friends we haven't met yet, then most straight men's anuses are just their new favourite place to do sex-things that they haven't tried yet.

Obviously if anal sex with a woman is what floats both of your boats, and you're all up for it, then bum away, my friends, with all my joyous blessing. I could not be more delighted about the botty fun you are having. However, as an old – possibly 'traditional' – woman, I would like to take a moment to re-pitch 'the vagina' as the main place heterosexual sex happens. It's low-maintainence, it's designed for the job – it's a faithful old pal that rarely lets you down. Honestly, if you're tired of fanny, you're tired of life. A vagina is an incredible thing – it has G-spots, it can ripple from multiple orgasms, it is self-lubricating, it is endlessly malleable and adaptable, and – when we take humanity as a whole – it is the cradle whence all life on earth has sprung.

But, on top of that – and, perhaps, most importantly – there is no poo up there. I can think of no greater recommendation. In a well-balanced sex diet, you definitely want a lot of fanny on your plate.

We Are Very Polite and Don't Want to Tire You

We are horrified, more than you would ever imagine, by the idea that we might take 'too long' to come. We don't want you to get tongue-cramp; we don't want to be labelled a 'hand-wearier'. The fact that, after you come, and need half an hour to recharge – while our vaginas could come again, over and over, for an hour, solidly – is something we constantly try to downplay, or ignore. We never want to feel 'too much' for you, sexually. We know that, if you feel like you're 'not enough', your erection might die of sadness – and so we try to give the impression that, when it comes to our sexual hunger, we 'eat like a bird'.

If you ever want to know why women seem to have a mystifying soft spot for men who come across as maniac shag-bag sex-addicts – 'bad boys' with tattoos, etc., etc. – it's because within their personas is the implicit promise that they're so fanny-crazed their tongues *never* get tired, their fingers go at 140 rotations a minute for two hours without pause, and they will only finally ejaculate on the third day of solid, non-stop pumping.

If more beta males want to break the sexual market dominance of the 'bad boy' – who is, as all women will admit, wearying in every other respect outside the bedroom – then they should begin a well-oiled PR campaign, promising that 'a cardigan and glasses' is like the 'handkerchief code' that gay men used to employ: guaranteeing you a diligent, luxurious and dedicated muff-diver/ fingerer. Or, at the very least, someone who *absolutely without question* knows how to use a variety of vibrating items, and feels they've short-changed themselves if their sexual partner comes less than four times.

On the Other Hand . . .

. . . The vagina, vulva and clitoris are made of very delicate, thin skin, and 'chafing' can often be an issue. On top of this, we might want to get the whole thing done and dusted in 20 minutes or under so we can get back to watching *Curvy Brides' Boutique.* Communication is key. Think of sex like giving a mate a lift. Sometimes, they want to get home as soon as possible. Other times, they want to go 'the scenic route', and pick up chips on the way.

Also:

When you're fucking us very hard, or deep, we're worried we might wet ourselves. Your penis is pressing on our bladder. Half the time when we say, 'Come now! I want you to come!', it's because we want to go for a wazz.

And:

If we're very 'vocal', and loud, during sex – 'YES! YES!' – it *might* be because we're aware we're doing fanny-farts, and don't want you to hear the party vag-sounds that are happening 'down there'.

But Now, Over to You

As 'they' say, the secret of great sex *is* communication, and there are a couple of questions I would be intrigued for men to ask either their partners, or themselves. For instance, when it comes to pornography, women have watched so much of it – all shot from the men's point of view – that, often, when we're fucking, *we're pretending we're you.* Because: that's the view we're used to. That's the majority of sex we've seen. We're imagining how amazing our arses must look while you fuck us from behind; how pleasing it must be to just collapse into us.

We can't see any of it, of course – but we're imagining how amazing we must look *to you.* We're getting off *on ourselves.* So, next time you're fucking a woman, ask her if that's what she's doing? Any reply's going to be interesting.

A question for you, now: I wonder, do you ever pretend you're *us*? Have you ever wondered what it's like to have a cock inside you; what it's like to have someone much bigger than you on top of you? A common Cool Girl line is talking about how awesome it would be to have a big cock; to be able to *stick it in* somewhere, or something, or someone.

But I have never, *ever, ever* heard a single man *ever* say they have imagined what it's like to have a vagina; to be fucked; to come all night. Have you *never* thought this? Why? I find it very, very odd – suspicious, really – that in this apparently sexually freewheeling age, this isn't a 'thing'.

Anywhere. I would be fascinated to listen to men being encouraged to really dig deep on why this idea seems so unthinkable, and unappealing. Purely on facts alone, you should crave a vagina – they're the things that have multiple orgasms! So is it that you have seen so many uncomfortable, awful, degrading, unhappy things happen to vaginas that you gallop away, terrified, from even beginning to imagine what *yours* might be like, and what might happen to it if you were a woman? Does the idea of having a vagina, and being fucked like a woman, make you feel uncomfortable? Scared? Sad? I think this is such a key question, for understanding sex between men and women. Honestly, if *I* were in charge of *Question Time*, instead of Fiona Bruce, I'd debate this literally every week, with every panel of guests, for the entire show. I think somewhere in this issue is a *lot* of truth we're overdue kicking around a bit.

Another, no-strings-attached question: if you really think about it, are you, maybe, *also* pretending to be the man? The man watching this fuck? The vertiginous rise in men wanting to film sex – and subsequently sharing the footage with friends – suggests that, maybe, pornography is making *everyone* involved in this fuck pretend they're actually the guy in the porno, or the guy watching it. And none of us are actually in the room, having this sex, at all.

In which case, ultimately, who is the Sex Daddy we're doing all this fucking *for*? Are we just turning ourselves into pornography? And why?

Chapter Seven

The Pornography of Men

The first feminist argument I ever got into was about pornography. Specifically, pornography with regards to boys, and men.

It was a room full of doughty old-skool feminists, and I was still but a mere young, gobby liberal, when the conversation turned to how damaging seeing extreme, violent online pornography was for women, and girls.

'It is *destructive*, and fills young girls with *fear* and *self-loathing*!' a woman in a hat said, animatedly. 'Imagine a *young girl* seeing extreme online pornography! A girl of *nine*, or *ten*, watching a violent double-penetration video! She would be *horrified*! It would *destroy* her view of what sex actually is!'

'Yes! Yes! I agree!' I said – before adding, mildly, 'but, let's not forget, also upsetting for young *boys*, too.'

I started to describe how worrying I thought it would be for a young boy's first experience of actually seeing sex to be some averagely unpleasant porn: some giganto-penised, moustachioed individual, violently bumming a crying woman. It wouldn't seem very . . . *nice*. It wouldn't seem terribly – *do-able*. I don't think there are many young boys who would immediately think, 'That's the future for me! Can't *wait*!'

For starters, children just tend not to like seeing people crying.

'NO! NO!' the lady in the hat shouted. 'A BOY wouldn't be upset about watching violent porn – because he'd enjoy watching A MAN BEING IN CONTROL!'

Several years later, I wrote about that afternoon in *How to Be a Woman*: 'I think of all the ten-year-old boys I know – Sam, say – who still gets a bit nervous about the skeleton pirates in *Pirate of the Caribbean*, and I thought, I don't think he'd be exhilarated by seeing a man "in control". I think he'd be scared of seeing a man who looks like an Angry Burt Reynolds, bumming a very sad lady across a landing.

'I really hope that, by the time Sam comes of age to start watching porn, we've started making, for the want of a better phrase, *free-range*, ethical, *nice* pornography: something that shows sex as something potentially wonderful that a man and a woman do *together*, rather than a thing that just "happens" to a woman. Something where – to put it simply – *everyone* comes.'

How to Be a Woman was published in 2011.

*

It's 2021. I'm on holiday with the Sam who I suggested would be scared to watch hardcore online pornography, because he was ten.

Sam is 20 now, because = time has flown. Jesus Christ, how has this happened? He's taller than me, drives a car, regularly stops in a doorway, hooks his fingers over the frame and casually does 20 pull-ups.

Earlier in the day, I had watched Sam hack at a tree trunk with an axe while smoking a cigarette, *without* letting the smoke get in his eyes – which is a skill I still haven't mastered in my forties. I can tell you exactly how it feels to have known someone since they were three years old grow up into a huge man chopping wood and smoking a fag: you feel like a 101-year-old Eastern European nanna swaddled in a black crocheted shawl, murmuring, 'You are strong like lion now. You make old lady proud.'

Later that evening, we're all sitting around a campfire in the garden – made from the axe-hacked logs – smoking and drinking beers. It's idyllic. We get quite pissed.

The conversation turns, after a while, to a subject that often comes up, in the modern era: therapy. We've all known each other a lifetime, and so it's easy to talk about who's had therapy, or is on a waiting list to have therapy. It's most of us. We are all twenty-first-century people, trying to understand our medieval monkey brains. And then Sam – with a confidence and calmness that is a notable trait in his generation – says, 'Since I had therapy, I'm two years clean, now.'

As he has a beer in one hand, and a cigarette in the other, I make a confused sound that means, 'Tell me more?'

'I'm two years clean from using pornography,' he says.

'I . . . I got in a bit of trouble with it. It got really dark. It was fucking horrible. And once I started getting help with it, and started being able to talk about it with my friends, you know what? Most of them said they had problems with it, too. Not just the guys – girls, as well. But mainly the guys. I'd say, 70 per cent? I mean, I think I only know one guy who *didn't* have a problem with it. But yeah – I'm two years clean, now. Haven't really watched it since 2019.'

Later that evening, I'm in the kitchen with Sam's dad, fetching more beers, and he says – looking utterly stricken – 'Yeah. It got really bad. I used to have to get into bed with him to help him sleep, because he was so distressed. He couldn't be alone. He would cry for hours. He really suffered.'

It looks like, by the time Sam came of age, we really hadn't started making 'free-range', ethical, wonderful pornography.

It looks like that, in fact, we just threw them to the wolves.

A couple of months later, when we're back from our holiday, I ask Sam if he'd be willing to have a proper chat about his previous problems with pornography. We both work very hard, in the initial phone call, to not make it seem in any way weird that the middle-aged mum of one of his nursery friends is asking him to come over and talk about porn, and I think we do very well. Sam really is an exceptionally sensible and wise young man.

That afternoon, I finally realised just how big a problem

the advent of endless, free, online pornography has been for Sam's generation. This gigantic, multinational, trillion-dollar business – so lightly regulated that you can be watching 'crying teen rape' 30 seconds after you start looking for it – arrived when they were children, was being waved in their faces on the smartphones of the 'edgy' kids in class years before their PSHE lessons had gone anywhere near sex education, and their parents just . . . didn't know what was going on.

I didn't know what porn was out there. *I* didn't know how regularly watching pornography, as a child, or young man, can act like a devastating explosion in your head: rewiring all your still-forming sexual thoughts and impulses until normal, real-world sex leaves you utterly numb, and you can only find any spark of excitement by clicking on something fantastical, extreme, impossible, illegal and, ultimately, a piece of cold, calculating business that will do anything to keep your attention. Even if you're a child.

'Where did it start?' I ask Sam, as we sit in my garden. We smoke like chimneys throughout the conversation – the only sign of Sam's anxiety, other than his repeated, politely murmured, 'This bit's horrible: I'm sorry.'

Sam was ten. 'It's funny – because by the time you wrote that thing about me and the other boys, in the book, I'd already seen my first porn. It was already happening.'

He was alone with the family computer, which was in the loft-room. 'I don't blame my parents – because there's so many ways to see it. I mean, even when they blocked the Wi-Fi, I got round it without any problems. Let's face it – most young people know more about the tech in their house than their parents do.'

At the time, Sam didn't know what pornography was. 'I didn't even know it was called "porn".'

This is borne out by what he typed into Google: 'Big bum sexy woman naked' – a search-string which stands quite strongly, I think, as a candidate for 'the most ten-year-old thing ever typed into Google'.

As you might expect from 'big bum sexy woman naked', the first stuff Sam saw was 'pretty vanilla, really – tame. I'd go on YouTube and it's pretty much censored, and monitored, so it would have been, like . . . *erotic dancing*. Stuff like that.'

Things escalated when Sam discovered actual pornography. This was Year 7, Year 8 – 'early teens kind of thing'. Groups of friends would watch it around each other's houses. It was just exciting – 'a bit of fun'. But it went from 'nought to a hundred really quickly, with the weird stuff'.

The weird stuff would be what was talked about at school – 'Freaky stuff would go around, and everyone would be talking about it.'

Classic stuff – almost designed to go viral in a school full of kids competing to find the weirdest thing, like **Two Girls One Cup**, in which the plot revolves around two girls, and one cup, being repeatedly filled and then emptied of shit and vomit. The infamous 'Blue Waffle' – a picture of a vagina so diseased, I feel it can be scientifically captioned as 'the most unlucky vagina ever recorded'.

'But now, even that all seems quite innocent, really, compared to the stuff I started watching that caused all the problems.'

Understandably, Sam doesn't want to discuss the actual

details of the porn that ended up making him so fucked-up and anxious that his dad had to start putting him to bed at night, like a scared and overwhelmed child.

'I was never *addicted* to pornography,' Sam is at pains to point out. 'My main problem was my OCD. But the porn worked like pouring petrol on a fire. Because it gave my intrusive thoughts this whole new thing to get obsessed with. Porn felt massive, and overwhelming, and dark – and my OCD *loved* that. It would spiral.'

Basically, the porn Sam got into started making him feel he might be a bad person. The line between 'watching porn' and 'being the kind of person who then actually *did* the things you see in porn' got blurred in his head. Even though he never, ever did any of the things he was watching – 'Christ, no. No!' he says, looking genuinely horrified – his OCD meant that, essentially, his brain and body couldn't tell the difference.

'I would be torturing myself, day in, day out: telling myself, what the fuck? Because you're into this kind of stuff, *this is who you're going to be*. And honestly, the stuff I was into wasn't even the worst stuff out there. I know people who were watching *way* more extreme stuff. I mean, I've never even *tried* to find the Dark Web. I don't even know where it is, hahaha. No – what I was watching was all considered "normal", mainstream porn. RedTube. YouPorn. The big porn platforms.'

During this time, things eventually got so bad that Sam broke up with his girlfriend, and dropped out of uni: 'My self-esteem was zero. I thought, I can't do anything. I need to be alone. I distanced myself from my friends. It was a fucking shitty time, to be honest. I was stuck. Because I was having constant, intrusive thoughts about porn, and what kind of person I was because I watched it.'

It's distressing hearing Sam, who I've known since he was three, and playing the donkey in the nursery Nativity, say these things. His family are very close, and very emotionally open: he's one of those young human beings who have been put together and tended with proper wisdom, love and care. Whenever I've heard my daughters are going for a night out with him, I've done that relaxed, parental sigh of, 'Oh, *good*. I don't need to worry *tonight*. Sam will take care of them.' He's the kind of young man you'd put a bet on succeeding at anything he put his mind to.

In the midst of his porn-addiction, however, this wasn't a bet Sam would have put on himself. He already thought he was ruined. His body was shutting down.

'I had erectile dysfunction. Porn-induced erectile dysfunction. Basically, my brain was telling me that when I'm with a woman, that's a situation so alien to me, I would think "This isn't normal", and my body would shut down.'

Because . . . ?

'Because "normal" was watching porn, having my laptop and my right hand. I'd be having sex, and my brain would be saying, "This *isn't* sex."'

Because sex is . . . porn?

'Because sex is porn. That's what I'd basically trained my mind and body to think – without realising it.'

It was at this point Sam started getting therapy, and during sessions, he was encouraged to look back over his whole sexual development. This was where he realised that, with the first three sexual partners he'd had, he hadn't been able to come – 'I could never get there' – because his sexual imagination was so wired into pornography, he couldn't 'be present' when sex was happening in real life.

'I was young, I was watching all these guys with gigantic knobs, so unrealistic, banging away for hours, and going "How the hell can I do any [of what I'm seeing on screen]?"'

Sam has talked to his male friends about erectile dysfunction – a sentence that reminds us that, whatever I might say elsewhere in this book about men being unable to talk about their problems, Gen Z are doing things 100 per cent differently, and better: my 52-year-old husband assures me that such conversations were *not* happening in the playground of Yardley's Secondary School in 1983 – and found that they, too, had found their first sexual experiences had ended with them being similarly over- whelmed, and unable to get either a hard-on, or be able to come.

'It seems it's quite common. The ideal body type [in porn] is to be as big and hench and alpha as possible. All the porn stars have this image of the perfect man, you know? And the dicks . . . like, if a guy has a slightly "small" penis, or a different penis, we're saying what a "normal" penis is based on by comparing it to porn. And that can fuck you up, too. You just constantly worry you're not normal.'

In as much as there can be an 'ending' to a story when the storyteller is only 21, this story has a happy ending.

'In a way, I think I was lucky that I had OCD,' Sam says, philosophically, 'because it made my relationship with porn so bad, so quickly, that I realised I had a problem with it. I think a lot of guys watch a similar amount of porn and *don't* realise it's fucking up their idea of sex – because they never reach the crisis point my OCD gave me. They think their view of sex is normal. That it's *normal* to not be able to come with your girlfriend; that it's *normal* to be thinking of something else – extreme porn – while you're fucking.'

Having had 'a bunch' of therapy, Sam is now in a stable, happy relationship with his girlfriend, and feels he's got a healthy understanding of how porn affects him. He wants to help other young boys, and men.

'I think I'd like to make a film about it, or start going into schools and talking about it. Just preparing kids for what they're going to find, and what might happen. Like, it's not *wrong* to watch porn. You just need to be aware it might end up being more . . . *complicated* than you think, when you click on that first website.'

How so?

'You might be about to start on a journey that will really, really affect you – and I don't think young people are aware of that. They're like, "Rargh, porn, funny, hahaha, every-one watches it." My own personal relationship with porn now is that I really try not to watch it. But even now, if I'm bored and I have absolutely nothing to do, a couple of times I *have* watched it, but the difference is now, I'll watch it and I'll be like, "Fuck, what have I done? I've let myself down." Because it will start me feeling bad about myself again.'

What Sam is describing about his personal experience – albeit one he's come to understand through a ton of therapy and hard work – is the central fact about pornography that we, as a society, have yet to properly acknowledge: for children, teenagers and young adults, there's no such thing as 'just watching' pornography. It's not something you can just pick up and put down at will. Sexual imagination is like a honeysuckle – *it will grow up around whatever it can cling on to.*

As puberty fires up your brain and body into a sappy, blossoming hot mess of thought and feeling, tiny little tendrils of sexual longing reach out – and then encounter the branch, or a wire, or a nail of something seen on TV (a gang-bang, a rape, a hole in a stocking), or in a book (Billy in *Riders* going down on Janey in the bluebell wood; James Bond fucking Pussy Galore), or in porn (choking, slapping, anal, old people, teens).

These become your ideas of fucking, because – that's the fucking you've seen. You have to start building your sexual imagination *somewhere* – and *obviously* the majority of it is going to be based on whatever scenes, images and sounds you have access to in those hot, formative, hungry, wet-clay years.

The simple truth is this: *when you look into the pornography, the pornography looks back into you.* It's not a passive act. It's absolutely a two-way street.

The first time you start clicking pornography – alone and excited; or giggling, with friends – you have no idea that what you're about to see has a massive potential to be *in your head for ever.* This is something that is never discussed, or thought about. The first time you smoke a cigarette, there's *guaranteed to be* one person in the room going 'You might get hooked!' But no one has *ever* said this about porn – despite the fact you are about to consume what we might refer to as 'Proust's Wankeleine'.

And porn has a high likelihood of causing a permanent affect – because you are also having a profound physical and chemical reaction to it. Your body is pumping adrenaline and – if the porn makes you come – oxytocin into your body. You're aroused. You know you're watching stuff society deems to be important, or secret, or shameful, or extreme – so there's a massive dopamine kick, too. As you see stuff you've never seen before, your synapses are going crazy – building whole new neural pathways basically labelled 'MY IDEA OF SEX'.

The drunkest conversations I've had with my girlfriends – real 4am stuff – have involved them admitting that their most primal sexual dreams and fantasies revolve around stuff they wouldn't ever admit in public: having sex with dirty old men, or tramps; rape; dogs; lions. Stuff that's very hard to square with being a well-balanced, sex-positive feminist.

None of the women have ever actually *done* any of these things – but, when they get drunk, the thoughts are confessed. This stuff is just *there*, not from choice, and buried really fucking deep – wired in when they were *very* young – which, when we talked about it more, could all be traced back to formative moments: a nature documentary. A rape scene in a movie. Being told not to wear a short skirt, or suffer the consequences of the 'dirty old man' who hung around in the alleyway by the school.

Currently, we would label these confessions as 'sexual

fantasies' – but they're not that. Not quite. Instead, they're sexual *beliefs*. The first information these women received about what sex is, how sex happens. *What their sexual future would be.*

And it's our sexual futures that we tend not to be thinking about when we're eight, and watching two lions banging in a nature documentary – or ten, and clicking on pornography for the first time. Because, in these moments where we're inadvertently training our sexual preferences to be tramps, or rape, or lions, or golden showers, or gang-bangs . . . well, what are the chances we're ever actually going to get that sex, once we go out there in the world?

Without the intervention of porn – watched by women *or* men – most consensual sex in the world comes down to two average-bodied people who like each other rolling around a bit, making silly noises, half-falling off the bed, having a panic about whether the condom's come off or not, getting a fit of the giggles at one point, and, hopefully, coming.

The madness of pornography is that not only is realistic content like that quite specialist – requiring you to sign up to 'ethical' porn sites like makelovenotporn.com, sssh.com or frolicme.com, and pay a subscription – but that it *also* has a tendency to make 'normal' sex feel, as Sam described earlier, 'weird'. Pornography *uninvents* actual sex, and replaces it with 'pornography', instead. Because, if your thing is now getting widdled on by Mexican twins, the only place you're ever going to find it – let's be honest – is online. Porn has given you a hunger that, in turn, only porn can feed.

And that, when it turns into addiction, reveals the cold,

dark business-bones at the core of pornography. With the estimates being that between 60 per cent and 99 per cent of men regularly use porn – Sam: 'I genuinely don't know *any* man of my age who doesn't watch it. Not one' – between 3 per cent and 6 per cent of those go on to become addicted to it.

And for both those who are clinically addicted to it, and those whose sexual preferences have been strongly shaped by it, pornography becomes a perfect, awful, escalating business model. Capitalism at its most breathtakingly effective.

For while one of the joys of sex between two – or more! – consenting adults is that it costs you nothing, pornography comes along and inserts BUSINESS right on the end of your dick. Now, you need THIS MULTI-NATIONAL PORN COMPANY in your sex life. Now, some MILLIONAIRE TECH GUY is in the bed with you.

If porn has fucked you up so much you can only come by watching porn, then it's just made itself a new, repeat customer to sell to its advertisers. It got you when you were young, and now you *need* it. All your fantasies are someone else's – they belong to a big company off-shored in a tax haven somewhere.

And now – while you might be going on Black Lives Matter marches, and Tweeting #StopAsianHate – your sex life involves giving over your subconscious to a platform that has categories like 'Ebony', 'Big Black Beauty' and 'Asian Teen'. And that's *before* we talk about the statistics of the number of women involved in the sex industry who come from backgrounds of sexual abuse, and mental illness, or sex-trafficking.

And you got signed up to all of this when you were ten – because, when you first, very naturally, started wanting to know what sex was, the internet gave you porn, instead.

'I was chatting to someone at my uni literally yesterday,' Sam says, 'and he was saying, "I'm going back to my girl-friend's house and she's going to want me to have sex – but it's just an *effort*. I just want to have a wank and watch porn. I think I prefer it." And at the time, I said "Fair enough", but I was thinking – we're just this generation where sex is so fucked up.'

And Sam is aware of just how wide the tendrils of this business model spread. Having had therapy for his problems with porn, and how it triggers his OCD, he is now hyper-vigilant about what we might call 'porn baiting' – in the same way those who've overcome eating disorders can clock a fellow patient posting seemingly innocent 'body-checking' photos on their Instagram, or using pro-ana language.

'I really want to talk about the way the algorithms work,' he says, keenly. 'Because they keep trying to get you back into porn. So, TikTok, right? I watched a BBC documen-tary about this, and it was true to my experience: if TikTok knows you're a young man, without even searching for erotic videos, within five minutes of you going online, there will be videos of girls with thongs on – basically just expli-cit, but in a soft-porn way. And then there's a link in the bottom corner – click on that, and it's straight to OnlyFans, or the links to actual porn.'

So you can't get away from it?

'It's fucked! It's completely preying on people's vulner-abilities. We're all victims to it. It's the main reason I deleted TikTok in the end, because there's, I dunno, girls on there doing sexual stuff all the time, and I'd be watching it going [Dracula impression] "This is arousing", and you start hav-ing the urge to watch porn again. And I just can't be arsed going down that tunnel any more. So I don't ever go there.'

Of all the things Sam told me during our conversation, this was the one that had the most long-term effect. As a middle-aged woman, my social-media algorithms are sol-idly driven by footage of spaniels, kitchen conversions, inspiring feminist moments, and, due to one drunken night when I listened to it on repeat, The Tamperer featuring Maya's 'Feel It'. My TikTok, meanwhile, is dominated by hairstyling make-overs – all leading me to a chilled belief that social media isn't as bad as some people say. After all, mine's pretty benign.

After this conversation with Sam, however, I started ask-ing my male friends what *their* social media algorithms were showing *them* – and I was astonished how different it was. On one dog walk with James, he showed me his Instagram: every third post 'suggested' was of some young woman, being a bit fruity in lingerie.

'I can't tell you how much this isn't because of my pref-erences,' he said, blinking, as we watched another lush beauty showing us her yoga leggings with some suggestive poses. 'I only follow about 50 people, and they're all accounts to do with politics, the Scottish referendum, or . . . George Ezra. This stuff just *appears*.'

I showed him my social-media feeds. He seemed astonished.

'Yeah – this isn't how mine looks,' he said. 'This is bananas. Totally different worlds.'

Even though it was a lovely sunny day, in the woods, with our two dogs joyfully sharing a piece of fox poo, I found it quite eerie: how utterly different the worlds of men and women were, without us knowing. We presume social media is a communal area: but from the first day, men and women are being presented with radically different worlds, *and we don't even know it*. Until we talk.

Back in my garden, Sam and I have finally run out of cigarettes, and Sam wants to show me his new electric scooter, so we start to wind up the conversation.

'Basically, watching porn pretty much destroyed my dopamine-release mechanism, and it's taken the last few years, and a lot of work, to get myself right again. I can't imagine a world where boys and men don't watch porn – like, they'd genuinely have to live in a cave. And I don't wish I'd never seen it – I don't think I would be any better of a person if I hadn't – but I do wish I'd *understood* it. My generation are the first to have had this crazy access to a lot of shit, online, and it's really noticeable that there's never really a *chilled* option to pornography. Humans always want bigger, better, greater, crazier, more extreme – and so porn's got like super-skunk. You know? It just gets stronger and stronger, because young people are always like, "Give me the most extreme thing", and so that's what sells.'

He sighs.

'I've tried to find, like, "intimate couple sex" on Pornhub, and there's some stuff that's actually quite romantic – and that's one of my favourite things to do with my girlfriend – to be in our own time, our own space, and be completely in our own little world. I love that. But whenever you're looking at "intimate couple sex", there's always a link at the bottom of the pages that says 'Brazilian massive arse crazy face-sitting', so, you know.'

He stands up. 'I think I just want to go into schools and say, "Porn. Ask me anything you want to know." Sex education in this country is all wrong. It's too late. By the time you're getting sex education lessons, all the boys in that class have already seen porn – and then they don't even talk about porn in sex-ed classes anyway. Porn *was* my sex education. Personally, I'd be talking to kids about it when they're in Reception. They do in, like, Sweden, and Holland, don't they? And it's just normal. Not weird at all. Me and my girlfriend have thought about doing it together – going into schools – so you have the male and female view. I just want to get across the fact that – especially at such a young age – your brain is so pliable, and this stuff is going to stay with you for the rest of your life.

'I think a *lot* of guys worry about this stuff, but they won't ever talk about it, and that scares me. We're allowed to, you know? We can talk about this. No one's really going over the edge and talking about it, and bringing it into the light, out of the dark realm, because they're worried it will make them vulnerable, or awkward, and it's just more comfortable to sit at home and have access to anything you want to see, instead.

'Ultimately, I got scared, because I was like, "I don't want to be a literal wanker! I don't want to be someone who just sits there playing Xbox, watching porn and wanking all the time! I want to . . ."'

By this point, we're out in the street, where Sam's new electric scooter is parked. In his excitement, he forgets the end of the sentence – jumping onto the scooter, immediately accelerating it up to 20mph, doing a really flashy turn, and then coming back to us, beaming.

Over the road, a group of schoolkids, waiting for their bus, have a classic 'younger kids watching a cool older boy smoking a fag and riding an electric scooter very fast' reaction: they all look like John Gordon Sinclair watching Dorothy play football.

Sam puts his cigarette in his mouth, and prepares to scoot away. 'Did I say "dark realm" earlier?' he says. 'Hahaha! "Dark realm." That sounds rude.'

And off he goes, waving, down Banner Road.

Chapter Eight

The Friendships of Men

Here they come, around the water, past the reeds, on a perfect late-spring morning. Paul Whitehouse, now 61, employs a purposeful stride, despite a slight limp from a cruciate ligament injury, and is carrying a fishing rod that has the discreet air of 'serious gear'.

Meanwhile, beside Whitehouse, Bob Mortimer, 59, chugs along at a more 'amiable stroll', managing to carry his fishing rod like he's holding someone else's for a while. It's not actually upside down – but Mortimer carries it as if it were.

They arrive under the willow tree where I am waiting.

'Hello! Hello!' Mortimer says. 'Lovely day, isn't it! D'you want a falafel?'

He pulls a tray of eight falafel out of his coat pocket. He then points at the other pocket.

'Or – I've got nuts?'

As Mortimer proffers his pocket buffet, chatting cheer-fully, Whitehouse is eyeing the water with a calculating squint.

'We should be over there,' he says. 'Under that tree. That's where they're rising. We should go over there. Bob? Bob?'

But Bob is busy doing an impression of Nicolas Cage, kung-fu fighting.

It's 2019, and I am spending the day fishing with Paul Whitehouse and Bob Mortimer, at a lake in Surrey.

In Britain, one of the biggest TV sensations of recent years has been the BBC's *Mortimer & Whitehouse: Gone Fishing*. It's spawned three spin-off books, regularly gets ratings in the millions, and has gained something of a cult following.

Initially, Bob Mortimer and Paul Whitehouse – two of the country's National Comedy Treasures – pitched a show about, yes, fishing. Whitehouse is obsessed with it, and very good at it. Mortimer – Mortimer is more of a 'hapless enthusiast', devoted to pissing about and eating endless snacks. As evidenced today.

At first, they didn't know what the show would actually consist of.

'We had no fucking idea,' Whitehouse says, preparing my rod, 'when we started shooting the first episode. No fucking idea what we were doing. When the BBC commissioned it, they were like, "We haven't done a show this way. You're just going to talk – with no promise of content or 'narrative'? The only objective is that you might catch a fish?" '

'On the first day of shooting, we didn't have a single idea of what would happen,' Mortimer agrees. 'I love reality TV – I always have done. *Big Brother*, *Ramsay's Kitchen Nightmares* . . . I watch them all day. So, we'd planned nothing.'

'No, that's not right – you had those fireworks,' Whitehouse says.

'Oh yeah – the fireworks!' Mortimer says, beaming.

'We thought we should plan something, so Bob had all these fireworks in the boot of his car, and set them off to celebrate catching a fish. But he nearly took out a cameraman. Practically killed him.'

'They were pointing the wrong way,' Mortimer admits. 'Huge bang.'

Whitehouse hands me a rod.

'Right? You ready?'

I have never been fly-fishing before. Twenty seconds later, I stare at the pile of tangled fishing line, at my feet, as Whitehouse – and, presumably, the fish – laughs at me.

'Hmmm, you see, you're kind of – *throwing* the rod around,' Whitehouse says, sternly. 'Be less . . . *jazz hands*.'

'You're a natural, Cate,' Mortimer says, supportively, taking a bag of Monster Munch out of his pocket, and starting to eat them.

As the filming for *Gone Fishing* went on – seemingly aimlessly, with the shooting going on for hours – Mortimer and Whitehouse realised what the show should actually be about.

'Two blokes, just talking absolute bollocks,' Whitehouse recaps, now. 'Just two old pals, shooting the breeze.'

At first, they just thought it would be 'banter' – two comedians trying to outdo each other. Essentially improv comedy, but with the occasional carp.

'Yeah – our relationship is pretty abusive, verbally,' Whitehouse nods.

'Mainly you to me, though,' Mortimer points out. 'Look at my phone.'

He gets out his phone, and shows a series of recent texts from Whitehouse. If Mortimer has left it more than 20 minutes to reply to a text, Whitehouse has hit him with a barrage of abuse along the lines of, 'Well, FUCK OFF then, you not-replying cunt.'

'A high percentage of Paul's messages are the c-word,' Mortimer says. 'Have you seen this? It's the best use of technology I've yet witnessed.'

He highlights the word 'cunt', and presses a button. The screen suddenly fills with thousands of 'cunts', floating around the screen like confetti, before exploding. 'That's basically a conversation with Paul,' Mortimer says. 'They made a Whitehouse Cunt app.'

However, as time went on, they noticed that what they were *mainly* talking about was: their lives. Both middle-aged, both with health issues, both married with children, they found their conversations started to be about big stuff: childhood violence and bullying. Angry fathers. Failure at school. Love. Depression. Work. Anxiety. Fear of mortality.

Bob had recently had a triple heart bypass – an operation so serious, he'd been told to make his will – and Paul had basically coaxed him out of the house, post-op and fearful, to fish. This was why they'd ended up pitching the show in the first place.

And so they realised that the show was, in the end, about *friendship*. Male friendship. Men talking to each other about their lives in a way British viewers had never seen before – and this is why it was a small sensation, in the country of stoicism, and the stiff upper lip.

As the commissioner at the BBC, Patrick Holland, put it: 'I had no idea until those first episodes started to come back just how special and touching it would be. And open and difficult, in the way both of them approach subjects that men of their age might find hard to discuss.'

Or, as Dr Anand Patel, a men's health specialist at the Centre for Men's Health, put it, 'With male friendship, it's not about saying: do you want to come and talk? It's like: do you fancy coming and doing something – the cinema, the pub, fishing – whatever your bag is? Bumping along shoulder to shoulder rather than necessarily face to face seems to be important; it takes the pressure off talking.'

This is why, in its own, gentle, tench-based way, *Gone Fishing* was a quiet revelation to many of the men watching. After each episode, Twitter would be full of men saying things like 'This show always makes me happy,' 'Lovely to see two friends just chatting together,' and, slightly heart-breakingly, 'Wish I had a mate I could go hang out with like this.'

*

It's funny that, when I was talking to men, one line many of them repeated to me – when talking about *women* they were friends with, was the quote from *When Harry Met Sally*: 'Men and women can't be friends – because the sex bit gets in the way.'

Because there is no equivalent wisdom about why men find it hard to be friends with other men – which is, I think, 'The *man* bit gets in the way.'

The recent film *The Banshees of Inisherin* is basically about male friendship, and how catastrophically it can fail. It's about male friendship struggling and floundering because men become quite *panicked* if a relationship becomes emotionally intimate – and it sparked dozens of think-pieces.

As psychotherapist Adrian Wilson-Smith put it, in the *Guardian:* 'There are a lot of men having functional rela- tionships with other men – I know this guy because he can help me out with my business idea. Or partying – these are the guys that I go out with for a drink or a line of coke. But enduring friendships, of the kind seen in many female-to- female friendships, are not something that most men over 40 see any need to have.'

I have a pretty equal number of male and female friends – and the difference between the two groups is astonishing to me.

For starters, the female WhatsApp group – Team Tits – exchanges upwards of a hundred messages a day. From how we've slept, and what we're having for tea – all the way through to wars at work, parenting struggles and episodes of mental ill-health. There's a constant, low-level ticker tape of conversation, sharing, advice, jokes and pictures of Adam Horowitz of Beastie Boys, looking fit, deployed whenever there's a Morale Emergency.

On top of this, we schedule The Ladies' Quarterlies: in reality, far more frequently than four times a year. Sleepovers, or whole weekends, where we go away from our partners, and/or children, and tackle the *really* big stuff: existential crises; divorces; and whether or not to get a Quooker hot-water tap – punctuated by walks, curling up together on the sofa like puppies, sharing double beds and gossiping until 2am.

Whenever an emergency strikes, within the hour, home-made curries are left on the doorstep; Valiums are delivered; contact details for solicitors are pinged over; furniture is cheerfully humped up staircases.

It feels like having a second heart, or family; the safety net of both care and long-running in-jokes is enormously comforting.

Essentially, with my female friends, I do not fear ever having a massive brain injury, and totally forgetting who I am. They are my external hard drive. They could come round and download the back-up me that they have collectively stored – and I'd be back to full functionality by 9pm. They know *everything* about me.

With my male friends? Well, the main difference is, when I tell them about all this – what female friendship groups are like – they seem . . . envious.

'Yeah – I have nothing like that.'

'I have *never* gone away for a weekend with my male friends.'

'My wife does stuff like that – but I never seem to get round to it.'

'Over the years, our social life as a couple has mainly turned into *her* friends coming round regularly. And then I'll maybe see my friends a couple of times a year, in the pub.'

'I have two male friends who I would say I'm very close to – and I realised, last time I was with them: I have no idea if they have any siblings; or what their dad's job was. Really fundamental, basic stuff.'

'It's perfectly normal for it to take a few days for another man to reply to a text.'

'Obviously, I have never "snuggled on the sofa" with my male friends.'

And, in the most upsetting case: 'I've spent whole evenings in the pub, genuinely feeling suicidal, and never mentioned it.'

Here is a scenario you might recognise from your own life:

A man returns home after a night out with a close male friend.

Wife: 'Good night?'

Husband: 'Yeah – really lovely. Great to catch up. Really nice.'

Wife: 'So, how's Simon?'

Husband: 'Seemed fine.'

Wife: 'Did he say anything about Anna's mum's operation? Or the new house? How's his work going? Oh my God – did they ever find their dog?'

Husband: 'Oh – we never really got round to all that.'

Wife, astonished: 'You were with him for *five hours*. What did you talk about?'

Husband, suddenly slightly awkward: 'Oh, you know. This and that.'

Wife, exasperated: 'I'm going to call Anna, and actually find out what's going on in their lives. The *dog* is *diabetic*.'

In this scenario – which, I suspect, is familiar to many couples – as we can see, no information has been gathered. Or, at least, the information a *woman* would seek out in a conversation with another woman, or man. Unless there is a woman involved in a conversation, information about mothers, operations, house moves, life events, hopes, dreams, histories, emotions and insulin-dependent dogs will almost certainly neither be requested, nor offered. That stuff is to be . . . ignored. Forgotten. It is not on the agenda.

Instead, men talk about – well, what do they talk about? *Other* informations. Men informations.

'Simon has found a new record shop in Bromley,' Pete offered, finally. 'It had a whole box of British jazz rarities on Decca from the late sixties. It's amazing.'

I observe, in my interactions with men, over the years, that there is something about being around other men that stops them steering the conversation off the – absolutely delightful! Really funny! Thoroughly warm and enjoyable! – road of Male Chat, and onto the rough yet necessary grassland of Sadness, Worry and Disclosure.

It's not that it *never* happens – I have seen both 2am Glastonbury conversations and dinner-party chats that have bravely gone off-road onto this more . . . unstable turf.

The big difference is that I have *never* seen a conversation between women that *didn't* – in any discussion lasting over 40 minutes – go there. It's absolutely conversationally standard. Women would think it utterly abnormal – indeed, a 'failed' conversation; a 'weird' night – if there weren't inquiries and follow-ups on mood, health, anxiety, love, child-rearing, depressions, feuds, panics and crises. We don't even need to be asked: we volunteer it, as being a staple of the conversational buffet. It's no biggie. It *is* conversation. That's the *real* shit.

Men, on the other hand, seem to see this kind of stuff as . . . a limited-entry deal. As if you maybe only have three or four tokens – *in your whole life* – that you can pop into this conversational slot machine, marked 'Difficult Stuff'. So you should only play them when things get really desperate. You have to hoard them. Until you're desperate. Until you're . . . suicidal. And, more often than not, you can only use them when you're around a specialist in this kind of thing, i.e. a woman.

Although I was interviewing Mortimer and Whitehouse about their TV show *about male friendship*, on that day, all

their conversation between each other was banter. Endlessly entertaining, world-class banter, yes: banter from
professionals, which frequently made me cry laughing. But
banter, nonetheless.

Two years later, I interviewed Bob Mortimer on his own.
We went back to his home town, Middlesbrough, while he
told me stories from his childhood. Although a great many
of these stories were breathlessly funny – 'That's the changing rooms [of my school], where the kid's penis retracted
fully back into his body. To the astonishment of all who saw
it' – a huge amount of them were very, very upsetting. Loneliness; his father's death; terrible social anxiety.

At one point, we stood with our faces up against the
gates of his old school, staring out across the playground,
silently.

'What are you thinking?' I asked, eventually. He looked
impossibly boy-like, and sad. 'What are you remembering?'

'Just crying, I guess,' Mortimer says, shrugging. 'Walking across the playground, and crying me eyes out.'

He looked on the verge of tears.

'Bob, I'm afraid I'm going to have to hug you,' I said.
'It's all too sad, and I need to give you a hug.'

I put my arms around him. I think he was a bit confused. A car went by. The driver – seemingly oblivious to
the look on Bob's face, and the fact that something had
happened which was, clearly, so upsetting we were hugging, at 11am, outside a school – leaned his head out,
beeping his horn.

'BOB! Love you, man! UVAVU!'

*

During the pandemic lockdown, I was aware that three male friends were particularly struggling. As soon as it was viable, we assumed the Classic Covid Socialising Situation – sitting outside somewhere very cold, two metres apart, huddled in layers of coats and hats, and smoking furiously to keep warm.

In all three situations, we started as we always did – with nerdy music talk, or industry gossip, or theories about politics – basically BlokeChat, in which I am fairly fluent.

And then, after this 20-minute warm up – the B-reel – I looked them in the eye, and said, 'Dude – I know you're going through a tough time right now. Do you want to talk about it?'

There then followed a combination of these things, in a variety of orders:

ONE: High-pitched, awkward laughter and the words, 'HA! Emotions! Those guys! Pesky fellas! ARGH!'

TWO: Some truly agonised face-pulling/gurning – like the bit in *Who Framed Roger Rabbit?* where Roger runs through 'all' the emotions, facially, for comic effect.

THREE: 'Ah – it's boring. You don't wanna talk about this.'

FOUR: 'Ah – it's nothing, really. Just the usual bol- locks. I just need to snap out of it.'

FIVE: 'Shouldn't we be doing this at 2am, pissed? Or on pills?'

SIX: 'I honestly feel like it's been better in the last couple of days – it was just a blip. I'm actually over it now.'

SEVEN: 'Argh, I'm just being a miserable cunt – ignore me.'

EIGHT: 'Men dumping their emotions on women is such a *cliché*, and I refuse to do it.'

NINE: 'You know what – *nah.*'

TEN: 'I feel like I'm *always* dumping on you.' [He isn't. We had *one* emotional chat, *once, seven years ago*.]

ELEVEN: Immediately bursting into tears.

Once the men had finished running through all their various methods for avoiding actually talking about how they felt, we finally got into The Big Stuff. Not to minimise anything these men were feeling, but it was all absolutely standard: career struggles; unhappy children; marriage problems; fractious relationships with parents; financial constriction; physical ill-health.

The biggest problem by far wasn't the actual problems – which were all quite solvable, or deal-able with – but *the way the problems made the men feel*, instead.

At one point, during the conversation with my most unhappy friend, his eyes filled with tears as he said – in a voice so quiet it was obvious he'd never said these words out loud before, but had thought them so often that they terrified him – 'I keep thinking . . . what is the point of me, any more?'

I admit that, at that moment, I broke social distancing guidelines, and we hugged for quite a long time.

The most notable thing about all three conversations, though, was that, when they were over – when we'd done all the heavy emotional lifting, and crying, and came out the other side into what I like to think of as 'the conversational recovery phase'; similar to how, after a very intense massage in a spa, they pop you onto a reclining chair in some pleasingly dimmed vestibule, while you gradually get your shit back together – all three men said variants of the same thing, while we relaxed, started joking again, and lit new cigarettes:

'That's the best conversation of my life.'

'I've never had a conversation like that.'

'Have *you* ever had a conversation like that before?'

Although I wanted to take the compliment – which suggested I was a Golden Empathy and Chat God, possessed of borderline supernatural powers – I was honest with them: outlining, as I did above, just how *normal* these conversations are for women.

My friend looked thoughtful.

'I have tried to talk to male friends about this,' he said, eventually. 'I went to the pub with B——, and said, "I'm feeling quite bad at the moment," and he said, "Ah mate, that's tough" – and then started talking about work. It was very clear he wanted the conversation to end there.'

We both know B—— very well. What *I* know, and my friend doesn't, is that I had a very similar conversation with B—— a year or so ago, where he talked about how furiously he has to hide his emotions, and how he often feels despair.

Back then, B—— said – which I find both resonant, and utterly heartbreaking – that when he tried to talk to my friend about how he felt, my friend 'clearly felt very uncomfortable – and then changed the subject'.

My friend and B—— have known one another for longer than *I* have known either of them – but they have not yet found a way to talk to *each other* in the way they talk to me.

Almost as if he guessed this, my friend joked, 'I guess men just need to make more female friends. Then they could enjoy all this "cathartically crying in someone's back garden" more regularly.'

It is an automatic assumption that if a man wants to have an emotional, vulnerable conversation, his best chance is while talking to a woman. I remembered how David, back in Chapter One, and my tour of the World of Boys, had confessed how, 'If I were ever to cry at school, I would have gone to the only woman who was there – Mrs Victor. Not because she was enormously Earth Mother-y and compassionate, but just because she was a woman. The only woman.'

And this is enormously damaging.

Not for women – as I said before, this shit is our bread and butter. We will happily talk to you about all your sadnesses, with absolute love for you. It really is no biggie. And we do it all the time.

No: the damage is that, if you believe you can only talk about these things with women – if you observe, as you become adult, that the only men who are being regularly emotionally cared for are those who have got close female friends, girlfriends, or wives – you will know a terrible truth: you cannot relieve your anxieties, and fears, until you 'get' a woman who can do this for you. It's like lancing a boil on your back that you cannot reach alone. You need an external pair of hands – female hands – for that job.

And for some men, struggling with their unhappiness, this belief – that you can only be emotional and vulnerable with a woman – leads to dark places. For if you cannot find a woman to love you – if you are rejected; if you are awkward and unpopular; if it's just not *happening* for you right now, romantically – then this awful, shameful, unrelieved need can, very easily, turn to anger. Because, until you get a woman in your life, willing to listen to your problems, here is your situation: you will remain, essentially and fundamentally, just half a person. You *need* a woman to be emotionally complete. Men cannot complete you.

It's a dolorous thing, but when we look at the 'manosphere', Men Going Their Own Way and Incel culture – ideologies which it is estimated that 70 per cent of young men have clicked on, read, or been exposed to – this *fury* over, basically, women not being interested in them, makes sense. It's not *just* about sex, or status. They don't *just* want a girlfriend to fuck, or show off about, or prove their masculinity.

It's far deeper and more existential than that: these boys, and men, feel they will get no comfort or relief – that they will be condemned to walk around with all their fears and anxieties and insecurities inside them, for ever – as it is only women they would ever be able to open up to. And there are no women in their lives who love them. Indeed, they have vowed to give up on women.

The irony, of course, is that when they spend their times on these radicalised, man-only websites, the truth of this only seems confirmed. For all the other men on there are communicating with such anger, hatred and nihilism – suicide is a regular topic: 'rope' for hanging, 'LDAR' means, simply, 'lie down and rot'; encouragement to take your own life is frequent – that it is obvious that no *man* could ever let you be vulnerable, or cry, or hope, or change. There is no help here. They all feel the same, too. Women are your only hope. And you do not have one.

This, then, is the ultimate tragedy of those who veer off into misogyny, and a hatred of women. Those who believe that women have something – a 'power', or something 'innate' – that men could only get access to if they, in turn, had power over women. If they possess them. Like some pagan belief that you can gain the powers of a lion by eating a lion's heart. If they can 'get' women.

For they do not know: you don't need to 'have' women to gain *anything*. Everything that, culturally, is seen as 'female', is something *anyone* can have. These are all things anyone can learn. These are all things *anyone* can gain. Women weren't *born* knowing how to be amazing friends – having super-deep conversations about anxiety, and sorrow. Personally, I just learned how to do it from watching *The Golden Girls*; and then, latterly, from noting what questions my therapist was asking *me* – as I was so surprised at how the simplest of questions were, often, the ones we are all least-often asked.

I think that, sometimes, what holds men back from being vulnerable with each other is a belief that doing it is, some-how, a *skill*. Something you need to learn, and which takes years to perfect – but which, if you did it wrong, some kind of cataclysmic Chat Emergency would happen. And that you would both maybe *die* from having Wild Emotions suddenly unleashed, which you are both too amateurish to deal with.

But honestly? Having Deep Conversations is something any dum-dum can do. In essence, it just consists of a list of very simple questions and comments – often used over and over again, in a very prosaic way: 'How you doing?' 'What's going on?' 'How's that making you feel?' 'What do you worry will happen?' 'Has this happened before?' 'What happened then?' 'What's the worst-case scenario?' 'Have you talked to anyone else about this?' 'God, that sounds tough.' 'I'm so sorry this is happening to you.' 'You've dealt with stuff like this before brilliantly.' 'It's going to be a shag, but you'll get through it.' 'Is there anything I can do to help?' 'What would make it better?'

I think one advantage women have is allowing them-selves more leeway in saying things that aren't memorable repartee, or witty banter – but which employ two different modes, instead: 'Fact-Finding' and 'Soothing'. And which, ironically, often lead to conversations which *are* more mem-orable, and witty: after all, you won't forget an evening when someone you love told you something they'd never told anyone else.

And for those – and I am one of them – who can often panic at the idea of a Serious Conversation, wherein humour ostensibly appears to be off the table: well, until you've had an evening where you are talking about all the Big Ticket subjects – death, mental illness, abortion, troubled children, divorce, existential crises – you won't know how unexpectedly and reassuringly often you *will* end up making jokes, even when you're crying. Some of the most enjoyably raw, dark material I've ever heard isn't in a Chris Rock routine, but during a 1am Crisis Chat. There is something about two people being really open and honest with each other that allows some manner of Super Humour to happen – which is why, I suppose, it's ultimately no surprise that two of Britain's greatest comedians seemed to 'invent' the whole idea of confessional male friendship, on *Gone Fishing*. Humour is, after all, the magic room we invented, where we can go to say anything, no matter how forbidden or raw.

In the last year – since I started writing this book, and talking to friends about male friendship and how it differs from female friendship – I've noticed something fascinating: men basically *copying* women. Realising they were slightly envious of female friendships – and subsequently being inspired by them.

The man who said 'I have *never* gone away for a weekend with my male friends'? He organised a weekend, hiking in the Lake District with some other dads, and came back saying, 'I should have done this *years* ago – we're going to make it a regular thing.'

The man who said 'My wife does stuff like that – but I never seem to get round to it'? He now has a monthly Pub Meet-Up with his mates.

The man who realised he didn't know if his best friend has siblings? They went for dinner together, and spent the whole evening talking about their childhoods – which unexpectedly resulted in him not only learning his best friend has two siblings, but also that he has a vestigial tail.

'We thought about going to look at it, in the toilets – but decided not to, in the end.'

The most affecting was my husband, who read a rough draft of this chapter, and then came on a dog walk with me.

'I think I've realised – me and my best three friends *do* want to meet up more, but we never really know how to say it,' he said, thoughtfully, as we tramped around Finsbury Park, in the rain. 'They say things like, "Yeah, I never really see anyone apart from you, and two other friends, all separately," and I'd just think it was a statement – but I see now, they were *really* saying: "I'm in my forties, or fifties, and the friendship group I thought I'd have hasn't really happened. And I don't know why." And because I'm in exactly the same boat, I knew why: you just have to schedule it, don't you? Friendship is . . .'

He thinks for a minute.

'A verb. Friendship is a doing word.'

Chapter Nine

Men Talking to Women

I first heard about Pickup Artists from my friend Hugo.

He'd come over to the house for one of our classic evenings of Reasonable Fun – two beers and a whisky – and we'd spent the first half-hour engaged in the more important business of our friendship: discussing which birds we'd most recently seen. We are both competitive ornithologists, and I am still very jealous of Hugo's unexpected nuthatch.

Once we'd finished our bird-chat, conversation turned to 'weirdest journalist jobs we've ever done'; and, in the course of the anecdote-exchange, he revealed that he'd once had to spend all weekend with a world-famous Pickup Artist. Someone who specialises in being able to get any woman into bed.

It had been, apparently, a truly eye-opening experience.

'We went to some club in Leicester Square. To just . . .

get women. There are techniques Pickup Artists teach you, whole scripts and routines – and the maddest thing was that they totally worked. By the end of the evening, after I'd basically just done what I'd been taught, there was a woman who seemed genuinely interested in me. I hadn't said a single spontaneous thing to her all night – I was absolutely pretending to be someone else. And she would, I think, have got off with me, if I'd wanted her to.

'It was . . .' and here Hugo considered, for a moment, the exact words to say, before settling on, '. . . *really* horrible.'

Since Eric Weber wrote *How to Pick Up Girls!* in 1970, and sold over two million copies, there has been a succession of male authors – and, now, YouTube stars – taking advantage of the fact that young men don't know the language of women. These tutors promise to teach them the tricks and hacks to bluff their way through it. For over 50 years, now, we have had Pickup Artists.

In theory, of course, there's nothing wrong with this. These tutors are merely addressing the fact that, for most people, going up to someone you fancy and starting a conversation with them is a terror on a par with throwing your heart into a volcano; or taking GCSE Maths, naked.

If there are older, wiser dogs giving out some 'chat advice' to the younger, nervous pups, then this is, as a general concept, all to the good. We all have to learn somewhere; and if young, horny modern men *will* refuse to watch the classic screwball comedies of the 1940s and

50s – wherein they could learn to flirt like Cary Grant, or Gary Cooper – then a more lumpen and prosaic handbook it must be, I guess.

Sadly, in practice, the advice Pickup Artists give anxious, inexperienced men is, ultimately, often terrible. Much of it works as a fairly comprehensive list of all the things women fear the most: strange men approaching them in the street, or touching them within minute of introducing themselves. 'Going kino' involves *biting* a woman who you've only just met.

And, more alarmingly, some of it verges on borderline criminal: there are many tips for 'breaking down last minute resistance to sexual intercourse' – or, as a jury might later hear it framed, 'being a bit rape-y'.

The bible of Pickup Artist manuals is, of course, *The Game,* by Neil Strauss – the Pickup Artist Hugo had spent the weekend with. First published in 2005, *The Game* was a worldwide bestseller, and became a key reference for a certain kind of noughties man. Strauss – who, in his Pickup Artist days, was known as 'Style' – begat a host of other Pickup Artists, all with similarly Marvel Universe names: Mystery, Gambler and 'Tyler Durden' – named after the (can I say it? Frankly unmarriagable) character played by Brad Pitt in *Fight Club.*

Although they all have their own innovations and tricks – much squabbled over, amusingly – the general idea is still the same: talking to girls, and getting them into bed, is, as Strauss's book title suggests, a game – and if you learn a couple of rules, *any* man can do it.

Indeed, Strauss goes out of his way to describe how he

and his fellow Pickup Artists are not classically 'hot', or charismatic, or, indeed, pleasant: 'I am far from attractive . . . to say my hair is thinning would be an understatement . . . My eyes are small and beady . . . I am shorter than I'd like to be and so skinny that I look malnourished,' Strauss writes in the opener to *The Game*. He describes Mystery as looking like 'a computer geek who'd been bitten by a vampire', and Tyler Durden as 'snotty . . . ungrateful . . . the palest non-albino human being I had ever seen', with orangey-blond hair stuck straight up like a troll doll. All Tinder profiles that could do with a slightly more upbeat rewrite. It sounds like *someone* needs a hug.

At the beginning of the noughties, these Pickup Artists formed a loosely bound gang who traded 'tips', 'games' and 'strategies' with each other. Twenty years later – post #metoo, the rise of Incels, and half a dozen misogyny-inspired mass shootings – reading them is an uncomfortable experience; particularly if you are a woman, or have daughters.

'Negging' is a key factor – approaching women who 'think they're too good for you', and shaking their confidence by mildly insulting them, in order to 'level the playing field', and 'intrigue' them with your apparent mild disapproval.

'You kinda have *man's* hands.'

'You *blink* a lot.'

'Is that a *wig*?'

'You have beautiful eyes – can I touch them?'

'Ewww – you have eye-crusties!'

Strauss does not detail how to respond if, say, your

'target' *is* wearing a wig because they're currently undergoing chemotherapy; or if they burst out crying when you reopen an old, old psychological wound – in telling them they have hands like Grandad. Knowing women, I would imagine if any of these 'openers' *did* deeply distress the 'target', they would have just politely covered it up; or mentally pop the comment in the always-open 'Jotter of Internalised Self-Loathing', under 'hands (grandad) (again)'.

Having 'opened' the conversation, you should then 'display value'. Amazingly, in 2005, the methods favoured by Pickup Artists were to *either* perform close-hand magic, *or* to introduce some mad, woo-woo theory. Strauss's favourite was to analyse women's *teeth*, to conclude what personality type they had.

One of the things I find most amusing about the world of Pickup Artists is how . . . *Light Entertainment* they are. This is the kind of stuff you more often see in the audition episodes of *Britain's Got Talent*, from the acts who get gonged off after 30 seconds. It's not the stuff of true Sexual Legends: I can't imagine Casanova pulling the flags of all nations out of his bum-hole in a nightclub while hoping for a bang. Frankly, my only interest in a man doing any of this stuff would be in possibly booking him for a five-year-old's birthday party – although the fact he's wandering around a nightclub with a semi, trying to analyse women's teeth, would, ultimately, put me off this engagement.

The chapter titles of *The Game* run you through the next stages: 'Isolate the Target.' 'Extract to a Seduction Location.' 'Make a Physical Connection.' 'Blast Last-Minute Resistance.' 'Manage Expectations.' The glossary includes, winningly, 'Caveman (verb): to directly and aggressively escalate physical contact.'

If anyone has watched the sitcom *It's Always Sunny in Philadelphia*, they will find the whole thing brilliantly parodied in the episode 'The D.E.N.N.I.S. System', in which Dennis – the most problematic of a bunch of problematic characters, with a permanent, faint whisper of 'rape' around him – takes the rest of his gang through his pickup game: '**D**emonstrate value, **E**ngage Physically, **N**urture Dependence, **N**eglect Emotionally, **I**nspire Hope, **S**eparate Completely.'

It culminates in the line: 'Wrong! Wrong! Wrong! Wrong! You were supposed to let her get stabbed, hope that it hits a major artery, and then as she's dying, you nurse her back to health – thereby making her totally dependent on you. *Before leaving her.*'

In the scope of Neil Strauss's career, it seems weird that he – a nerdy Jewish *Rolling Stone* writer with a bright knack for a one-liner – didn't end up in the writers' room for *It's Always Sunny in Philadelphia*; but was the butt of the Alpha Comedy Men's satire, instead.

But then, as *The Game* makes clear, Strauss had other priorities: by the end of the book, Strauss and his gang have fucked literally thousands of women using their version of The D.E.N.N.I.S. System. They have moved into a Hollywood mansion with a floating harem of women, and even though it's very clear that everyone in the mansion is quite unhappy – drinking, pill-popping, arguing over housework, riddled with jealousy, aggressively fucking each other's girlfriends in order to 'make a point', and squeamishly trying to avoid all the used condoms in the Jacuzzi – the conclusion is still clear. Pickup Artist techniques *work*. If you want to fuck a lot of women, this is a proven, and borderline magic, way of achieving it. And a lot of people heard that message: *The Game* has, so far, sold 2.5 million copies.

Do you know what hasn't sold 2.5 million copies? Strauss's 2008 follow-up, *The Truth*. This is a shame, because *The Truth* is, well, the truth. Strauss explains, several years post-*The Game*, that learning a borderline magic trick to get women to fuck you does not, in the end, make you happy.

Being able to get a woman into bed with you, half an hour after meeting her, might be fun for the first, say, thousand fucks – but then, after that, you start wanting something else. To maybe stay in a bit more, watch TV with someone you find amusing, have a life partner who you can hang out with when you both have flu. To not go to some horrible, loud club and act like the presenter of a daytime TV game show in order to bang a semi-drunk model who's as emotionally unengaged as you are.

You start thinking about the next 20 years: how can you fit in a family around all these one-night stands? Who will be with you when you die? Who can you talk with about subjects that aren't a) your dick and b) where she's going to put it? And will you *ever* be able to stop doing close-hand magic?

In *The Truth* – which is a brilliantly readable, fun book – Strauss details how he finally realised that he was a sex addict, with low self-esteem, depression, anxiety and ADHD, and that, in compulsively finding and fucking women, 'My thinking was, "If this woman's going to be naked with me, I must be OK." *But it doesn't last.*'

In *The Truth*, Strauss recounts how he had, finally, fallen in love with someone – Ingrid – but that he was frequently unfaithful to her – and so she, understandably, left. That happens in Chapter Three.

The rest of the book is Strauss exploring every kind of therapy to understand why he has destroyed the love he so desperately craved – and it's one of the most vividly honest and illuminating examinations of male emotion and sexuality I've ever read. I can't recommend it enough – primarily because it reads almost like a myth: Strauss *has* gained a magic power, but it has terrible consequences. It's like Midas's ability to turn things into gold – *amazing* for the first ten seconds; a living nightmare ever afterwards. For, if you're Midas, the first time you go for a wazz, your magic gold-making hands turn your cock into a glittering yet numb sausage – and then it's all downhill from there.

For Strauss, meanwhile, *his* bad magic is trying to solve his low self-esteem with a years-long Hollywood fuck-fest – and then realising he's spent every night with women who don't know the real Strauss, nor care about him, and who he's tricked into bed. He's used the wrong spell. He's gained the wrong magic. His cock is, metaphorically, glittering – yet numb. He is, ultimately, a lonely wizard. No one loves him, after all.

So what *is* the solution? How do you talk to girls, and make them want to have sex with you?

It's hilarious and yet awful that so much of young men's time – and money: most Pickup Artists also run seminars, or online courses, starting at $99 and upwards – is spent asking that question of each other, when I can tell you for a *fact* that this is the question that young women ask each other about men – and spend their time and money on, too.

Here's a fact about humanity: we *all* want someone to take our knickers off and tell us we're smashing. *Everyone* is up for an evening of sexy good-times with someone they like the look of. If there were a microphone installed in the sky over every village, town and city in the world, the main sentence it would pick up, over and over, is people wailing, 'Why can't I find someone who likes me enough to munch my genitals?'

And here, we must circle back round to what we discussed earlier. Why is it so difficult for men to approach women? Why don't men know what to say to women? 'One of the world's greatest mysteries is the mind of a woman,' Mystery – one of the OG Pickup Artists – says, grandly, in *The Rules*.

'Our parents and our friends had failed us,' Strauss continues. 'They had never given us the tools we needed to become fully effective social beings.'

Women are mysterious. Society does not give you the tools to converse with them. There is no way to know what women like to talk about.

Here's a list:

Love Island. The classic MGM musicals. *Legally Blonde*. Jane Austen. The best cute/rescued animal videos on the-dodo.com. 'Fight Night' on *Big Brother* series five. Whither

Zoella? Judy Blume. Lizzo's reality TV series, *Watch Out for the Big Girls. Meet Me in St Louis. Bridgerton. Girls.* Beyoncé's *Lemonade*. Which member of The Beatles would you trust to cat-sit? Can Girls Aloud perform without Sarah Harding? Sisters. Toni Morrison. Does 'dry clean only' actually *mean* anything? The worst bitch you've ever worked with. What parts of feminism you hate. Which alcoholic drink – having thrown up on it before – can you now not drink? What is the king of potato formats: crisp, chip, roast, baked, mashed or, for the pervert, dauphinoise? Worst-ever holiday. Best-ever holiday. Is there an acceptable hat a man can wear? Most annoying advice your parents keep giving you. Weird things your nan eats. Riskiest wee/poo you've ever done. Unlikeable children you've known. Dogs. *Cats.*

Those are all off the top of my head – there isn't a woman in the world who wouldn't respond to at least five of those, as conversational topics. Because the answer to 'Why does it feel so difficult for a young man to talk to a young woman?' isn't 'Because you haven't yet learned some tricks, or close-hand magic, to get her attention', it's: 'Because you aren't talking to her about stuff *in her world*.' Do you *know* her world?

And it is that simple: we all know the cliché-because-it's-true fact that straight women and gay men can, more often than not, chat away all night – and that's because gay men are more likely to engage with the stuff in women's worlds. They're more likely to have watched the same TV shows as us, read the same books as us – and, plus, we can bond over which men we fancy.

Of course, you might get lucky and find a woman whose

primary interests are football, shots, *The Fast and the Furious*, *Call of Duty*, shagging women and 'bantz' – one of those 'Cool Girls' that Gillian Flynn so effortlessly parodies in *Gone Girl*. One of those code-switching girls who is at home in the world of Men's Things. But the simple and most effective way to be able to 'talk to women' is to know about the same stuff that they do. *All* the best conversations are those where you both hit on a topic you feel passionate about – whether it's how much you *hate* guinea pigs ('They're just a giant face and nothing else') or how much you *love* Linda from *Bob's Burgers*.

If you're going to 'learn' and 'study' how to talk to women – if you're going to invest all that *time* – why not skip the Pickup Artist tricks, and actually learn about, and study, *women*, instead? The actual thing you're interested in? It's as easy as just 'asking them questions about themselves', it doesn't require that you suddenly bite them in a nightclub, and if it doesn't lead to eventually getting a fuck, it might lead to eventually gaining a friend. Who might have *friends* you could fuck. 'Getting to know someone' is rarely a wasted effort. And you really might enjoy *Meet Me in St Louis*.

The bottom line is, the world is full of billions and billions of things to talk about, and everyone wants to get laid. Men and women are on the same side, here. Our interests run concurrently. It is a shared quest.

There is, however, *one* tip, or technique, that I wish someone would run a seminar on, or write a book about. Just one.

Admittedly, the seminar would be three minutes long,

and the book a single page, but it is this: rather than learning chat-up lines, or 'negging', or 'value display', learn the rules of improv comedy, instead.

Specifically, 'Yes – and'.

Everyone needs to know 'Yes – and'. It is the secret to all good conversation. And it is, merely, this. In improv comedy, when someone comes onstage and says, 'Hello! I'm a doctor – why are you in my waiting room with a saucepan on your head?', you *don't* reply, 'You're not a doctor, and I don't have a saucepan on my head.' Because all the comedy just died, and now everyone wants to go home, and you will now be known as Scene Killer for ever.

Instead, you say, 'Yes! I have a saucepan on my head – *and* you should see what inconvenient kitchen item I have stuck in my pants!'

Your improv partner can now ask you about the problematic contents of your pants, you can get them to guess ('I figure the worst thing might be . . . a blender?'), and so you can trundle on, building the scene.

As in improv comedy, so in conversation. I have watched so many conversations die because people did not know the magical secret of 'Yes – and', and so destroyed a fledgling conversation.

Instance: you're in a group of people, but the one you're standing next to at the bar is someone you've never met before. The silence is becoming awkward. Finally:

'Do you want a drink?'

'No – I'm having a Dry January.'

RIP this chat. Enjoy the next five, uncomfortable minutes of silence.

If you live by 'Yes – and', however, it would have gone like this:

'Do you want a drink?'

'Yes – fizzy water, please, and could you get me a packet of crisps? Someone told me this place sells the worst crisps they've ever eaten, and I want to see if it's true. Which of those flavours do you think will be the *most* unpleasant?'

And there you go. If that doesn't see you through at least ten minutes of chat about crisps, other awful foods you've eaten, the worst pubs in your home town, the *best* crisps, and, then, once you're loosened up, maybe *why* you're not drinking – possibly because, during this Christmas just gone, you got so drunk you tried to climb up a chimney, shouting 'I'M SANTA!' – then that chat was never going to work in the first place. You can simply move on. Because, at the end of the day, who wants to fuck someone who *doesn't* want to talk about crisps?

On the night where Hugo told me about his weekend with Neil Strauss – King of the Pickup Artists – I obviously had a million questions to ask him. But the main one was: 'Was there anything actually useful, or good, about the techniques he taught you? Is there anything *of use* in Pickup Artist tricks?'

He looked thoughtful.

'It taught me that you can actually *learn* to be better at conversation – to have interesting stuff to say, to be a better version of yourself, etc. – *provided* you know what to take from your lessons, and what to ignore like a sexist plague.

And it can be useful even when *not* chasing "poontang". I remember being taught that the way to feel comfortable and attract people at a party is to make everybody else feel like you are the centre of whatever is going on. One way to do this was to form a circle with your friends, that other people wanted to see inside. I went to some ridiculous awards thing – music industry, I think – and spent the entire time roaming around it in a loud rotating circle with two friends, and pointing at celebrities, to try to lure them in.'

He pauses.

'It didn't work, mind you – but was more fun than getting quietly pissed in a corner.'

Chapter Ten

The Advice of Men

I once had a revelation in a bookshop in Hay-on-Wye. It was two years ago, and I'd spent the last hour in the vast section marked 'Women and Feminism' – because that's my jam: also, I like to check if they have my books – before I finally tired of the genre 'Vag Advice' and decided I needed a palate-cleanser: men. So I went to look for books about men.

It was one of those delightful, higgledy-piggledy bookshops – like a corn maze of paperbacks – and laid out over three storeys; so I'd been clomping up and down the tiny wooden staircases for a good half-hour before I finally realised, with a shock: I would not find this section. Ever. Because: *there is no section called 'Men'*.

Not just in this bookshop – in *every* bookshop.

I have *never* seen one.

We might have sections about astronomy, cookery, walking in Portugal, foraging, boat-building and cats: but there is no section for men – because there is no *genre* called 'Men'. It simply doesn't exist. There are sections on *sub-categories* of men: I found a 'Gay Men' section, and another, even smaller, section on 'BAME Men' – but when it comes to straight white men, despite them being, in our culture, the default, they are, oddly, flying under the radar when it comes to actually being described, analysed, chronicled, discussed or advised. They are so much the default, no one can see that they are just a category, like any and every other.

Meanwhile, judging by the shelves surrounding me, 'women' are the third-most written-about subject *in the world* – after cookery, and the Nazis.

It took a while for it to sink in just how odd it is that there is no 'Men' section in libraries or bookshops. Or, when I checked later, on Amazon – and Amazon even has a sub-section called 'Erotic Recipes'.

'Why do you think this is?' I asked Pete, later, as we walked down by the river. It was a slightly disjointed con-versation, as the dog – despite technically being a 'water dog', descended from two breeds that specialise in hunting wildfowl – was being chased by an angry duck, and we had to intervene with some 'dominant quacking'.

'I dunno,' Pete said, once we'd seen off the enraged mallard, and checked the dog still had both eyes intact. 'I mean, maybe it's just business. Women buy most of the books, don't they? Isn't there that stat, that men read, on average, five books a year – and women read ten?'

'True,' I said.

'So I guess as men have less interest in books anyway, writing books *about* them is a bad business model?'

'That figures,' I said. 'How many books about "being a man" have you read?'

'Erm, none?'

'Can you name any?'

He looked blank.

'I think the only advice I've ever read was the problems page in *Just Seventeen*,' he said, eventually. 'That's where I learned about periods. And herpes.'

'I literally can't name how many advice books I've read about being a woman,' I mused. 'Given that I would also include both *Riders* and *Jane Eyre* in that. They taught me you can break your hymen riding a horse, and that if you fancy a really rich married man, you just have to wait until his castle burns down, killing his wife, and leaving him blind. Love's all about *the long game*.'

As I spoke, I was googling on my phone – I'd half-remembered an interview with Jonathan Coe, author of *The Rotters' Club*, who'd come to some conclusions about how men and women look for different things in books.

'Found it!' I said, before reading aloud: 'Coe said: "I dislike generalisations, as a rule, but [statistically], the male reader's choice is more thrillers, or fantasy, while women are more likely to go for 'literary' fiction. That suggests to me that women read books to understand themselves – and men, to escape themselves." That would explain why there is no "Men" section. Who wants to write books analysing men – if men just have no interest in analysing men? If men only read to forget their problems, while women read to solve them?'

We continued our walk, in silence. I was absolutely consumed with pondering this whole revelation. It was one of the most striking disparities I had come across when considering the difference between women and men. Women *inhale* books about being a woman, mainly non-fiction: in the last decade alone, there have been the massive bestsellers *Women Don't Owe You Pretty, Bad Feminist, Everything I Know About Love, Feminists Don't Wear Pink, We Should All Be Feminists, Hood Feminism, Invisible Women, Lean In.* The basic, gigantic question – 'What *is* a woman?' – is constantly debated, *and changed.*

And that's before we include all the self-help and advice books that aren't *specifically* aimed at women, but kind of *are*: Marie Kondo, *Why Has Nobody Told Me This Before?, The Book You Wish Your Parents Had Read, The Subtle Art of Not Giving a F*ck.* Women are constantly looking to understand and improve themselves. To understand and improve life – even if it's just their sock drawer. They are taking on hundreds and hundreds of hours of advice, from a variety of self-proclaimed 'advice givers', across almost every aspect of their lives – save 'Erotic Recipes' – every year.

Men? Men – not so much. There isn't anything like the full-time, industrialised Advice-Giving Economy that women live in the centre of. So when a book *is* written that is intended for men, it tends to arrive without a context, rivals or peers. It comes not out of a movement, or a wider discussion – but seemingly out of nowhere. It's a one-off. A mad phenomenon. And because there isn't the constant *competition* or *market* for male readers, those books – like Soviet-era cars – tend to be of poor quality. When you kick them, pretty quickly, the wheels fall off.

And so the male reader – absorbing perhaps his first *and only* book of analysis, and advice, for men – understandably finds it more difficult to judge whether or not, to be frank, the book is absolutely batshit or not.

As Thomas Aquinas said, '*Hominem unius libri timeo.*' I fear the man who has read a single book. He meant it about the Bible.

I mean it about Jordan B. Peterson.

If, and when, there is a section invented in bookshops called 'Men', Jordan B. Peterson would be far and away its best-seller: his combined back catalogue has sold over 7 million copies; his various YouTube lectures have 520 million views and 6.5 million subscribers; and, in 2019, *Time* magazine named him 'the most influential intellectual in the world'.

I first became aware of him as the 'make your bed in the morning' man. In 2019, his *12 Rules for Life: An Antidote to Chaos* was well on its way to selling its eventual 7 million copies, and the first and main thing everyone was discussing was how his most sensational piece of advice was: 'Every morning, make your bed.'

'My sense is that if you want to change the world, you start with yourself and work outward because you build your competence that way,' he expanded. 'I don't know how you can go out and protest the structure of the entire economic system if you can't keep your room organized.'

Of course, we may note that here that Peterson has found a 'fancy' professor's way to say, for £25 in hardback, what everyone's mums have been saying to them, since they were born, *for free*. Who knows how much more effective it would have been if our mothers had conflated our dirty duvets with the continuation of neo-liberal capitalism – and, indeed, the entire validity of organised protest. Perhaps our mothers were, at the time, too busy simultaneously loading the dishwasher and worming the cat to 'go there'. But, still – can't argue with making your bed, right? No one gets hurt by a guy who wants tidier bedrooms? With his dapper waistcoat and Kermit-tinged voice, Peterson presented like a Henson Workshop Bright Uncle. He's just ultimately a common-sense guy. Also, he's Canadian. Canadians can't be *bad*, right?

Over the next year or so, I lost count of the people – predominantly young men – who said, 'Have you read Jordan B. Peterson? He's got a lot of interesting ideas. Really got me thinking. I wonder what you think of him?'

I started with one of his most successful podcasts – in which he and Russell Brand discussed the topic of 'Masculinity'. It was . . . odd? I'd expected to hear some smart analysis; playful debate; historical context; pertinent anecdotes, gleeful conclusions. I was ready to be both educated and entertained by two very famous, clever public speakers getting stuck into masculinity. I actively wanted to have all my beliefs challenged with some top-notch tussling.

Instead, after three-quarters of an hour, all that had been discussed was how *difficult* Peterson was finding fame – a conversation during which he cried several times.

There was nothing positive about masculinity. There was no celebration of what is wonderful about boys and men – no enthusing for his own team; no castles-in-the-air daydreaming for how men could be happy in themselves; take pride in themselves; sell to a currently sceptical world how underrated, essential and lovely the inherent traits of men could be.

Instead: the complaining. The crying. I found this so astonishing that, three days later, I was at a literary event with several very well-known, very successful feminist authors/campaigners – all of whom have tussled with the difficulties of fame – and mentioned that I'd just listened to it.

'Oh my God! So *weird*!' one said.

'I just didn't . . . understand. I can't think of a single female author who would come on to debate a subject, and then just talk about themselves, and how hard their success was, and then *cry*,' another said. 'I mean, there was just so much *waffle*.'

'Obviously it's not bad to cry, or tell the truth about your life,' the third said. 'But – he's at *work*? Can you imagine if any of us were invited to talk about our work – and just spent it crying?'

In the room were an anti-FGM campaigner, a notable feminist, and a woman who has written a great deal about violence against women and girls. All have had rape and death threats: two have panic buttons in their houses. One has never even mentioned that she has children – as the police told her there was the very real possibility that, if the knowledge became public, there would be threats made against the children's *schools*.

Of course, as discussed before, there is no hierarchy of feelings – if you feel sad, you feel sad – and in so many ways, it's all good work when a public male figure feels comfortable enough to discuss feeling overwhelmed, or depressed, or fearful. All truths are useful for someone, somewhere.

But I'm always slightly alarmed when someone who is very confident and vocal about telling people *how to be*, and *what to do*, is themselves apparently struggling with just such a thing. When their Rules for Life appear not to be working *for them*. Additionally, for Peterson to become so emotional when talking to Brand – there was a real sense of the floodgates opening – suggests that this isn't a thing he's been able to widely discuss in private, with family and friends. Perhaps Peterson hasn't yet learned to 'do' friendship, either.

Peterson generally presents as a loner preacher-man – one voice in a wilderness of modern, woke madness. This point feels like the right moment to mention Moran's Rule Number Three:

By and large, don't *listen to a loner preacher-man*.

Who wants to be a loner preacher-man? Why have you had to become a loner preacher-man? And how does that work out, day to day? It doesn't sound like much fun for you, or the people around you. After all, no one ever said, 'I feel a bit blue, and down, today. I know – I'll go and get a hug from the loner preacher-man.'

I bring up just how happy Peterson's own life is because, well – I wouldn't buy shoes from a cobbler wearing two plastic bags on his feet. Similarly, I wouldn't accept rules – not even 'advice', or 'thoughts', but *rules* – for life from someone who appears quite sad, and lonely. Because, ultimately, what are you buying when you buy his thoughts and theories? Something that seems not to be working terribly well for him right now. To the point where Peterson appears quite fearful about simply being alive: famously, in 2018, Peterson revealed that he lives by a *very* strict diet, which consists solely of 'beef, salt and water'.

I am not being flippant or dismissive when I say this sounds like a very serious eating disorder – and eating disorders tend to stem from very unhappy, anxious people who feel they need to exert more 'control' over their lives. The subtitle of *12 Rules for Life* is *An Antidote to Chaos*. I would suggest someone who fears 'chaos' so much they've removed 90 per cent of all possible nutrition from their diet, losing 60lbs in the process, might not be terribly well.

On top of this, in recent years, Peterson has been incredibly vocal on social media, peddling anti-vax propaganda and climate-change denialism. When you fly in the face of overwhelming scientific evidence and agreement – when your feelings and emotions about a subject are so strong you start both denying, and campaigning against, *facts* – then you're not really an academic. You're not rigorously and intellectually examining possibilities. You're doing something more . . . medieval, and primal.

Anyway. Finally, I read *12 Rules for Life*. And there is some good stuff in it. Peterson's step-by-step advice for how to properly 'argue' with loved ones, and come to an agreement that is satisfying to both, is undoubtedly good advice: as it was when psychotherapist Carl Rogers originally came up with the method in 1951. Similarly, Peterson is good on how the basis of society is sharing and delayed gratification; how a person is defined by the ideas they have; and how it's a good idea to both 'make your bed every morning', and 'stop and pet a cat in the street'. The first of those observations is from Freud, the second by Jung and then Popper, and the last two can be found on either Instagram or TikTok any time you want to look – and often presented as an amusing lip-sync, rather than a densely typed Bible-quoting rant. What I'm saying is, whenever Peterson hits on a truth, it's usually someone else's.

However, the ultimate reason why I fear for any man in a crisis turning to Peterson is that he comes across as a severely depressed man, crushed by a belief in fundamentalist Christian teaching, busily building bridges so that other people might join him in his depression – and thus make himself less alone. If you want to have a night where you blitz your liver to oblivion, play the Jordan B. Peterson *12 Rules for Life* 'Suffering Game': taking a shot every time Peterson intones, like Puddleglum in C. S. Lewis's *The Silver Chair*, that life is about suffering and/or misery, and that human beings are evil.

Page 58: 'We are fallen creatures.' Page 61: 'Life is awful – worse than that of an animal. Only gods can bear it.' Page 125: 'Violence . . . is no mystery. It's peace that's the mystery.' Page 149: 'Everyone is destined for pain.' Page 161: 'Life is suffering.' Page 174: 'Pain and suffering define the world.' Page 174: 'Self-conscious Being produces suffering.' Page 177: 'Life is nasty, brutish and short.' Page 227: 'Life is suffering.' You get the gist.

Now I'm not one to belittle anyone's Bad Times – Peterson is right, no one is immune from suffering – but there are two points here.

The first is: this absolute belief that life is terrible, and that we are all here to suffer, is an awful thing to repeatedly tell your readers.

I do wonder if a lot of his gloom stems from, well, believing an absolute bunch of useless cobblers. Literally. For if *12 Rules for Life* has one, overarching theme, it's that life is harder for men, because . . . lobsters.

The very first page of *12 Rules* dives into Peterson's now-infamous Lobster Theory: explaining that studies have found that the more aggressive male lobsters have more serotonin, while the less aggressive lobsters have less serotonin – and so are presumed to be 'depressed'. The logic follows that *unless* men/lobsters are *constantly* aggressive, they will turn into Ian Curtis from Joy Division, and die. Again, I'm not being flippant: Peterson cites how if a male lobster loses *a single fight* against another male lobster, the chemical changes are so profound that *the loser lobster's brain starts to melt*. 'Its brain basically dissolves. Then it grows a new, subordinate's brain – one more appropriate to its new, lowly position.' Lobsters – and, therefore, human men – must *always* be aggressive, fighting and winning, or else turn into cabbages.

Christ, that's a depressing thing to believe. Imagine actually thinking you'll become *brain-damaged* if you lose. And, also – it's horseshit. Humans aren't lobsters. We're very, very different. For starters: we do not have gigantic, delicious hands. Also: we diverged evolutionarily from lobsters 500 million years ago. Also: we don't piss out of our eyes, like lobsters do. Also: our brains *don't* melt when we lose. If they did, every single sporting competition in the world would be a death-sentence for half the people playing. The Olympics would be a killing fields. Even the average Christmas game of Boggle would see massive casualties in every family in the world.

This is all, obviously, a pretty classic example of 'wilfully misreading a single instance from the animal kingdom – and then concluding it tells us something about all core, primal human behaviours'.

I do find it extraordinary that, in the twenty-first century, people will still pick out the behaviour of one, single species – and then use it to confidently deduce something unchangeable and vital about *all human behaviour*. Dude, there are *eight point seven million different living things on earth*. There are bees that can vibrate so fast they can cook a hornet to death, and lizards that squirt blood out of their eyes, and fish that live in the butt of a sea-cucumber. Male giraffes drink female giraffe piss, to see if they're fertile – you know what I mean? Animals do crazy shit. I'm not sure randomly picking one, and then basing your entire life's theories on it, will hold much water, logic-wise. Or if you ever bump into a qualified anthropologist on a train.

Indeed, if I were to coin a Moran's Rule Number Four, it would be:

Be immediately distrustful of someone who uses an example of a single animal to explain what all men are really *like, in their 'natural' state.*

When you hear someone do this, you are invariably about to hear someone who is, tldr, cherry-picking a single animal to – essentially – explain why they're being a cunt.

My main alarm with Peterson, however, comes back to Thomas Aquinas, and *hominem unius libri timeo*. I fear the man who has read a single book. Peterson hasn't just read a single book, of course – *12 Rules for Life* credits over 30 different works in its end matter. But Peterson has definitely read very *narrowly*, because both the title of the book and its central thesis seem to come from a book called something like *The Usborne Book of Wiggy Feelings Goblin Kings Discuss in Private*, and would have been easily challenged and disproved if Peterson had read *any* books by *any* feminist in the last hundred years; or even talked to a reasonably bright nine-year-old with Google. And it's this:

'Order is symbolically associated with the masculine. Chaos is symbolically associated with the feminine.'

Well, okay . . . this is a Yin and Yang thing, right? Men are order, and women are chaos – but they're *both* equally good/bad and necessary? This is the balance? We're all in this together?

Well, 'order' is certainly good: 'Order is . . . the structure of society. Order is tribe, religion, hearth, home and country. It's the warm secure living-room where the fire glows and the children play . . . It's the greatness of tradition . . . the place where all things turn out how we want them.'

Sounds pretty cool! I'm glad you men got order! Can't wait to see what the ladies got. What's 'chaos', then? It's gonna be some other awesome things, right? Maybe the end of 'A Day in the Life'; or the Big Bang; or the techni-coloured swirl you can see through a kaleidoscope – allowing the untrammelled visions of the mind?

'Chaos is the domain of ignorance itself . . . It's the rustle in the bushes in the night-time, the monster under the bed, the hidden anger of your mother, and the sickness of your child. Chaos is the despair and horror you feel when you have been profoundly betrayed . . . the place you end up when things fall apart; when your dreams die.'

Huh. Well, I can't lie – one of these 'elemental forces' *definitely* sounds better than the other. It's bad news for the ladies, and no mistake. Obviously we're not gonna make a fuss right now – we'll just say 'thank you!' and then go bitch about it later, in the Ladies toilets – but I just want to check: this is all *based* on something, right? The order/chaos men/women thing? There's some kind of, erm, *facts*, or something?

'It has always been so.'

Where?

'In mythology.'

And, here, really, anyone who wants to save themselves from reading the following 370 pages could usefully clock out. I'm all for a bit of mythology, and collective subconsciousness – I'm all up in my Joseph Campbell, and Jung – but you can't claim to have come up with actual *rules* for life when you don't only not believe in science, and facts, but also genuinely believe that the fundamental, baked-in, born-with-it essence of women – all women! Even Angela Merkel! – is that we are ignorance, chaos, fear, sickness, things falling apart and dreams dying. How can you *possibly* say women are chaos? *Based on mythology?* We're the uptight fuckers moaning about how messy the kitchen is; posting up pass-agg 'housework rotas' on the fridge; shouting 'Don't drive so fast!'; hating jazz – 'it's all *over* the place'; and planning our weddings aged six, and holidays two years before they happen. If I was going to reductively stereotype half the world's population, I'd go all-in on *men* being chaos – fun, creative, bold, disruptive, innovative chaos! – and women being the Fun Police wet blanket of 'order'.

But once you know this is Peterson's idea – that women are chaos, and chaos is bad – then the subtitle for *12 Rules for Life* becomes, well, alarming: *An Antidote to Chaos*. Peterson sees femaleness, and femininity, as the main problem of men. *Women*, basically. And men need an *antidote* to it. Chaos/women are *poison*.

Hence, in further chapters, the deeply disturbing pages where he recounts seeing a female patient, while working as a psychologist – and absolutely doubting her account of having being raped. The weird leap in logic where he praises male 'bullies' – Nelson Muntz in *The Simpsons* is a tough 'corrective' to the 'touchy' Milhouses and 'chocolate-gorging children' – but female 'nags' are always bad, because 'If men are pushed too hard to feminize, they will become more and more interested in harsh, fascist political ideology.' So, hitting someone is fine, but asking someone to clean the toilet is bad. And will turn a man into a Nazi. Fine, fine.

And then there is the final *coup de grâce*, of where women fit into Peterson's world. Giving his 'advice' for being 'a good husband', Peterson talks about the greatest revelation he ever had about his wife: 'Treat her as if she were the Holy Mother of God, so that she might give birth to a world-redeeming hero.'

So in this scenario, Peterson's wife is Mary – a virgin – and their child might be Jesus, which makes Peterson . . . God?

Blimey.

I remembered again the words of Jonathan Coe: men want to 'escape themselves'.

These books aren't, ultimately, advice and understanding, then: they are escapism. Into a fantasy. Into the past. Into a myth. Into the idea that you might be a god. Into – ironically – intellectual chaos.

Also: eat some fibre, Jordan B! Your bowels must be shot.

Of course, Peterson wouldn't be the only author in the putative 'Men' bookshop section. There are others – the most successful and numerous being books written by ex-Army, SAS and Marines men. You'll have seen them: they all have a picture of the author – ripped, frowning – on the cover; arms like hams crossed, as if saying, 'Yeah, I wrote a book. But WITH MY FISTS. Like a man.' The background is usually grey, with silver writing – grey like the still-clearing cordite from a grenade explosion; silver like the glinting rocket launcher they appear to have stuffed down the front of their trousers.

I've read a half-dozen of these books: most of them are by current, or ex, presenters of *SAS: Are You Tough Enough?* They usually take the form of memoir – troubled childhood, joining the army, being hazed, learning the value of a team, going on a couple of missions that are still classified – interspersed with musing on how military life teaches a man larger lessons on life: how to be organised, disciplined, tactical, stoic, strong, loyal, always on alert for danger and ready to defend those he loves.

In theory, all of this is gravy. There almost certainly are things you can learn in the military that will better prepare you for life: particularly if you come, as most of these authors do, from troubled, violent, unloving or disrupted backgrounds. It's no bad thing to learn that you should keep your mess-tins clean, polish your boots, take care of your mates, and be constantly prepared to lug a 60kg 'Bergan' up a mountain and back down again, in the rain, if needs be. Besides, the stories *are* exciting. So long as you ignore the fact that a lot of people, eventually, die in them.

However. I would point out one thing about this vast *literal* army of authors using their former military training to hand out general life advice to a readership in whom the vast majority has never been in the army, and never will be. And it's this: soldiering is, by and large, a vanishing business. Since the 1980s, the US Army has declined from 2.2 million to 1.3 million; in the UK, from 330,000 to 150,000. Across most Western countries, the decrease is similar. Broadly speaking, we don't *need* soldiers as much as we used to.

It is odd, then, that an increasingly old-fashioned business, so rapidly in decline, should be telling us how to live. It's not happening in any other sector: we don't have dozens of barrel makers, or town criers, or falconers, all writing barrel/shouting/falcon-based life advice.

On top of this – and I hate to point this out – all the ex-military men writing these books are . . . *ex*-military men. The *primary* skills they're *actually* displaying now are a) writing and b) waiting in the green room before appearing on *The One Show*. Simply by writing a book, they're acknowledging the fact that there's more money and demand for art, and showbiz, than there is in military stuff.

Finally, when it comes down to the real fundamental skills taught in the military – the ones of immense physical fitness and endurance – I'm constantly aware, particularly when seeing them demonstrated on *SAS: Are You Tough Enough?*, that the *real* audience who needs these skills almost certainly isn't watching it. Falling backwards into freezing cold water, then standing in it for hours; going up and down mountains without knowing when they will be allowed to stop; having abuse screamed at them; and knowing very few will still be on the course when it ends? I know literally only one demographic that's of use to: refugees. An eight-year-old Syrian kid will actually use those tips. A man with a beard in Chester who can tell the difference between an IPA and a lager – perhaps not.

You know how – cliché alert! But cliché because it's true! – when a woman's car starts making a weird 'clunking' sound, or 'pulling to the right', she often wants to bring a male relative or friend – you – to the garage, as she's worried about being patronised or 'ripped off' by the men in the man-place, taking advantage of a woman? That cars are still, generally, seen as a man thing, and so it's best to take a man along for the ride, just in case?

I think the same is true for advice books for men. Advice books are still, generally, a woman thing – we have stacks of them, by the bed! We specialise in this shit! – and so we have a diligently honed sense of which ones hold up, and which ones don't. When a woman advice-giver comes along who, say, ignores science, and facts, and peddles a load of woo-woo horseshit, there is an almost immediate pile-on from other women – in blogs, TikToks, columns and Tweets – pointing out what horseshit it all is. I refer you to the constant debunking of Gwyneth Paltrow. Thousands of women have been on to her from *day one*.

If, and when, a 'Men' section is ever invented in bookshops, and you hear a weird 'clunking' sound coming from a paragraph, or find that the ideology is 'pulling to the right', maybe . . . bring along a female friend, or relative. She can finally pay you back for the whole 'garage' favour. She can stop you being patronised, or ripped off.

And this is the final point of all this. For being an advice-giver is, often, ultimately, a grift. A shopfront for merch and lucrative corporate speaking circuits. In her time, Gwyneth Paltrow has sold 'jade vagina eggs' (£55) and 'psychic vampire repellent spray' (£22). Jordan B. Peterson, meanwhile, has sold 'The Lobster' hoodies (£41) and 'Personality Tests' for $10 a pop. The 'self' in 'self-help' is often a clue. Often, it doesn't refer to the reader. It refers to the author.

Jordan B. Peterson is worth $8 million.

Chapter Eleven

The Manosphere

'I found out who Andrew Tate was on Christmas Day,' a friend says.

Oh, that sounds . . . festive. How?

'I had my nephew over, who's having . . . a difficult time. We were talking around the table, and I noticed my daughter was becoming distressed. I took her into the bathroom and asked why, and she said he was doing the Andrew Tate Hand Gesture.'

The . . . what?

'There's a hand gesture Andrew Tate does. He puts all the tips of his fingers and thumbs together, into a kind of . . . steeple.'

She showed me. It's the thing elderly professors do when they're about to make a very pointed comment about e.g. Minoan history.

'What does it mean?'

'Well, my daughter said it just means he supports Andrew Tate. It's a way of saying, "Shut up, women." And he was doing it *at* her. She knew what it meant. It really upset her. And then she told me who Andrew Tate was, and it upset *me*, too. On Christmas Day! Just before pudding!'

My friend seemed very upset.

'I don't understand! He's 15, and he seems *immersed* in this really right-wing, misogynist culture – but his parents are so *nice*! They're just ... classic, left-wing, liberal, *Guardian*-reading nice people! I don't understand how they have a son like this!'

I paused for a minute. I knew why.

'Why?'

'Well, it's *because* they're lovely, left-wing, liberal people, isn't it?' I said. 'Like, do you think they ever say things like "This is classic, straight white male behaviour", or "Typical men!", or "Ugh, toxic patriarchy!"'

My friend thought.

'Well, of *course*,' she said. 'They live in Hackney.'

'That will be why, then,' I said. 'If he's grown up hearing that straight white men are awful – if he's been made to feel shame, and guilt, over who he is – if there's a lot of conversation about how most of the problems in the world are down to men – then of *course* he's going to be attracted to a man who says, "Don't be ashamed! Men are great! We need men! Men are the best! Fuck woke-dom!" I mean, why wouldn't he? That's a classic piece of dumb, teenage rebellion against parents. What were you talking about, when he started doing the Hand Gesture?'

She thought.

'Gender-neutral toilets.'

'Well, there you go.'

Andrew Tate is the 'King of Toxic Masculinity'; one of 2022's most-googled people on earth; banned, on and off, from Facebook, Twitter, Instagram and YouTube; and a self-proclaimed 'trillionaire'. Although, as he noted, 'in Zimbabwean dollars'.

During the writing of this book, Andrew Tate went from one of the most popular male influencers in the world – 4.5 million followers on Instagram, 600,000 subscribers to his YouTube channel, 'Tate Speech' videos viewed over 14 *billion* times on TikTok – to a man under arrest in Romania, as part of a rape and human-trafficking investigation.

By the time you read this, he could either be in jail – or the case could have been dropped. In a way, it doesn't matter, because the big question is – why is a man who is so radically misogynist so appealing to young men? So appealing, they're willing to ruin Christmas dinner over him?

In January 2022, following his arrest, the *Guardian* ran a big piece, detailing how prevalent Tate's world view was in schools. It was described, repeatedly, as 'grooming on a massive scale'. Michael Conroy, whose company Men at Work trains school staff on talking to boys about these issues, had run sessions in over 50 schools about online misogyny – and teachers had raised Tate's influence in every single one.

In one session Conroy discussed the sexist meme 'make

me a sandwich', used by some men on social media to belittle women. 'A female teacher said: "I've got a lad in Year 10 who always writes MMAS at the bottom of my homework,"' he says. 'She hadn't known what it meant until then. But he was trying to humiliate her.'

One Monday morning, I asked on Twitter if anyone involved in education/working with young men had found their pupils were fans of Tate, and had had their behaviour influenced by him, and the replies flooded in. In the end, I had over 300.

'I work in a secondary school, and have a number of male students aggressively defending Tate. I've spent the week crying in the staff room at breaks because of their behaviour.'

'I get this from boys in Year 7 to 10 on an almost daily basis. It's extremely draining, frustrating and offensive.'

'I think we all have! We've had the police teams in, done assemblies, had staff training, but still the rot is there with young people (not just boys!) defending AT to the hilt. Misogyny was here first; AT has channelled it.'

'I've seen half the boys in my class doing that Tate Hands thing while I'm trying to teach them. It's weirdly intimidating.'

'I have Year 11 boys who ask me if I *allow* my wife to go out on her own.'

What world view is Tate selling? Well, he's an undeniably good-looking, very fit, very confident dude who has a lot of sports cars – or, *did*, until they were all impounded by the

Romanian police – who suggests any man who follows his advice can have the same; and who presents himself as a defender, and champion, of 'beleaguered' boys and men against 'woke-dom'. To an angry, insecure young man, with no real ideas of how to get by in the world, the basic appeal is obvious.

Having started out as a kick-boxing champion, Tate ended up on the British *Big Brother* – before being removed from the show when footage of him beating a woman with a belt appeared online. Although both Tate and the woman involved claimed the beating was consensual, and part of their sex lives, British police subsequently opened an investigation into rape claims other women made against him.

Off the back of this sudden notoriety, Tate opened a website – Hustler's University – offering 'training courses' on how to accumulate wealth, and manage 'male–female interactions'. It gained over 100,000 subscribers, at $49 a month, despite being described as 'a pyramid scheme'. With his brother, Tate then started a webcam business – employing as many as 75 lingerie-clad women, who perform 'erotic acts' for clients – and claimed to have made millions of dollars.

It's usually his views about women that get the headlines. He has described himself as both 'absolutely a sexist' and 'absolutely a misogynist', and said that women 'shouldn't be allowed to drive', should 'bear responsibility' for being raped, that women are at their 'peak' 'between 18 to 19 and 25' because they 'haven't had too much dick', and that while he would never be faithful in a relationship, he would never allow a woman to be unfaithful. He claims he doesn't let partners out on their own – 'I won't allow them to go

out with female friends – they all hate me. Or male friends –
they all want to fuck her. If she wants to talk to a man, she
can talk to me. Or my brother. Or my dad.'

Most famously, he re-enacted what men should do if their
partners accuse them of cheating: 'Bang out the machete,
boom in her face, and grip her by the neck. Shut up, bitch!'

Aware that everything I knew about Tate was from
second-hand reporting, I spent one very sad afternoon listening to his podcast, *Tate Speech*. Even though I had a fair
idea of what he was like, there were several occasions where
I had to take my headphones off for a minute – so bleak was
Tate's world view.

First of all, his chat-style is SHOUT MODE. He's not
a gentle conversationalist – everything was pitched as if
he was trying to reach the people at the back of a theatre,
without a microphone. It's quite wearying on the ears.

Secondly, I had no idea how ... racist he was. The
misogyny had, unfairly, hogged all the headlines. The phrase
'Soon, there will be no white, Christian people left' was used
repeatedly; he fretted about 'borders' disappearing; Tommy
Robinson is 'a solid guy with a good heart'; the n-word was
used repeatedly. Fair fucks – his 'anti-woke-dom' covers
every wicket. He hasn't missed any out.

But the main takeaway was just how nihilistic and joyless
Tate's view is. Not just on women: on sex. Love. Human
interaction. The world. And, ultimately, men. But all seen
through the main prism of belittling and controlling
women. Women are referred to by numbers – 'a seven', 'a
ten' – based on their attractiveness. Tate wearily described
how, these days, now he's rich and famous, he finds

attracting 'tens' easy – but as he now has 'so many' women (he claims *22* have his name tattooed on them), when he sees a new, attractive woman, he doesn't think about fucking her any more. 'It's too much effort.' Instead, he thinks of how much money she could make him, if he recruited her as a cam-girl. He 'hooks' her by giving her attention – then 'moulds' and 'dominates' her, until she's 'a good girl'.

On the podcast, his interviewer – presumably talking on behalf of Tate's fans – asks if it's true: are there still places men can go, in Eastern Europe, full of hot tens who will fuck any guy? How *can* a young man get sex?

'Dude, I always get asked, where's the best place to get laid – and I always say, the north of England,' Tate laughs. 'Liverpool. Because the women there are fucking *stupid*. They'll fuck you just because you make them laugh, or because you'll smoke weed and watch Netflix with them. Women in Eastern Europe won't do that! They have a sense of their own value! They'll only fuck powerful guys, or guys with money. Because – they don't have money! They can't get a job! All they have is their beauty – and they're gonna use it!'

I found it unbearably sad that Tate had just dismissed women who will fuck a man just because he makes her laugh, or smokes weed and watches Netflix with her. Surely, for most people, that's the dream – women *and* men. For a big proportion of Tate's male audience, that would have been why they started seeking out his 'male–female interaction advice' in the first place: to overcome all their anxiety, inexperience and low self-esteem, bang a giggly chick, then smoke a doob while watching *Curb Your Enthusiasm*. I mean, that's one of life's finest prizes. That's happiness, right there. And yet, it was being dismissed – as if cheerful, horny young women who laugh at your jokes and want to fuck you were to be looked down on. Despised. A *problem*. As an outside observer, it was as if Tate was smashing up the Yellow Brick Road his young male listeners so desperately needed to be on.

But it was only towards the end of the podcast – when Tate had been talking for over an hour and a half, and what sounded like the 'clink' of a whisky glass had become quite frequent – that some of Tate's deeper psychology became apparent. Asked if he wanted, eventually, to be a father, Tate replied, 'Eventually, sure!' Becoming a father didn't mean becoming 'trad', and giving up fucking other women. Or even being around much. 'Being a dad isn't a full-time job,' he said, emphatically. 'It's a part-time job. You can do it, like, one day a week – and still carry on with your crazy life.'

This, Tate went on to reveal, was the relationship he'd had with *his* father. A champion chess player, Tate Snr was rarely around – 'I never saw him! He was always off, at chess tournaments. He'd ring me on Wednesday, hear what I'd been up to, say, "I'll beat your ass for that on Saturday" – and then he would! With a belt!'

I googled 'Emory Andrew Tate Jr', International Master, and found him described as 'an absolute trailblazer for African-American chess'. Tate's racism took on a new, complicated, daddy-issues edge. He himself is mixed-race. What was all his fretting about 'white, Christian' people being 'out-bred' about? It's way beyond my paygrade.

But it was when Tate sketched out his vision for

fatherhood that the biggest flaw in his world view – the massive, emotional black hole at the centre of all his febrile charisma – was revealed.

'Two sons,' he said, over and over. 'I'd like two sons. To replace me. Two sons.'

A simple truth never seemed to occur to him: he has a 50/50 chance, every time, of becoming a father to a daughter.

He might *only* have daughters.

As he continued to talk about fatherhood to these two imaginary sons – 'I'll teach them to be good' – it became apparent: considering the possibility of having daughters is simply something Andrew Tate cannot allow himself to do. Because he knows: they might end up dating men like Andrew Tate. Men who've learned everything they know *from* Andrew Tate. Men who won't allow them to leave the house on their own; who will beat them with a belt; who will make them work on sex-cams; who will 'mould' and 'dominate' them; who will be, as Tate refers to himself, constantly, 'their pimp'.

And that, ultimately, is the problem with misogyny – with peddling a world view where women are innately inferior to men, and need to be controlled by them – half the world is female. Your sisters, your mother, your nan. The female teacher you write 'MMAS' to on your course-work: she might be the only person who can coach you through your exams. The only person who will give you a job might a woman. The person who saves your life in A&E might be a woman. The female cousin you do the 'Andrew Tate Hand Gesture' to, on Christmas Day – she might end up being your only possible kidney donor. Or, just, the person who introduces you to her best friend, who you fall in love with.

And, one day, you might look down at the person you love most in the world – someone who was born 30 seconds ago, and already makes you feel like your heart is now an external thing, in their tiny, starfish hands, which will be destroyed if something bad happens to them – and it might be a girl.

And then every time you ever belittled, hurt, betrayed, terrified or humiliated a woman will come back to you, and you will truly know what hell is. It's what you did – now happening to your daughter.

Of course, it's not just misogyny that Tate peddles. As mentioned before, the primary emotion he actually taps into is a fear that men are not valued any more: that the problems of everyone else – bitches, non-white Christians, 'fags' (I'm quoting Tate here) – are prioritised over straight white men.

'Men like me have a hugely important role in society,' he told Hugo Rifkind of *The Times* in 2022, 'which is being removed, destroyed and demonised and decimated. There are more invisible men than invisible women. That's been proved. Scientifically.'

He goes on to point out that, in a nightclub, almost all women would be able to find somebody willing to have sex with them, while many men would not.

'They are the gatekeepers of the sexual marketplace,' he asserted.

Of course, these are all things we have already addressed, earlier in this book, and without having to be massively misogynist. Or, indeed, at all. You really can talk about the problems of men without concluding the answer is to make 75 women work on your sex-cams.

But the fact remains, in the centre of Tate's world view, there is a tiny kernel of truth. There's a little nugget that chimes with nascent fears, and anxieties, in young men. The great pity is that it comes encrusted with all this hate-filled, counter-intuitive, bleak, dangerous stuff – and boys are consuming it at an age when they are least able to analyse it, evaluate it and understand just how damaging it is for both them and the people around them. Eleven to fifteen – those seem to be the years boys are most vulnerable to being radicalised and groomed.

'By the time they're 16, boys seem to . . . grow out of it,' said one teacher on Twitter.

'As they get older, other boys start standing up in class and telling the Andrew Tate fans they're talking bollocks.'

'People start laughing at them, or using "Andrew Tate" as an insult.'

But why do these influencers strike such a chord for younger men? For Tate is part of a wider picture, of hundreds – possibly thousands – of radicalised extremists, on the Manosphere, who peddle conspiracy theories: about 'Feminazis', 'the Great Replacement Theory' and, biggest of all, 'Red Pill/Blue Pill'.

Red Pill/Blue Pill refers to *The Matrix*, where, to be Pauline Kael for a minute, Ted from *Bill & Ted's Excellent Adventure* is informed that everything he has ever known is a lie, and he now faces a choice. He can either take the Blue Pill – like most of humanity, the idiots! have chosen to do – and continue to live in a lovely, dumb fantasy.

Or he can bravely take the Red Pill – and finally see what the world is *actually* like. Which is: a brutal place controlled by a shadowy organisation he needs to overthrow, yadda yadda yadda.

In the right-wing, radicalised, online world, 'Red Pill/ Blue Pill' is beyond a standard reference. It's *the* reference. Those on the Blue Pill are sheep, idiots – they don't realise what's *really* going on.

Those on the Red Pill – they are the heroes. They have now a power – the truth – which will help them overthrow the shadowy forces ranged against them. Reality, and their quest, has now been revealed to them.

In the US, it's the underpinning of QAnon.

The teachers on Twitter, talking about Andrew Tate, mentioned the Matrix and 'Red Pill/Blue Pill' with alarming regularity:

'I had a boy in Year 10 telling me that PSHE [sex education] lessons were all part of the Matrix.'

'I gave an assembly on misogyny – and the first question from a male pupil was "Are you on Blue Pills, Miss?" All the other boys laughed – they knew exactly what he meant. And it was his way of trying to intimidate me.'

Most worrying of all was a support teacher who works with 'impressionable, vulnerable' young men, who tried to start an open conversation about Tate, and why many people thought his advice was harmful.

'A young man replied that Andrew Tate had predicted

that people would say things like this – that they would try to question what he said – and that it was all part of the Matrix.'

Indeed, Tate's words to the waiting camera crews, as he was arrested in Romania, were, 'The Matrix has attacked me.'

In one move, Tate had brilliantly booby-trapped any attempts to analyse him, or bring him to account, because: those doing it were part of the Matrix. It was all a conspiracy theory against him. Against his fans. Against men. It was proof he was *right*.

Red Pill/Blue Pill

Why does this all seem so *plausible* for young men? Why are young men so open to this idea of revelation: that, in their confused, early adolescence – 11 to 15 – they might suddenly discover the reason why their lives are so difficult; why they struggle to fit in; why they feel like outsiders? And that it's all because of a huge, secret conspiracy, which they have now, finally, learned the truth about – a truth that now makes them powerful. It makes them part of a movement. It gives them their quest.

As I pondered this, I suddenly remembered talking to all my male friends, about what stories they had read, and watched, when they were younger.

'Comic books.'

'Comic books.'

'Sci-fi, and comic books.'

'Nothing about ordinary teenage boys, trying to learn how to become happy, normal men?'

'No. Stuff where they find out the *truth* about their world; are told about their superpowers; realise they are *not* like everyone else.'

Maybe, I thought, this is why conspiracy theories feel so *likely*, so *comforting*, so . . . *expected* for young men, as they go through their wilderness years.

After all, every teenage boy they watched, or read about, when they struggled at this age, suddenly found out they were from another planet; or had lasers in their eyes; or were born to something different. Something that *explained* why they were finding life so hard. They discovered that there *is* a shadowy organisation, running everything. *They* all get the Hero's Call, from an older, wiser man – and then go out to overthrow the current world order.

This was, basically, the storyline template being tapped into by those radical, online misogynists, 'grooming' younger men. There had always been a deeper truth, all along. And now they were being told it. Right on schedule. In the middle of their teenage years. Like Superman.

Ultimately, everyone – boys and girls, men and women – finds their teenage years difficult. We *all* feel that we're not fitting in; or that no one really 'gets' us; or that the future is so scary and unimaginable, it crushes us. We *all* sometimes feels like the world is stacked against us, and is against 'people like us'. We *all* crave hints, tips, advice, role models. No one is more likely to hand over their cash, time, belief and fandom than a lonely, struggling teenager who desperately wants to believe that 'These Three Life Hacks!' will suddenly make everything better. Make everything make *sense*. Make their adult years, finally, begin. It was on this basis that I both started trying to 'get into' jazz, and got a perm.

But when it comes to advice, there are, I think, two things that are worth bearing in mind. Yes – I am about to give advice *on advice*.

The first is Maslow's Hierarchy of Needs: the idea that there are eight things that human beings *need* in order to feel safety, and contentment, and to generally enjoy being alive. They are:

ONE: Basic physical stuff. Shelter. Warmth. Food. Water. Sleep. A toilet.

TWO: Safety. Emotional security. Financial security. Good health.

THREE: Love and belonging. Family. Friends. Intimacy. Trust. Acceptance.

FOUR: Esteem. To be both valued by those around you, and to value yourself.

FIVE: Understanding. To be educated, and to be able to educate yourself. To learn. To understand the world.

SIX: Aesthetic needs. Beauty. Nature. Some clothes you feel happy in. A bunch of flowers. A picture you like.

SEVEN: Self-actualisation. To become the person you want to be. To be good at your job. A good parent. A good friend. A good partner.

EIGHT: Transcendence. Which means – a spiritual
element, whatever that means to you. Being able
to help others. Feeling part of the world. Feeling
awe at amazing things. Feeling joy, and thankful-
ness. Feeding the birds, and going, 'Wow – look
at their tiny little legs, and wings. How the *fuck*
do these guys fly?'

By and large, if the person you're taking advice from only
concentrates on one or two things – money and fucking
women, say – but isn't talking about hanging out with your
sister, feeling happy about a new jumper, or paddling in the
sea, they're nowhere *near* to having all the answers you
need. Note how things like 'a toilet' are in the first, and
most essential, category. If your role model can't honestly
talk about the joys of going for a good poo, I wouldn't
trust them. This is the basic, key stuff of being human.

But the second, and possibly most crucial thing, is this:
are you taking life advice from someone who is actually having a nice life? In the end, those are the only people you
should really be listening to.

Jordan B. Peterson seems so beset with fear, and
sorrow – 'Life is suffering' – that I cannot believe he is
someone who has *really* cracked this whole 'being a human'
thing. Very notably, and presumably due to his constipation-
inducing 'meat and salt' diet, he never once talks about
going to the toilet.

And Andrew Tate had to go and live in a CCTV-riddled
complex in Romania – because, in Romania, 'corruption is
accessible to everyone' – surrounded by armed guards, and is

regularly questioned by police. I don't want to be a party pooper, but it seems like being the world's most-googled man isn't really a viable lifestyle for most men. How does that work out, long term? What does he do at Christmas? Does he take all the women *with* him, back to his mum's? Who sits on the edge of the bath and 'keeps him company' when he's got food poisoning, and is puking his guts out? What happens in the future – when he's a 70-year-old man living in an Evil Lair in Romania, with 75 cam-girls?

Suddenly, he's a pensioner, basically running a Lady Zoo.

And – because women 'pass their peak' at 25 – you're having to go out, night after night, to find replacements. No woman has known you long enough to have in-jokes with you. She doesn't know the TV shows you're referencing. She doesn't remember that year you really got into model airplanes. You have no one to share your world with. You are building in future loneliness.

And, if you believe women are inferior, but you still need 75 women in order to carry out your life plans, that presents something of a paradox.

If there is one overriding theme with all misogynists, it's that they can only ever frame the idea of male power *in relation to women*. The only way a man can prove he is powerful – worthwhile – is by pointing to all the women who are inferior to him. *Or*, how things are unfair because women are more powerful than him: academically, sexually, culturally.

Guy! Guys! This is such a weird framing to pick! If you want to feel *real* power, then it's only ever, ultimately, in

relation to yourself. Learning new skills; becoming physically happy; creating a beautiful world for yourself; seeking
out awe; enjoying your relationships; helping others; feeling part of something meaningful. Being better tomorrow
than you were yesterday. You don't ever have to bring
women into it. Just – go for a run with a mate, then make
yourself a nice stir-fry. Learn to make yourself happy. Like
they say, wherever you go, there *you* are. *You* are the
quest. You don't need to bring 'dominance over women'
into it. That's *way* too complicated.

And what's *best* about only ever seeking power over
yourself is, it never ends with a knock on the door from the
police.

Final, last point: When I googled the 'Most Loved Men in
the World', I got a load of returns for 'Most Influential
Men in the World', instead. It's almost as if, culturally, we
do not value men being loved – merely influential, or
admired.

When I finally found a 'Most Loved' list, it was notable
none of them believed that life was suffering, or had been
accused of sex-trafficking. They were Michael Palin, Barack
Obama, Martin Luther King, David Attenborough, Prince,
Nelson Mandela, Harry Styles, Paul McCartney, Lewis
Capaldi. The Rock – sitting there, while his daughter put
pink stickers on his head. They were loved for being smart,
hard-working, kind, joyful, sexy, funny, brave, groundbreak-
ing, world-changing, patient, stoic, relaxed, confident.

At the end of two days of people on Twitter contacting

me about Andrew Tate and his influence on young people, a New Zealand masculinity activist and educator called, magnificently, Richie Hardcore, DMed me. Hardcore is *also* a martial arts champion – ripped, tattooed – but has spent the last 20 years giving speeches and doing school visits, talking about masculinity, pornography, mental health and healthy relationships.

'Last year Tate became a constant feature of the conversations,' he wrote. 'You ask boys "What stereotypes do you think of when you think of masculinity?", and they used to yell out "being tough", "not crying". Now they just yell out [Tate's catchphrase] "Top G!" Tate is very much a walking archetype of a very limited idea of manhood, but is hugely popular – I think in part because boys are desperate for relatable role models, and partly because he is "anti-woke", and a lot of boys feel under attack in the culture war.

'If we want to make positive changes when it comes to masculinity, we can start by highlighting the myriad of powerful yet relatable male role models out there, who aren't blatantly disrespecting women.'

In other words, the best way to stop boys being 'groomed' and radicalised by misogynists isn't to attack their heroes – but to promote better heroes, instead. And, in this, we need to give young men a viable off-ramp from their more damaging fandoms.

I was contacted by Josh Spears, an educator at a technical college – 'sport, IT, bricklaying' – where, he told me, 'the name Andrew Tate started to come up'. Josh decided to take a more discursive method on addressing him:

I explained to them that Tate was someone who was really good at showing young men that they are worth something. We talked about perceptions of masculinity, and how Hollywood teaches us that men are only worthy if they have money, muscles and Megan Fox. How men compete with one another for top dog status; how any other male is a sidekick. We challenged together whether that view is actually a healthy one, and where it comes from.

At this point, the lads began to quieten down. Mobile phones (usually the safe haven from boredom) were not there. They were listening to me.

We talked about how these role models in life shape us, guide us, give us little fragments of our growing sense of self. How it's not a bad thing to have men in your life that you respect and learn from.

I then talked about Kevin Spacey.

None of them knew who he was. I explained that for many years Kevin Spacey was a hero of mine. A fantastic actor, brilliant speaker, patron of the arts, which all mean a lot to me.

I then explained that allegations of sexual assault came out about him – and I was heartbroken. A hero of mine was now a villain.

I explained that I had a choice to make. I could either let my heart be broken and cut that part of me, the fandom, away – or, I could double down on my support, essentially supporting his actions.

I told them: I made the choice to allow my heart to be broken. I believed in his guilt. And I told them it was one of the hardest and more painful things I had to do. I questioned, then rejected, a hero. I explained that if they could master that process, they would grow. It was part of being a good person – of being 'a man'.

I finished by telling them what I thought the measure of a man was. A man was someone who helped and contributed to their community. A man was brave enough to say no and confident enough to say yes. Finally, a man was someone who was honest with those around him, and could tell those he loved that he loved them without fear. Admittedly I stole this triplet from a video by Ordinary Things. But it rang true with my thoughts anyway.

I asked the boys if they had any questions and they said, as they usually do when their mind has begun to change, 'Yeah – I can see what you're on about.'

Some people don't understand modern teenagers. But they are embedded in two worlds – the digital world, and the real world. And, like a tick that's burrowed in, if you just tackle one side of that, the other will still be there. Young men lack role models with the same digital skills as Tate, or Peterson. They don't have the funny quips. There is a . . . Cultural Poverty.

It was one of the most intelligent and inspiring things I've ever read: a properly loving, patient and wise understanding of just what it is to be a young man in the modern world, and how simply screaming 'YOU'RE A FAN OF A CRIMINAL!' will, ultimately, get us nowhere. We always need stories to lead us into new ways of thinking – and Josh's was perfect.

In the 'Most Loved Men' lists that I found, there was one man who topped the charts, over and over again: Keanu Reeves. Which felt deeply poignant – for, in *The Matrix*, he is Neo – the man who takes the Red Pill. The radicalised misogynistic far right's ultimate hero.

By way of contrast, however, the *real* Keanu Reeves is a tireless philanthropist who founded a cancer research institute after his sister got leukemia, has suffered immense personal tragedy, and is estimated to have given away over $125 million of his earnings to charities, friends and lower-paid crew members on his movies. He has campaigned in support of the Dalai Lama, sees the world as 'beautiful and bountiful', and is, by all accounts, the nicest man in Hollywood. He spent his fortieth birthday sitting outside a coffee shop, giving free coffees to anyone who wanted to talk to him. He lives a life that is the absolute opposite of every Manosphere grifter and radical misogynist – and it has made him loved, wealthy and happy.

If you are the kind of person constantly referring to Blue Pill/Red Pill, and quoting *The Matrix*, and Neo, I guess you have to pretend the man who played him doesn't exist at all.

Chapter Twelve

The Fatherhood of Men

'I think, contrary to most beliefs, fatherhood is where it all gets easier, with regard to being a man. It's the home stretch. *Easier.*'

I am in the playground with my friend Johan, drinking coffee from paper cups. As the father to two children – one four, the other six months – he doesn't, I have to say, look like the *embodiment* of an easier life. He has the new-parent, baked-in, bone-deep tiredness that's like a palpable ache: his eyes are red, his reaction times are slowed to treacle; there are a couple of times where I would bet good money that he has actually, momentarily fallen asleep, with his eyes open, while talking to me. And been so tired he hasn't noticed.

Nonetheless, he is stalwart in his beliefs.

'It just . . . *is,*' he says, with the Zen-like simplicity of someone who hasn't slept a full night since 2019. And is also too tired to add to that sentence.

The topic has come up because we both saw a Tweet that we sent each other at the same time.

'I just drafted a Tweet connecting "dadness" (dad dancing; dad jokes; dad-bod) with radical self-acceptance. I will be leaving it in drafts – but also I'm a genius. Have a nice day.'

'It's true,' Johan says, now. 'When you become a dad, you can kind of . . . relax into . . .'

And here he casts around for the right word. Clearly, the exhaustion has taken its toll – so I try to help him.

'Your normalness?' I try. 'Your "just enough"-ness? Some essential sense of not being *amazing* at what you do – dancing, telling jokes, being ripped – but just really enjoying it anyway? And having a Zen amusement over how average, but happy, you are? Like, you're in on the joke, and the joke is *you*, and so you have assumed Ultimate Dad Powers? You are liberated from trying to compete, or be cool. You are . . . *content*.'

'That's the monkey!' Johan said, pointing at me. '*Exactly* what I would have said, if I wasn't a man whose brain don't work so good no more.'

At that point, his daughter fell over into a puddle – and so he had to start the long and difficult process of changing her dress and knickers, while also having a six-month-old baby strapped to his chest, in a papoose.

I gave all the help I could – several supportive 'thumbs up', while taking advantage of the baby being on the other side of the playground to have a fag.

It's what he did for me, when I had small children.

It's what friends are for.

I have to say – the fathers of my generation are some of the most under-celebrated heroes of our time. Because: they didn't have a lot of inspiration from *their* fathers to go on. Generation X might have many descriptors, but 'over-fathered' isn't one of them.

Look, for instance, at the most famous father/son story we were raised on: that of Darth Vader and Luke Skywalker.

Like many terrible Baby Boomer fathers, he was 'tetchy', prone to bouts of pointed heavy breathing when particularly vexed, and too 'busy with work' (building a Death Star. Three times!) to be around much. When he *did* spend time with his son – engaging in ill-advised 'horseplay' – he pissed about so much he chopped Luke's hand off, and then used this – the least suitable moment *ever* – to drop a massive emotional bombshell ('Luke, I am your father!') and then try to convince him to join the family business ('Together, we can rule the galaxy!' No mention of Luke's presumably massive arterial haemorrhage – as, let's face it, a mum would. Mrs Vader would be right in there with the first-aid kit. The kindest critique I can give here is: 'extreme carelessness').

At the end of Darth Vader's storyline – three movies of terrible parenting later – he even does another classic 'bad dad' thing: of using his deathbed to lay on a massive guilt-trip. Saying 'sorry' *only* at the point where he is too knackered to be evil any more, and just wants people to give him 'a nice hug' before he dies.

And it worked! We remember him as a *redeemed* character now! He came through *in the end*! The fact it was just *six minutes* before the end would be an 'uncharitable' thing to point out, because: that's just what *our* dads were like!

Given this role model, the general, notable goodness and desire to 'be a good dad' in Gen X dads is apt to make women feel a bit tearful.

I am surrounded by good fathers – almost without exception, the men I know put everything they can into fatherhood, bring energy, imagination and tenderness to the job, and are also feminist enough to report back to the women every time mums at the school gate say, 'Ooooh, you *are* a good dad!', just for dropping their own kids off at school. To quote the great Chris Rock routine on parenthood, 'That's just what you're *supposed* to do, you low-expectation-having-motherfucker. What do you want – a cookie?'

What I find particularly heartwarming about good modern dads, however, is that they have, essentially, sorted all this shit out themselves. Obviously. They didn't learn to be great dads from either Darth Vader or *their* dads – while my generation's fathers weren't actually building a Death Star (three times!), they were the guys who tackled childcare by parking the car outside the Red Lion and occasionally posting a bag of crisps or a bottle of Coke through the driver's window, while beerily hissing, 'Don't spill it.'

Or, as a special treat, getting all the kids to sit on the bonnet of the car while they drove it, at what I would describe as 'a medium speed', around the caravan site, shouting 'HOLD ON!' over the sound of Mungo Jerry's 'In the Summertime'.

When people who were kids in the seventies and eighties are asked to describe their fathers by people younger than them, every conversation inevitably ends with the younger people whispering 'Why are you not in therapy?' and looking visibly upset, while the older people say 'It was just a different *time*' in an oddly nostalgic voice.

Back then, it was perfectly normal to have a dad who kicked dogs, 'thumped' children, complained that they 'can't see the telly!' as their exhausted wives hoovered around them, and panicked at being left in charge of the children all day while e.g. their wife went into hospital to give birth to another one. Dads telling their hospitalised, postpartum wives 'I'm knackered!', while eating all their Special Hospital Grapes, and drinking their Special Hospital Lucozade, was a staple of Visiting Time, 1986.

I think my generation is kind of *proud* of how shit our dads were, compared to the modern-day ideal of fatherhood. It proves that, whatever we have achieved, it was definitely not with the help of an engaged and empathetic patriarch. Whatever else we have, we do not have 'great dad privilege'.

But that oddly proud sense of 'I figured out how to be a better dad *on my own*' leaves modern men at a distinct disadvantage, compared to their female partners.

One of the most recurrent phrases I hear from men of

my generation is 'I figured out a lot of who I wanted to be – both in my marriage, and as a father – by remembering what *my* dad had done: then doing the exact opposite.'

If you ask them if they had any *other* formative notions about being a dad; or how they and their friends talk about being a father, they look at you rather blankly.

'Do you talk to other dad-friends about being a dad?' I asked my friends, and then Twitter. 'Do you swap tips, talk about what it's like – the highs, and the lows? Actually – what *do* you talk about with other dads? I've never sat in on a Dad Chat.'

I guess I'd vaguely assumed Dad Chat was like when mothers get together – 16 hours of swapping escalatingly horrific and disgusting birthing stories ('The baby came out, right, *eating a poo*'), endless hints, tips, advice, gossip, confessions, crying, hugging, product recommendations, life hacks, reassurance-sessions and story-swapping, and – for those not used to them – startlingly bitchy and brutal assessments of your child's social group ('That Daisy, right, might only be four, but she's a *stone cold bitch*, and I'm sorry, but you can tell even now that Finn is going to end up as a twice-divorced crypto-bro.')

The truth for dads, it turns out, is a little different. 'Football.' 'Football.' 'How tired we are.' 'Pubs we miss going to now we're so tired.' 'Pop trivia.' 'Whether or not we could have been professional sportsmen if we hadn't had kids, and were now so tired.' 'Who looks/feels the oldest.' 'Taking the piss out of each other for things that happened 30 years ago.' 'How great things used to be.' 'Football.'

The general feeling was summed up by Mark Orrell-Davies, on Twitter, who said: 'Usually [we talk] about the groups of mums, wondering what on *earth* they can find to chat about for so long.'

It concluded with Tom Keenan's mock-surprised: 'You're allowed to talk to other dads, now? When did this rule-change occur?'

The conversation had been going on for *37 minutes* before I got this, from Alistair Bayliss: 'What do I talk about? How the f*** do you do a plait on a moving target, without PTSD, tears, or clumps of hair?'

This was notable because – in over 1,200 replies – it was the first that addressed any actual, practical topic of parenting. Or, more specifically, *fathering*.

Mothers, of course, have known how to plait hair since they were four.

Obviously my Twitter timeline is a self-selecting echo-chamber – people who follow me are probably mainly middle-aged, working- and middle-class feminist white dads with a soft-spot for *Ghostbusters* – but the replies seemed wholly in line with the general societal dad-vibe: modern dads really love their children, and their family; they're working hard at being – by all accounts – the most present and attentive dads yet known to humanity; but it hasn't changed their conversation. *There is no culture of fatherhood*.

There's no gang of dads, talking about dad stuff.

You're doing this shit on your own.

And of course, in a situation where there's no conversation about a subject – from 'I am incredibly depressed' to

'How the fuck *do* you plait hair?' – huge tranches of parenthood remain in the domain and control of mothers, just by default. It remains just as it was a century before, or more.

I didn't realise quite how rigid this all was until I read a throwaway sentence in *The Descent of Man* by Grayson Perry – the cycling, skating, hyper-competitive potter who's also spent a great deal of his life as his transvestite alter-ego, Claire, and so has one foot in both gender camps.

'Maybe we need to change not only the image of the dad, but the *practice*,' he suggested. 'Perhaps we need new styles of childcare arrangements that appeal to fathers: stock car racing with child seats in the back? A category in marathons for dads with buggies? Pubs with crèches?'

He's saying it half-jokingly – but he's also right. A lot of balls gets written, and spoken, about parenthood, but the truth is that the most important thing about parenthood is *making it as interesting as possible for the parents*. Parenthood is an *incredibly* long, exhausting grind, carried out for the benefit of someone who will be, on multiple occasions, the single most ungrateful and downright *rude* person you have ever met. Unless you're very unlucky, there will not be many people in your life who will shout 'I HATE YOU!' and punch you in the balls if you give them 'the wrong kind' of cheese. Maybe only if you work for Jeremy Clarkson.

In a parent/child relationship, meanwhile, these will be everyday occurrences for someone you are still supposed to love and adore very much.

So why *isn't* more of fatherhood enjoyable for fathers?

Because – believe me – mums are absolutely doing all

the stuff that makes parenthood more enjoyable for us. Decorating the nursery; choosing the cot/buggy/high-chair/car-seat; picking out the outfits; putting a hair-clip on a baby girl the *second* she has more than 3mm of skull-fuzz; carefully curating a toy box of items she deems delightful based on her own childhood (gotta put a vintage Sindy in there; and a Big Yellow Teapot!) and throwing out the disgusting loud plastic purple thing your mum bought, partly just because we hate your mum.

The blankets, the mobiles, the tiny duffle coat, the pink ballerina dress – mums form 90 per cent of the material world of a child, and it is pleasing to us, because we see ourselves and our tastes reflected in the primrose-coloured nursery and adorable vintage blankets. We *literally* buy into motherhood. Dads – you are allowed *one* (1) 'amusing' babygro reflecting your favourite band (e.g. Guns N' Roses, Neil Young). And that's it. Enjoy your singular freedom!

Similarly, toddlers. What would toddler fashion, mediated through millions and millions of dads who were totally in charge of dressing their kids, look like? I suspect it would be different from the tastes of women that we see on display. Isn't it weird that we don't know? Isn't it weird that this is a world that men are still, for various reasons, totally shut out of? As all parents – male and female – know, your child's world is tiny: it is absolutely made up of their favourite red shiny shoes; a quilt they love; the cushion they like to sit on to have stories; the carefully collected tea set, or collection of farm animals.

They have a doll's house – a small, perfect world; but *your* doll's house is *their* world: made and ordered and the centre of everything. With mothers being the default world-builders for children, when Daddy comes to play with the tea set; read the story; tuck them in at night, he can often feel like a guest star cameoing on a movie set made by someone else. A very welcome and loved guest star – but one who will have to ask the director (Mum) where the hot-water bottle is; or how the weird mushroom night-light works.

And of course, you might be saying, 'Honestly, Cat? I don't give a shit about the nursery, or the baby's tights. The missus can totally have charge of that.'

But it's nothing to do with your relationship with your wife. It's to do with your relationship *with your child*. It's about the relationship of all dads and kids. Do dads see their children differently? *Would they create a different world for them?* How would they deal with e.g. boys' T-shirts that say 'Here comes trouble!' and girls' T-shirts that say 'Future Heart-Breaker'? Women have been complaining about these things for years, because they're the ones buying the clothes. But what do *men* think about it?

Because what's 'just' a sexist T-shirt when they're four, a decade later, is your now-14-year-old girl attempting to leave the house in a see-thru babydoll dress. Are you going to say, 'I think you should talk to your mum about that' – or is the guy who was picking out her babygros now going to be able to handle this pivotal conversation about What Girls Wear – because he can? Because he's *always* been that guy?

And of course, nursery paint and babygros are just the easy-to-see, physical aspects of parenthood. But it's bigger stuff, too – like what your days consist of. All those minutes, and hours. At the moment, all the advice – all the templating and scheduling – is based on what's best for the *mothers*. Which is understandable if mothers did *all* the babycare. But if you have paternity leave? If you're taking it in turns? Then, as a father, you can be massively practically disadvantaged.

Take, for instance, those first few weeks of a baby's life. All the books and advice talk about how those 'first few weeks' after birth are all about 'nesting' and 'cocooning' in the house; basing yourself around the bed, or the sofa, so you can 'nap when you can', and generally being delight-fully withdrawn from the world, during your 'babymoon'.

The thing is, that works for *women* – who have just given birth, and who therefore feel generally disinclined to leave the house, since their fanny exploded/someone took a breadknife to their guts. For mothers, 'nesting' makes sense. They're physically fucked.

However, when dads are taking their turn with the baby – and 'turn' is the acceptable phrase, over 'shift' (too work-y) and 'sentence' (too jail-y) – it's actually far, far bet-ter for them to be *out* of the house. A baby being walked around the local streets in a buggy, or sling, is infinitely more likely to stay distracted, or asleep – crucial if, when it gets hungry or sad, all you have to offer is the crushing dis-appointment and wrongness of 'the Hairy Nipple', and a whispered, 'I'm sorry.'

With our first daughter, my husband walked hundreds of miles around our neighbourhood while I either worked, slept, or looked at the Hoover and cried. Theoretically, this mileage made up for the fact that 'getting to the gym' is very much not on the To-Do List of a new dad. In actuality, Pete used the strolls to sample every available item of fast food in the area.

When he finally returned home, and I removed the baby from the sling on his front, I'd be able to examine the top of her head – where bits of food had fallen – and say, 'Pop-corn, then?' or, 'Chips?'

On one occasion, I was quite confused by a nit-like infestation of sesame seeds, until he said, in a brisk, busi-nesslike manner, 'Whopper with Cheese.'

This *totally* worked for us – Pete taking the babies out – but in conversations with other dads, it seemed not to be 'a thing'.

'We're *nesting*,' they would say, in their front room, during 'Daddy Time'.

Even as the baby, who could see their mum on the other side of the room, *screamed* for her.

If a newborn baby *can* see its mother, it *will* scream for her – it wants tit! It wants mum-smell! – thus setting up, very early, that sad, common situation: a new dad feeling distinctly second-rate, and crushed, by his child's prefer-ence for its mother.

Dads – take the kid out! Away from its mum! When it comes to early fatherhood, your best bet is to try and work some benign version of Stockholm syndrome, while snack-ing as heavily as possible. This is the tactic that will work *for dads*. That's the origin story of a good father-child relation-ship right there.

When I asked on Twitter, 'What Do Dads Talk About?', aside from football, the two main themes were very notable, and totally linked: happy nostalgia about what things were like *before* kids, and longing chat about what the dads could start doing again *once the kids had grown up.* It was either the past, or the future. There was nothing about what life was like *now.*

It's almost as if fathers – unable to really talk about 'being a father', and aware that so much of 'parenting' is, still, 'mothering', but done by dads – are treating parenthood like something that's temporary. Or not even happening at all. How can you engage with something that you have very little practical say in inventing? In so many cases, Dad isn't 'Dad' – he's just 'Not Mum'. He's the person doing what Mum would do if she were here.

And so no wonder the dads were so nostalgic about their lives before they had kids, or were looking forward to doing stuff without the kids, because, let's face it: 'Daddy' is not seen as a great job. While 'dad jokes', 'dad dancing' and 'dad-bods' get affectionate press, by and large, the word 'dad', or 'daddy', is a harbinger of something, at best, laughable; and at worst, ominous.

Daddies are 'silly', daddies get things 'wrong', daddies are buffoons: the 'Daddy' in *Daddy Day Care* suggests chaos; Daddy Pig is always being patronisingly chided by Mummy and Peppa; the board books *Daddy Fartypants* and *My Dad Used to Be So Cool* are hardly morale-boosters.

Meanwhile, 'Daddy' in the title of an adult book is almost always the harbinger of some incredibly dark and fucked-up shit. *Daddy, We Hardly Knew You*; *Please, Daddy, No!*; *Daddy, Why Did You Steal My Childhood?*; *My Daddy – The Paedophile.*

In many situations, 'Daddy' sounds . . . wrong.

A case in point: when our children were younger, my husband used to spritz up normal lemonade by adding some lime and mint to it, and serving it in the 'fancy' jug, and the girls loved it.

Unfortunately, they called it 'Daddy's Special Lemonade' – and I can tell you now, when a six-year-old girl asks for 'Daddy's Special Lemonade' in front of a bunch of other parents, a certain . . . uneasiness is evident. The same uneasiness we saw when Dora would ask for 'Daddy's Special Tickle'. Even though the 'special tickle' was just under her chin, simply putting the word 'Daddy' at the front of it conveys a certain . . . menace. 'Daddy' is . . . scary.

Because, as is so often the case, the small number of bad men have hogged the majority of the bandwidth. In the absence of dadtrepreneurs and fathering memoirs, and in a world where Dadsnet has a fraction of the users of Mumsnet – and, rather poignantly, offers a crate of beer as an incentive for signing up as a member – the main times we hear about dads are when it's bad news.

Absent fathers; abusive fathers; emotionally unavailable fathers; workaholic fathers; alcoholic fathers; fathers with destructively fixed ideas of what their children should achieve.

Donald Trump saying his daughter is 'hot' and that he would date her if she wasn't his daughter; Michael Jackson dangling baby Blanket off a balcony; rapper T.I. sending his teenage daughter for yearly 'virginity tests'; Prince Charles making William and Harry walk behind their mother's coffin in front of a billion viewers; Ryan O'Neal not recognising *his own daughter*, Tatum, at Farrah Fawcett's funeral, and chatting her up ('Daddy, it's me!') – the terrible fathers hog all the headlines.

Meanwhile, in movies, even the good fathers don't do any actual . . . fathering? As a general rule of thumb, if a man in a movie has a child, that child will be a) kidnapped; b) murdered; c) used to introduce some kind of jeopardy that necessitates the father go 'on a quest'.

In movies, 'being a dad' means 'tracking down baddies', 'seeking revenge', or just doing all the usual cool stuff – blowing up cars/robbing a bank/hunting down the magic stones of Multiplatform-Franchisia. Apart from the opening scene – where it's established This Guy Loves His Kid, as our hero makes breakfast while engaging in a bit of Dad Banter ('Pancakes, buddy? I bet I make them better than your mom!'); and the end scene – where we see This Guy Has His Reward when he's reunited with his kid, who cries 'I love you, Daddy!' – movie-fathers don't actually spend any time *with* their kids. The kids can be the stakes, or the reward, or the MacGuffin, but *they're not the plot*.

And that's the problem, right there: if you are a father, a real-life father, your kids absolutely *are* the plot. They are what's happening – day after day after day. Modern dads are turning up and doing this work – beautifully, and brilliantly, and constantly – and yet there is a male reluctance to discuss this or admit that they take it seriously. A belief that talking about it, showing it, or somehow *drawing attention to it*, is against the rules of being a man. That to want more from it – or consider how you would change it – would be the start of something risky, or unfair.

Weirdly, 'being a dad' looks – to women, to your other halves – like something you are almost trying to keep secret; as if to talk about how it is confusing and dementing and heart-bursting and awful and amazing and the most most *most* thing you have ever done would be . . . cheating? Letting the other dads down? Making a fuss?

I know that it is the fear of all modern men that they are talking too much; dominating the conversation; making it about *themselves*; somehow crushing other people with their man-ness, and their goddamn patriarchy. But it's impossible for you to talk too much about being fathers. That whole field is empty, and it is infinite, and it is yours, and to not fill it makes it look, to us, like you are fathering two metres apart from every other father, and in silence.

As my friend Johan is, right now – standing near, but not talking, to the other dad in the playground.

I, meanwhile, have been joined at my picnic table by a mother who has also sneaked away for a fag, and we are – of course – discussing our Birth Stories.

'The doctor looked down and said, 'Ooooh, I've never seen one so hairy!', and I said, 'Yes, sorry – I didn't get time to wax,' and he said, "I *meant* the *baby*."'

Chapter Thirteen

The Illnesses of Men – or, Why Won't Men Go to the Doctor?

It's 2015. It's 3am. I am sitting in bed, wide awake. Beside me, my husband is dying.

Or, at least, that's what it sounds like.

This is real last-days-of-the-mastodons-like gargling. Honking, rasping and snorting.

And regularly punctuated by silences where he doesn't breathe for an agonising length of time – before, finally, just in the nick of time, gasping back into life again.

On the occasion of the fifth ghastly silence – where, surely, the beginnings of oxygen-deprived brain damage must be swiftly approaching – I gently shake his arm.

'Love. *Love.* You're doing it again. Wake up.'

He wakes up immediately – hair on end, spluttering and coughing.

'You're snoring again.'

'Sorry. *Sorry.* SORRY!'

'You keep stopping breathing. It's horrible. It sounds like you've entered the Tunnel of Light, and can finally see your grandma again. It can't be good for you. Every night seems like a struggle between life and death. You need help.'

'I'm sorry. *SORRY!* I promise I'll go and see the doctor. Tomorrow. *Tomorrow.* Sorry.'

It's 2019. It's 2.30am. I am sitting in bed, wide awake. Beside me, my husband is dying.

Since 2015, there have, inevitably, been developments in his sleep apnoea. In the same way Frank Sinatra's voice took on deeper, richer, more resonant tones as he aged – peaking around the sonorous genius of 'In the Wee Small Hours' – so my husband's snoring has taken on its own, brass-section-like resonance. There are trombones in his nose, saxophones in his epiglottis, and some mad, dissonant, rumbling synth effects – like the kind of stuff Hans Zimmer does on the *Inception* soundtrack – somewhere in his chest.

As his nasal orchestra reaches some Wagnerian crescendo, I not-so-gently shake his arm.

'Love. *Love.* The snoring. It's happening again.'

He shoots upright in bed.

'Sorry. *Sorry.* SORRY!'

I reach over and grab his mobile phone, which is on the pillow next to him. I open the recently purchased 'Snore-Lab' app, which records the noises snorers make during the night. In a nod to the music press in the mid-eighties, 'SnoreLab' gives the snorers' noises marks out of ten, and the most pertinent adjective for them.

I show my husband tonight's read-out. It reveals that he's basically Led Zeppelin, in their pomp. 10/10, and 'Epic', for the last two hours. SnoreLab calculates it's been so bad, he will only have had 20 minutes of REM sleep all night.

'I'm sorry. *SORRY!* I promise I'll go and see the doctor. Tomorrow. *Tomorrow.* Sorry.'

It's 2022. It's 4am. I am sitting in bed, wide awake. Since 2019, we have acquired a dog, Luna, who sleeps on the bed with us.

Lying on her back with her legs in the air, she is snoring, too – pausing only to occasionally issue a rich, meaty dog-fart.

Three feet up the bed is my husband. He has now not had a good night's sleep since 2017. Currently, he appears to be engaged in some kind of jazz-improv snore-duet with Luna – it's real Ella Fitzgerald and Louis Armstrong shit. Their honks and splutters sometimes syncopate, sometimes work on the off-beat: I'm pretty sure there are clubs full of hipsters who would genuinely dig it.

My husband's freeform gargling is all the more noteworthy because there is a strip of two-inch surgical tape across his mouth, supposedly glueing his lips together. It's a 'tip' I'd found online when googling 'How stop husband snore am go crazy' at 2am.

The fact that he is managing to make all these noises

through his nose only is, in a way, I guess, admirable. Life will find a way, and all that.

Because this is now *seven years* into this snoring debacle, the way I wake him is not so much a 'gentle shake' as a 'tetchy punch'.

'Why won't you go to the doctor?' I say, as soon as he wakes up. '*Why?* I'm not angry. I'm just *fascinated*. You know if I had a medical problem that was stopping both me *and you* from sleeping, I would have gone to get it sorted out on *Day Two*. And you are the kindest and most considerate person I know. You once carried my brother *on your back* from the bottom of Devil's Bridge gorge in Wales to the top, in order to catch the day's last-departing novelty steam train. *Why* will you not try to fix this? *Why* won't you see a doctor? *Why* are you currently solely working on advice, filtered through me, from a *Daily Mail* columnist with no medical training at all?'

He looks uncomfortable. He's obviously finding it difficult to put this into words. Possibly because he still has two inches of surgical tape over his mouth. I remove it.

'I don't know!' he says, eventually. 'I don't know! I don't know why I don't go and see the doctor! I will go and sleep in the spare room!'

Two days later, I talk to my daughter. She is in her first serious relationship, and has something she wants to discuss with me.

'Harry is very depressed and anxious – but he won't go and see a doctor. Should I make him? What do I do? Do I make the appointment for him myself? Why won't he go and see a doctor?'

I hug her.

'Darling,' I say. 'Congratulations. You are now nagging your partner to see a doctor. Today, you finally became a woman.'

'Men are notoriously bad patients. Compared with women, they avoid going to the doctor, skip more recommended screenings and practice riskier behavior. They also die about five years sooner, live with more years of bad health, and have higher suicide rates,' as a piece by Laura Landro in the *Wall Street Journal* put it in 2019. Or, as my GP put it, 'Whenever I ask a male patient why they've come to see me today, most of them don't list symptoms. They say, "*Because my wife/girlfriend made me.*"'

Why don't men go to the doctor? By which I really mean, why don't men take care of themselves? What is it about a man that means he will tenderly fit a new needle to a broken record player, take the weird 'clunking' sound from the clutch straight to the garage, or lovingly sit up all night with a dog that looks a bit 'sad' – but won't apply that level of care to himself?

Guys, we're *worried* about you. It can't be fun for you to have your girlfriends/wives/sisters constantly *nagging* you to go and see the doctor – not least because you must be knackered from dragging around the gigantic bulbous growth on your neck, roughly the size of a badger, that you've had since 2014.

Or hobbling from that 'knock' to your leg you got four years ago – which really is increasingly looking like it was a compound fracture, given that your leg has now healed at a sharp right-angle.

I went on Twitter one quiet Thursday afternoon, and asked a simple question: 'Men – I've just read a piece in the *Wall Street Journal* that says men are very reluctant to go to the doctor if they're ill, and only tend to go if their partner MAKES them. Why is that? What's going on there? Tell me!'

Over the next two days, I got over a thousand replies, full of utterly fascinating insight and honesty, and the reasons given broke down into roughly seven categories, the first of which was briskly summed up by one of the first Tweets I got, which was, simply, 'FEAR.'

The first was fear of judgement, or what might boldly be surmised as The Day of Bacon Sandwich Reckoning.

Fear of Judgement

'It's a fear of being chided by doctors.'

'I don't go because it's just another chance for my doc to tell me to lose weight.'

'Unless you totally lie about how many vegetables you eat and how much you drink, they look at you like you've made *yourself* ill – even if you go in with, like, corns.'

'Everything I say about my life makes them look very disappointed.'

No one likes being judged. That's why we don't have the saying 'As lovely and friendly as a judge'. And all the statistics on men's lifestyles – more likely to smoke; more likely to drink; more likely to be overweight; still really into those bacon sandwiches – mean that, when talking to your GP, you are very likely to be informed that almost every moment of your waking life is WRONG, and that you are simply a catalogue of lifestyle fuck-ups which, tldr, mean you deserve whatever illness you have. And, even if you're *not* told that – you fear it.

'I have a health condition that has worried me for three years, now. It almost certainly has nothing to do with my weight, diet or blood pressure – I have a side hustle as a hypochondriac, so I'm pretty certain about this. However, I will not go to see the doctor until I have lost at least a stone, and am doing regular cardio, and also have secretly had a "rehearsal" cholesterol test before my GP gives me a "proper" cholesterol test – because I haven't seen my GP for ten years, and I don't want my next medical record entry to be: "He's lost it." Basically, I won't see the doctor until I'm totally fit and healthy. Yes, I do know how illogical and insane that is.'

Given how recurrently this was mentioned, I do wonder if there needs to be research done on scrapping the targets GPs have for recruiting patients into weight-loss and stop-smoking programmes. It seems like a fear of being chided about lifestyle issues is preventing a *lot* of men from checking in for any medical help whatsoever.

And, as the stats reveal that only 30 per cent of men take up GP offers of e.g. weight-loss help, it does seem that this seemingly preventative initiative really *is* being preventative – it's preventing men from dropping into their doctors until their head is hanging off their neck by a single tendon.

The second fear was an all-time classic:

Fear of Death

'Fear. Of what? Fear that the illness might be terminal.'

'Because we're big old cowardy-custard chickens, and we're scared to find out something is wrong. Don't let anyone pretend it's because we're big and tough; we're feeble and terrified. If I'm going to die, I'd rather not know in advance, thanks.'

'Admit that I could be dying? No, thank you, ma'am.'

Well, this is a very basic fear, and I totally get it. After all, 'Finding out you have a terminal illness, then dying shortly after' is very likely to have been something men have witnessed in their own lives.

In previous generations – our parents, and grandparents, and all those dead uncles and aunts – the routine generally seemed to revolve around a relative calling you up, crying, and saying, 'Mum/Nan/Uncle Steve's just found out they've got the big C, and six weeks to live.'

And then, bang on time, six weeks later, you'd be wearing black, in a church hall, buttering 200 baps for the wake next to a bunch of crying aunties, who were only smoking *outside* 'out of respect' for the lung cancer.

I don't remember anyone before my generation having radiotherapy, or chemo. Or, indeed, any treatment at *all*. It was a fairly rapid trot from 'diagnosis' to 'grave'.

With this as a formative memory, it's very understandable why men are reluctant to go to the doctor. There is no 'five years of warning symptoms that could lead to early diagnosis and successful treatment' option in their heads. They are, essentially, *fatalists*. The medical world has still utterly failed in conveying the message that most people *survive* their illnesses – *so long as they get early treatment*.

If there is to be a male feminism, this would be a good issue to have as a primary campaign: a putative 'GOOD NEWS, MEN – MEDICINE CAN SAVE YOU!' message. It feels very different for women? It seems like half the women I know of my age have triumphed over serious illness. We almost have 'survive breast cancer' on our To-Do Lists, around the age of 50. Within ten minutes of feeling a lump, we've booked in to the doctors *and* googled 'sexy chemo wig'. We're *ready*.

If I were to be bold, I would suggest that it boils down to something as simple as this: women presume they will eventually survive a serious illness – and men don't. And that sucks for you. You can't live thinking you have only two options: 'Totally fine' and 'Dead'. Not least because, in not seeking early medical help, that's actually how you *are* living. And, then, sadly, dying.

This fear – based on previous generations' experience with healthcare – dovetails neatly into:

Stoicism

'You are brought up from an early age to put up with things and not to complain (because it is wimpish). (Incidentally, as a child I often had the "big boys don't cry" thing – but never from one of my male relatives; always mothers, grandmothers, aunts.)'

'Years of being told to "man up" or, in the words of my dad, "Don't be such a big girl's blouse." These things linger in your subconscious, I guess.'

'I'm not great with the old "fuss".'

Men are supposed to be tough, and stoic. Despite being made of the same blood, flesh and bones as women, and children, for some reason, their pain doesn't . . . count? Women and children first into the lifeboats. John McClane will carry on defending the Nakatomi Plaza, even though his feet are full of glass. Manchester City's Bert Trautmann broke his *neck* halfway through the 1956 FA Cup final – but still carried on playing.

How many times have you watched a male character in an action movie spend 90 minutes receiving the kind of repetitive, crippling blows that would, in real life, lead to instant unconsciousness, haemorrhage or death – only for them to shrug it off with some bantz, before having the Hulk thrown at their head?

And yet, still, they have to treat everything like it was a mere graze, because: they man up. They do not act like a big girl's blouse. The male body is *supposed* to endure a certain amount of pain. It is perfectly normal to be achey, injured, constipated, sleepless, limping or unable to lift your arm above your shoulder – but to never mention it, or do anything about it.

After all, you don't want to be accused of having Man Flu.

Worry That You're Not Really Ill At All – Just Weak

'I felt really, really bad – but went to sleep. Thinking it wasn't that serious, and that probably in the morning the symptoms would be gone. Only the next day, I went to the hospital when I understood it was not just fatigue symptoms. It was a stroke.'

'Once in agony with a cyst on my belt line which was the size of a lemon. The GP was aghast I'd put it off so long – then stuck a needle in it!

'Sometimes I've literally dragged my father to the doctor to stop him dying unnecessarily. He totally leaves it to the last minute and has nearly died two times as a result.'

'My ex-colleague walked around with a ruptured appendix for four days (yes, really) before he went to the doctors. He's *very* lucky to still be with us.'

When 'Toxic Masculinity' is discussed, this is the kind of stuff women mean when they explain that old ideas about 'real men' are toxic to *actual* real men. *Literally* toxic, if you've got septicemia, but 'don't want to be seen as weak'. The fear is, you're complaining over nothing. You are Man Flu Guy.

And of course, many men don't know what is 'normal', health or pain-wise, because, as one man on Twitter pointed out, 'As we know, men talk about rubbish with our mates – so no one ever tells us that whatever we might be going through isn't normal, and needs checking out.'

Where women will happily sit around discussing the symptoms of their twisted ovaries, or recreating their largest menstrual clots using a pile of mashed potato, men have not yet learned the great release and conspiratorial joy of discussing with *their* mates the various mad happenings of their bowels, balls or bums.

A lot of men seem to treat their bodies like their own personal Las Vegas – 'What happens in Vegas, stays in Vegas' – and keep all of its varieties and malfunctions as a terrible, shameful secret.

Men! Having recurrent, stabbing chest pains, or depression, is *not* the same as having banged a stripper while off your tits on tequila. *This is a story you can share with others. It's okay to complain!* And complaining might just save your life!

Of course, it's not just fear and shame that keep men from the doctor's door. There are practical issues, which often intersect with your class, and the healthcare system in your country. The fifth problem cited for men was:

Money/work

'My husband is self-employed and walked around for weeks with a broken leg (fibula) until he was forced to get it

X-rayed by me and the GP. A&E consultant was amazed as he marched up and down refusing to have it broken and reset or even plastered – because he had to work.'

'Self-denial and worrying that if it's serious, how would we cope not bringing a wage in to the family?'

'For me it comes from the American fear of the health-care system being expensive and intense.'

Men are far more likely to be self-employed (67 per cent) and in physical labour (in some industries, like plumbing and carpentry, up to 99 per cent of the workforce) than women – and so there is a real, practical and financial pressure to *their* stoicism. They simply cannot *afford* to be ill – their business, and family, depends on them doing an awful, modern version of that 'dance as if no one's watching' motto – they must 'work as if no one else will ever pay the bills'. Because – they won't.

And if you're American, and don't have comprehensive healthcare – well, what other option *do* you have, but ignore your pain?

In the long term, obviously, the answers to these problems are a) genuinely comprehensive healthcare in the US; b) campaigns for the self-employed to be provided with financial aid when ill; and c) better pay for the typical jobs of working-class women – so that, in a typical working family, Mum's pay packet is just as powerful as Dad's.

Remember: the thing about the Gender Pay Gap is that it screws men over *just as hard* as it screws women – if your partner is being underpaid, it's *you* that has to make up the shortfall, when the bills come in. You *both* live in that gap.

Obviously, though, these aren't answers for men *now*. You don't have *time* to completely change the economic status of women and the working classes across the globe – you've been constipated for three weeks, passing nothing more substantial than farts, and are seriously considering 'a Carol Vorderman' (from the Carol Vorderman Joke: 'What does Carol Vorderman do when she's constipated?' 'She works it out with a pencil.') You just have to think short term: that you wouldn't keep working with a drill that was breaking. You'd get it fixed. You are your own drill. GO TO THE DOCTOR.

Bums

Now you know the Carol Vorderman Joke, it's a happy synchronicity that the next most-cited reason for men not seeing a doctor can be summed up with 'Bums'.

'We're worried that they're going to poke their finger up our bumhole.'

'I'm worried about the finger up the bum. Worried about the following erection.'

'High risk of getting a finger up the arse from a stranger.'

When it comes to being a woman, I guess I tend to look on the bright side. Yes – I'm a 'vagina half-full' kinda gal.

Because while having the wildly complicated reproductive system of a woman – which might be briefly described as 'a mad trouble cupboard full of blood and bullshit' – is often a bit of a drag, it does mean one thing: women are *very used* to strangers putting their fingers in our holes.

Smears, IUD-insertion, pregnancy examinations – from puberty onwards, there is a lot of traffic in our vags.

If you're a woman, barely a week goes by without you being treated like a glove puppet by some medic – and sometimes, it's a real team effort. When I was giving birth to my first child, I had *11 people* in the room, all taking it in turns to look up my wedge, or have a good old rootle around in there, as if they were looking for the wine bottle in the bran tub.

On top of this, those of us who favour 'cock' in Mankind's Sexual Buffet often actively *encourage* things to be up our fannies, or bums, as and when the mood and preference strikes.

As a consequence, women are far, far more breezy about an anal examination than men. Like Otis Redding, it often feels like we're sitting on the dock of the bay, watching the boats come in, and go back out again. If by 'bay' we mean 'our holes', and by 'boats', fingers, medical spatulas, etc.

Although I am sympathetic with all the other reasons men quoted for being fearful of a medical appointment, I'm afraid that when it comes to 'Bums', I feel myself becoming a *little* brisk and Mary Poppins-like. Forty-four per cent of straight men have had anal sex with a woman. Frankly, if you've put your cock into someone else's bumhole simply because it's Friday, the 'do as you would be done by' rule insists a single finger in *your* bumhole, in order to potentially save your life, is merely karmic quid pro quo. I'm afraid you *do* need to man up, anally, here.

Besides – as your fear of erection attests – you might actually find out you like it. Or, as one man on Twitter put it, after seeing how many men had cited 'anal exam fear' as a reason not to go to the doctor, 'This is ironic, considering some of us pay good money for it.'

And if – when you look into your heart – the Finger/ Bum Fear comes down to a nagging worry about 'gayness', remember Moran's Rule Number One: '50 per cent of all straight men's biggest problems come down to a fear of being called "gay".' Honestly, once straight men have conquered this nagging fear, the world is their oyster. And their bumholes will hold no fear at all.

Nobleness

Do you know what's very, very underrated in men? How noble they are. How much they have absorbed the message that – simply by being men – they are the 'powerful', 'privileged' ones, and should therefore constantly seek to put the rest of the pack above themselves. There is a quiet element of self-sacrifice in men that I think men are often not aware of themselves.

'Our NHS services are under-resourced, I'd prefer not to add to that pressure unless I feel it is absolutely necessary. If this is to cost me dearly, that's on me. I'm OK with this, especially if it means others, who are in need, are being treated.'

'Is there a class, as well as/rather than a gender divide here, I wonder? My working-class parents always felt very guilty about "bothering doctors", who they thought were busy people with better things to do than, er, diagnosing cancer.'

'I don't want to waste the doctor's time. Like I went once for an allergy, but the waiting room was full of old people and babies and people who *needed* a doctor more than I do.'

'I always think that there's someone out there who needs that doctor's appointment more than me.'

Feminism has been very effective in campaigning for healthcare, tests and discussions about a range of female problems – from reproductive issues to breast cancer. My bitches have talked, networked, campaigned, legislated, got that funding and firmly established that 'running a marathon dressed in pink wearing a pair of balloon-breasts' is a normal part and parcel of helping our sisters.

However, as there is still no male equivalent – no general spirit of 'Let's do this for the boys!' – healthcare in general isn't seen as such a . . . man-thing. Because there are constant campaigns about the health needs of women – and the elderly, and children – there's a sense that men can only step forward for a piece of the healthcare pie *after everyone else has been served before them*. That it would be greedy to ask for help while there is even one more 'traditionally needful' person in front of them. That it would, indeed, be *wrong*.

I feel that there is a sense that men need, for want of a better word, to be *invited* to have their health treated seriously. To be able to raise a problem, safe in the knowledge that they weren't basically screwing over some disadvantaged minority demographic, simply by ringing to make an appointment.

Interestingly, in 2021, as part of National Men's Health

Week, an NHS clinic in Rochdale held a specifically publicised 'Young Men's Health Clinic' – the section of the population least likely to seek help.

As general practice nurse Caroline Lomax wrote, 'We attempted to engage young males aged between 18 and 24 years old and encourage them to take ownership of their own health and wellbeing. I myself have two sons in this age group, so I fully understand the need for them to engage with their own health and wellbeing, as well as the importance of normalising talking about health concerns and asking for help.

'The first clinic had an 80 per cent take-up. As a result of that clinic we identified several health issues – particularly surrounding mental health, low mood, depression and anxiety. In turn, patients expressed that these feelings have triggered other negative coping mechanisms such as smoking, binge drinking, overeating and lack of exercise.'

The pilot scheme was a raging success.

Given that 'not wanting to take away someone *else's* help' was such a surprisingly large factor in the Twitter replies I got from doctor-avoidant men – a good 37 per cent of the responses – I feel similar schemes, across the age ranges, could be very useful, in terms of men's health.

No one should suffer because of a chivalric impulse. No man should be so polite and self-sacrificing that they die. Men need to be invited to care for themselves. They can't just rely on being 'nagged' into going, by a partner/sister/wife.

Although we will absolutely totally keep doing that. You betcha.

Postscript

Two months after I wrote this chapter, my husband *finally* clicked on one of the multiple links I had sent him, giving details of a doctor, and went to get a general health check. His first in ten years.

'*Tell them about the snoring,*' were my last words, as he left the house. 'The snoring. *Promise me.* It's not normal.'

When he returned, two hours later, he looked as scared as I've ever seen him.

'They took my blood pressure – it's dangerously high,' he said, sitting at the kitchen table, looking pale: '220 over 120.'

I indicated that this meant nothing to me.

'Normal is, like, 100 over 60.'

'Christ.'

The doctor had explained that my husband's blood pressure was *so* high, he should immediately cancel all work, go straight to bed, avoid all stress, and wait until they could scan his heart.

We went upstairs, and got into bed together for a week – watching non-exciting TV shows, ignoring the phone, and silently holding hands – punctuated only by my husband saying, every so often, 'I've been so stupid. And I'm so scared.'

When, a week later, they did the scan, they found his blood pressure was so high it had caused damage: it had permanently enlarged his heart. That muscle had struggled so much that, even as he tried to stay 'healthy' at the gym, every day, it had become swollen.

The reality of this was brutal: at any moment in the last few years, he could have had a stroke, or a heart attack – and died before he got to a hospital.

We just stared at each other.

Two months previously, his father had dropped dead, without warning, in his bed – from a heart attack.

Our mourning clothes from the funeral were still hanging on the wardrobe door, waiting to be taken to the dry cleaners. The Order of Service was on the bedside table – the photo of his father staring outward. The fittest and most relentless 84-year-old we knew. Half of Pete's DNA.

Pete was prescribed a couple of bottles of blood-pressure medication, and told to lose weight – to take the pressure off his heart.

With the same stoicism that meant he hadn't gone to the doctor before, he now stoically followed orders. He changed what he ate; stopped snacking late at night; and started exercising again – once the blood-pressure medication brought his readings back to a normal level. Whenever we took his blood-pressure readings, to make sure he was as relaxed as possible, he would bury his face in my bosom, while I murmured things I knew he would find soothing. The track-listing to Orange Juice albums. The lyrics of Neil Finn. From deep in my bra-area, I would hear him say, muffled, 'I should have done it before. I should have just gone to the doctor before.'

It's now six months later. The heart enlargement aside – that will never go – Pete has a completely clean bill of

health. The weight has stayed off, his blood pressure is normal, and he regularly runs 40k a week. He was scared to go
to the doctor – for all the reasons outlined by all the men
on Twitter – but he did, and it undoubtedly saved his life.
It saved his life.

'I'm just so grateful I got the chance to make it better,'
he says, every so often, when we're walking the dog, or
watching the kids play together. Less so when we were
cleaning out the gutters, or doing the VAT return, though.

And – the final kicker – the snoring has vanished.
Stopped. Gone. It comes back if he eats late at night –
buttery toast at 10pm means being punched in the arm at
1am – but it is, otherwise, cured.

My desperate plans – for separate beds, in separate
rooms, on separate storeys, in separate houses – have now
been shelved. We will have a peaceful old age together.
Partly because I won't have to kill him.

But mainly because he won't be dead.

Chapter Fourteen

The Oldness of Men

It's *hard* to become an old man. There aren't many options on the table. Having a quick gander at the archetypes offered by popular culture, they seem to boil down to:

ONE: Continuing to be Tom Cruise – flying planes, banging women, jumping off buildings – even though you're 63.

TWO: Irascible, lonely widower, only emotionally revivified when taken on a fantastical journey by a Korean boy-scout and a talking dog (*Up*).

THREE: Over-knowledgeable man keen to tell everyone the shortest way from the M4 to north London ('You take the A312 cut-through onto the North Circular – but *don't* tell anyone about it, it's my secret rat-run').

FOUR: Golf.

FIVE: Mr Burns.

SIX: Man-child reliving teenage years with purchase of e.g. sports car, and unsuitable swimming-trunks.

SEVEN: A wizard.

One upside of the batshit biology of women is that we're used to transitioning though multiple physical phases. We're girls! Then we're bleeding! Then we're pregnant! Then we're breastfeeding! Then we're menopausal! We're all *over* the fucking place! We're Mr Benn! Every day, a new outfit, and adventure!

We're *used* to not being able to do things, or our bodies letting us down, or turning into something else. It's all part of life's mad variable flow.

For men, by way of contrast, old age can be something of a shock. A man likes to be able to lift a heavy object, right? He likes to operate a power tool, crack on with stuff on his own, drive his car and eat his red meats.

It can be quite devastating, then, to suddenly have your back 'go', find that a drill makes your hands feel 'all juddery', realise you nearly crashed your Fiesta because your eyes 'aren't what they were', or have a doctor chide you about your gout/prostate, and explain that Steak Night is going to have to become a twice-yearly event, max.

Men like to take care of other people. The idea of having to be cared for by others – in whatever way, small or large – can spark an absolute existential horror. And yet, its inevitability is never discussed.

I speak in broad generalisations, but, by and large, men don't like things to change. There is a pleasing consistency and constancy to the lives of men – once they have found a thing that works, they stick to it.

You only have to ask around your social group for 'Dad's Race at School Sports Day' stories to find ample evidence of men's unwillingness to confront ageing. There *will* be hospitalisations among them. 'I thought I'd still "Got It" until my Achilles tendon snapped.' 'Family X sent in a fucking *ringer* – a 22-year-old nephew – and three dads nearly killed themselves trying to keep up with him.'

My friend Dan wins this story round: watching the dads lining up at the starting line, he noted that Daley Thompson – two-time Olympic gold medallist – was in the line-up. And still over half the dads 'went for it' – and consequently blamed their lack of success on 'I was wearing shoes. If I was in trainers . . .'

The problem with men's otherwise enjoyable existential consistency is that a lot of it derives from fear of being mocked if they try something 'new'. E.g. you go back to your home town sporting a snazzy white polo-neck and, for the rest of the evening, the entire pub keeps asking you, 'How are all the other submariners?'

All fine when you *can* throw away the polo-neck and go back to wearing a Fred Perry polo shirt, as God intended: more problematic when you actually *are* changing, and need to do something about it, e.g. ageing.

Men Need a Third Act

The problem with men's lives is that there is no Third Act.

When women reach old age – post-menopausal, children raised and gone, reaching retirement – they often *blossom*. There is a story that women follow, and it's one of, basically, fun. It doesn't matter if they still have a partner, or they are widowed or divorced: those old ladies start attending evening classes, retrain as volunteers, take up a new hobby, learn to salsa, do up a caravan and go around East Anglia.

If you hike up any reasonably sized hill or mountain in Great Britain, halfway up – already knackered, even though you're only in your forties – you will almost certainly meet a group of women in their sixties and seventies, already on their way back down, chatting and cackling over a lifetime of in-jokes, and sharing a variety of pleasant-looking home-made cakes.

Ring your mum, right now, and ask her what she's doing this weekend – and prepare for a fully loaded itinerary speckled with the names of women you remember being around your kitchen table back in 1986.

Women nurture their friendship groups throughout a lifetime – so by the time they reach old age, they tend to be in a gang of similarly sprightly women having the time of their fucking lives now that Our Mackie is off to college, and Our Arthur has become a close-hand magician in Mallorca.

In my female social group, we have been discussing what we will be doing in *our* old age since our mid-thirties. Working on the assumption – based on statistics – that our male partners will die before us; we will club together to buy a large house; spend Friday nights having 'Back to the Nineties' DJ sessions in the kitchen; adopt roughly 6,000 spaniels; and take it in turn to do the gardening. The loss of our best-loved ones aside, we're kind of looking forward to it.

By way of contrast, I don't know any men who are making any such plans for old age. Maybe it's because they presume they *will* die first. Or maybe it's because it's too depressing to contemplate. In 2016, Britain's biggest charity for the old reported that over 1.2 million older men report feeling 'socially isolated', with 10 per cent 'chronically lonely'.

The crisis point is often the death of a wife – who will have been effectively running the couple's social life, or been the one who phones the kids, then 'hands the phone over to Dad to say hello'. Seventy-five per cent of men without a partner 'feel lonely', and one in four had 'less than monthly' contact with friends.

As any army general will tell you, every war needs an Exit Plan, and if life is a war – it is! – you must consider how you will exit 'youth', and enter your older years.

Currently, it's notable that, as far as men are concerned, our Third Act isn't a Third Act at all – it's a rerun of either the First or Second Act.

'The Classic Mid-Life Crisis'

A rerun of the First Act is the technical name for what we all more commonly refer to as 'a mid-life crisis'. And one of the great sorrows of being a man is that everyone finds the male Mid-Life Crisis simply hilarious.

Whenever women reclaim their youth – going all *Shirley Valentine* on holiday, banging a tennis coach, or getting a pixie-cut – everyone's like, 'Girl Power! You go! Bad-ass bitches still got it! Strong *Golden Girls*-on-the-razz energy!'

Should a man reclaim his youth, however, everyone falls about laughing. Remember David Dimbleby getting a scorpion tattoo? John Travolta's 'new face'? Harrison Ford's pirate earring? Tim Robbins abandoning acting to record an 'emotional' album about his life?

Motorbikes, leather trousers, hair transplants, attending festivals, micro-dosing, finding a shaman, suddenly having a musical side-project: the idea of *dads* feeling liberated from childcare and reliving their youth, now their children are grown, is treated with nothing but sniggering.

This is, frankly, piss – *why*, so long as they're not hurting anyone, is it so bad for a man to relive a bit of his youth? So long as he's not abandoning a long-suffering wife and twins in order to suddenly open a Hash Workshop in Leeds, why *can't* a man enjoy putting on some silly trousers and taking 'the Hog' down the A41 to Ketley while listening to Cream?

Of course, these things can get out of hand: there is a classic trope of Maverick Boomer Dads, now divorced, who move in with their uptight/long-suffering daughters, who repeatedly have to tell them to turn down 'A Whiter Shade of Pale', to stop growing marijuana in her greenhouse, stop living in her shed, and stop teaching the kids to say, 'Chill your boots, hot mamma.'

If men are going to relive their youth, they need to make

sure they're not inadvertently casting someone else as their mother. That's all kinds of Marty McFly wrongness.

But if it's 'liberating' and 'kick-ass' for women to dedicate their older years to freedom, fun, tattoos and rock music, then why is it seen as a bit embarrassing when men do it? I actually find it quite moving – because the reasons behind it often aren't simply that men are 'regressing'. They are, instead, catching up on undone business.

Why *Do* Men Have a 'Mid-Life Crisis'?

By and large, I've noticed that the men who want to 'relive their youth' tended *not* to have done all this stuff when they were *actually* youths. The classic mid-life crisis is usually the move of someone who spent *their* youth . . . not being a youth. They didn't piss about, or rebel, or bang around, or have a 'Hog': instead, they were building up a business; or taking care of ill parents; being ill/depressed themselves; or just being poor. Or studying hard – to the detriment of any fun.

Or maybe they were a fat teenage boy, or a spotty one, or one who was desperately shy, and insecure – and never took part in all that pleasing, rebellious, 'just doing it because I want to' young-man stuff.

In this instance, by having a 'mid-life crisis', they're simply living their life *out of the normal sequence* – and doing 'youth stuff' at 65.

To misquote Eric Morecambe, 'It's all the right life events – just not necessarily in the right order.'

Rerunning the Second Act: Trying to Put Right What Once Was Wrong

A rerun of the *Second* Act, meanwhile, is when a man either leaves his wife and family, or his wife and family leaves him – and he starts the Second Act, of fatherhood, again; with a new, and usually younger, wife.

It's absolutely standard for a man marrying for the second time, and starting a second family, to be met with a certain amount of derision. 'Trading her in for a younger model, huh?' 'Fucked it the first time round?'

While this derision is more understandable when a man has left a perfectly decent and loyal wife in order to shack up with the nanny, secretary or friend of his daughter, just because things got 'too hard' or 'too boring', I find it fascinating that no one 'deeps' the emotional impetus behind this.

Because, a couple of years down the line, when Act Two man has had a couple of kids with Wife Two, what is the most common thing he will say?

'This time, I'm really enjoying the kids being babies.'

'This time, I've been here for it all.'

'The first time around, I was too busy working to really appreciate being a father. I never really saw them. For these guys, I'm doing 4am feeds, nappies, school runs – I'm really *present* in a way I never was with my first family.'

Personally, I find this really heartbreaking: a combination of economics and inability to question traditional roles means that these men, when younger, in their first marriage and fatherhood, prioritised 'being the breadwinner' above all else.

At an earlier point in their career – and therefore when they were probably both poorer and more insecure – they didn't feel they could negotiate a proper work/life balance. They 'left the kids to the wife' – 'She kept the home fires burning' – and it's only now, older and wiser and maybe richer, that they allow themselves a second chance at being properly present fathers.

Often, there have been unpleasant revelations that have led to this point: older children, in their teens or twenties, that have turned around and said, 'You were never there for us. You loved work more than us. You *never* attended a single school play – we talked to your secretary more than you.'

Or else, there is no relationship at all: the children's primary relationship is with their mother, who is now reaping all the benefit of her close parenting in calls, visits and holidays with adoring adult offspring, while Dad hangs around awkwardly in the background, trying to start conversations with a nervous, 'So, how are you, bud?', only to be shot down with a brutal 'Oh, you fucking care *now*?' and a slammed door.

Little wonder, then, that there is often a wild urge to try to clean-slate it – start again, with a new wife and children, and finally do life *properly*: *enjoy* the babies, the silly songs, the bedtimes and school plays. To get to your deathbed knowing you finally *did* do all the vital stuff of the heart, after all: lay on a sofa with a tiny, hot baby sleeping on you; taught a kid to ride a bike; counselled a weeping, drunken teenage daughter, with mascara all down her face, that 'she's fucking magic, and so much better than that carbuncular wazzock'.

Oh, why can't we, in the twenty-first century, reinvent the idea of being a man – and put the option to parent fully and whole-heartedly at the centre of it? 'Blended families' might be a wonderful thing – but not if the main reason the first marriages didn't work is simply because Dad went out to earn the money, and Mum was left with a part-time job, or no job at all, and the baby. That doesn't work for *anyone* – mothers, fathers, or the children. It's insane that childcare is still seen as a 'feminist issue', when it's so obviously an 'everyone issue'. No father should be robbed of proper, engaged, bone-deep, 24/7 parenting.

As any parent will tell you, ultimately, it *is* all about the hours you put in. It's being there for the boring bits, the routine bits, the suddenly revelatory magic bits, which come and go like rainbows: you just have to *be* there when they happen. Stand under them and marvel, before they fade away again. No father should be having his children's lives reported to him, at the end of the day, when they're asleep. You don't want to be saying, 'Send me the photos.' You want to be the one *taking* the photos. Has Mr Banks in *Mary Poppins* taught us nothing? You just have to . . . go fly a kite.

And this is the main thing about getting old. We talk about retirement and pensions; investments and suitable housing. Keeping fit and finding hobbies. We're very good at making *those* kinds of plans and preparations. This part of old age, we are ready for.

But there is one part of getting old we're *not* so good at preparing for; one investment for which we *don't* employ specialists, to ready us. Or even discuss in the pub. And it's the pension plan of *memories* – our investments in mental souvenirs. We do not, it seems, regard the fact that, by the time we're 70, we will be as a dragon, sitting on a lifetime's hoard of hours and days. A dragon with four slightly dodgy knees, who doesn't get around as much, and so spends most of its time just sitting. Just sitting with the past.

I've watched old people, but men in particular, become quite agonised by what an inadvertent, unhappy, meagre memory-pension they've left themselves to live off, by the time they became chair-bound. Oh, the regrets! That they let work replace love; that they were unkind; that they didn't keep in touch with old friends; that they missed whole childhoods; that they let marriages fail; that they ignored their health. That they were too scared to grow up into the slightly weird, but amazing, boy they were when they were nine. Before all the weirdness got crushed out of him. Before, as Anna Calvi puts it, they 'beat the girl out of my boy'.

And when you talk to these men – the ones in the corner table of the pub; the ones who've had two whiskies at a wedding; the ones who suddenly strike up a conversation at the bus-stop, because it seems they can't keep these thoughts in any longer – they end their list of disappointments and remorse by shrugging, and saying, almost marvelling at their stoicism, 'But then, that's what it was like, back then. That's just what a man did. That's just what life is like.'

And this, ultimately, is what this book is about. No man should reach his final years full of regret, and abandoned ideas, and heart-aching disappointments, simply because he obediently played by the rules of 'what a man should be'. Because there *is* no science, or physics, or rules, of what a man 'should' be! You have signed no Man Contract; there is no one to report to. By the time you're 70, everyone whose disapproval, ridicule or disappointment you feared will be long gone, or dead. There is no one who will give you a medal for your sad dutifulness. The approval you wanted will never come. Rebel now! While you still have the time!

This is what feminism has done, for so many women, over the last few decades. 'The sisterhood' is as wide and nebulous a phenomenon as the Milky Way – a billion points of light, all so distant from each other that, even if you are *in* it, you still see it as a far-off thing, which you are not quite part of – but one of the things it has been excellent at is cheering on girls, and women, who say, 'I do not like *this* rule. I do not like *this* rule of being a woman, or girl.' And then simply broken it, and carried on. They have revolted into more freedom, and more happiness. More choice, and more power. More silliness, and more fun. Simply, *more*.

I think men should have more of this . . . *more*. I think every man should see how his 'normal' story of 'being a man' – when told honestly, and fully – joins up with a million other stories, all of which point to the same thing: you *do* want more. This often *doesn't* feel like enough. You want *different*. You want *options*. You want to not feel terrible guilt for both things you never did, and the things you did. You want 'being a man' to be a joyful, simple thing – and not this label that, so often now, seems to stand for everything old, awful and uncool.

You want . . . something to happen. Before you're standing in the pub, full of unhappy memories, with aching knees, sighing, 'That's just what a man did. That's just what life is like.'

Chapter Fifteen

What About Men?

This, then, is the last chapter of this book. I have spent a year going on my journey into the World of Boys, and Men – but I am aware that, as with any book, this is in no way a complete map.

As you will have probably noticed, I have followed all the roads *I* found intriguing, or had something to say about, and have carefully avoided all the topics I didn't really know, or care, about: like sport, violence, computer games, or why it is that all men can quote huge reams of TV and movie dialogue, particularly *The Godfather.*

By the way, I tried watching *The Godfather,* to see what all the 'fuss' was about, but my main takeaway was the scene where Marlon Brando is playing with his grandchildren, in the garden – and then, after three minutes, has a heart attack, and just dies.

I found this inability to play with young children, despite being capable in every other way, up to and including running *the Mafia*, chimed hugely with a great many grandfathers I know of the same age. Yes – they *would* rather just die than spend more than three minutes playing with their grandchildren. It's . . . so much easier.

So yes – this is a very selective, and very personal, attempt to answer the question, 'What about men?'

I will admit – a lot of my motivation for writing it was a very petty urge to be able to say, 'Well, no *man* had got around to writing a book like this, and so, as usual, muggins here – a middle-aged woman – had to crack on, and sort it all out.'

Of course, I have not sorted anything out at all. All I've really done is try to write a book that provides a starting point for, I hope, a lot of conversations, by, I hope, a lot of men. If there's one overriding theme in this book that I bumped into time and time again, it's the feeling that – angry Incels and Men's Rights Activists to one side – most normal, lovely, mediumly perturbed men felt it would be somehow *wrong* to start talking about men; that it might be seen as *impolite*, or complaining; that it might be seen as sexist; that it might cause a *fuss*.

To which I would reply: I found all the conversations, Tweets, emails, interviews and responses I had during the writing of this book both *deeply* fascinating, and also regularly, reliably, *very* funny. Men are absolutely aware of the absurdities of many of their problems, and have found – as girls, and women, do – that often, the healthiest way to start talking about them *is* to make a joke about them; and

I am a great believer in humour when talking about difficult or awkward things.

But, as I wrap up this book, and journey back to the World of Girls, and Women – I have a *lot* of washing stacked up, and my period is due – I thought I'd return to one of the comments that sparked this book in the first place:

'It's easier to be a woman than a man.'

Is it easier, in our culture, to be a woman than a man?

And the answer is, in some ways, *yes*. In certain respects, it *is* easier to be a woman than a man. And mainly because of one thing:

Feminism

We have feminism. If women, and girls, are 'winning', it's because they have feminism. That's the only real material difference in the lives of modern women and modern men right now. The only thing men *don't* have that women do is: a philosophy that questions gender.

Sometimes I wonder if the misogynist anger we see against women isn't because they believe women are inferior, as they claim – but is, instead, really *envy*. Envy that women can admit their vulnerability; articulate their needs; find support and appreciation in the sisterhood; be sexually desired; pursue things that give them joy; make their worlds pleasant and comfortable; self-soothe their fears and angers; be loved by their family and friends; and have real hope about their future.

I do not think any Men's Rights Activist, Incel,

Manosphere misogynist, or angry young man in Luton repeating slogans feels that they have these things in their lives. If they did, they wouldn't be angry. Anger is, after all, just sadness, brought to the boil.

My husband once nailed why Oasis are still, for millions of men, their favourite band. A band they love with passionate intensity. 'Noel and Liam grow up in a really violent, unhappy house. And then Noel starts writing what are really, when you look at them, very sad songs – songs about wishing you were somewhere else; feeling trapped in your home town; not knowing how to say what you're feeling – but then Liam sings them in a really *angry* way. With real *attack*. Everything you need to know about men is in the line, "There are many things that I would like to say to you/But I don't know how." Liam *howls* that. And there's something quite heartbreaking about watching 250,000 men singing it back to him – like they really mean it. You know when men are sad, and scared – because they get angry.'

There was a Men's Movement, once. Right alongside the Women's Movement, back in the 1960s and 70s. Alongside Women's Liberation, there was Men's Liberation, too.

Hippydom had happened – men were refusing to go to war, growing their hair long, writing poetry and wearing kaftans. Certain gender norms had starting breaking down. In this climate of change, men got together, talked about their biggest problems, and tried to come up with solutions for them.

There are pictures of these groups on the internet – there are a lot of beards, and patchwork jeans. They seem a very amiable bunch. The banners they hold on marches say things like 'MEN ARE MORE THAN SUCCESS OBJECTS' and 'LET'S SHARE CHILDCARE'. There's an adorable mildness to it all – the slogans recall the ones from the protest on *Father Ted*, outside a cinema showing a 'rude' film, which read 'CAREFUL NOW – DOWN WITH THIS SORT OF THING'.

There was even a magazine, *Achilles Heel* – full of thoughtful essays, including one that sighingly noted how hard the fundamental business of the Men's Movement was: 'Consciousness-raising could often be a frustrating experience – as we had mastered, over the years, the art of intellectualizing our experience as a way of avoiding having to share ourselves with others. It was difficult to escape the abiding feeling that other [men] would inevitably take advantage of whatever weaknesses we happened to show.'

In other words, the men were too scared to liberate themselves by admitting their problems – in case other men shouted 'ARGH! You girl!' and then hit them on the bums with wet towels.

Inevitably, given these fundamental problems, the Men's Liberation Movement didn't last long. As with all big break-ups, 'recollections may vary', but the biggest reason seemed to be that many fretted that Men's Liberation was essentially self-loathing. It disliked *everything* about masculinity – it was essentially *ashamed* of being men.

There was also a chunky dose of homophobia – or, as Wikipedia sadly notes, in a dry presaging of Moran's Rule

Number One, 'The fear of being seen as gay prevent[ed] boys and men from questioning, and ultimately abandoning, traditional masculinity.'

By the late seventies, the Men's Movement, and Men's Liberation, had fizzled out. The differences were too great. Men could not agree on what 'men' should be. Or what the problems were in the first place.

Of course, that wasn't the end of attempts to examine and reinvent what 'being a man' was: humans are restless, and we never entirely give up on an idea. In the eighties, there were New Men, and Metrosexual Men. In the nineties, there was Robert Bly's *Iron John* book, which spent 62 weeks on the *New York Times* bestseller list, and urged men, weakened by industrialisation and electric tin-openers, to retreat to the wilderness, reconnect with their masculine identity, and find 'the warrior within'. More recently, there's been Jordan B. Peterson's *12 Rules for Life*, with his bed-making; and the hyper-masculinity of Andrew Tate and the Manosphere.

While these have all been massive phenomena – sparking endless think-pieces, debates, book tours and, latterly, hashtags – they never turned into proper, identifiable movements. Not in the way that, say, the LGBTQIA+ rights movements, or the Civil Rights movement, inspired a sudden, global blossoming of language and thought. There was no sense of men reaching out, and really connecting with each other: organising campaigns for lasting, institutional change. There were no marches, or groups started in school and colleges; no legislation was drafted; no research was commissioned. No culture – books, TV, music, comedy – bloomed as a result of it. There wasn't even any adorable, man-based inspirational merchandise on Etsy.

All the ideas floated were things that, basically, a man could do on his own, in order to feel he had conquered his problems on his own, and then – that was it.

Meanwhile, Women's Liberation, and the feminist movement, conducted research, organised think-tanks, backed the election of female MPs, worked on draft legislation, opened women's refuges, formed charities, wrote petitions, camped out at Greenham Common, started micro-loan companies in the developing world, campaigned for free menstrual products, lobbied the UN, and invented Beyoncé.

What, then, *would* a successful Men's Movement look like? What would feminism for men be?

We know what the problems of boys, and men, are: in an unlikely turn of events, everyone is pretty much agreed on the core stuff. Whether you're a strident lady feminist, beardy New Man, or furious right-wing Men's Rights Activist, up to your tits in 'I HEART Andrew Tate' badges, the list is pretty similar, and based on inarguable statistical facts:

Boys underachieve at school, compared to girls.
Boys are more likely to be excluded from school.
Boys are less like to go into further education.

Boys are more likely to be prescribed medication for
ADHD/'disruptive behaviour'.

Men are more likely to become addicted: to drugs,
to alcohol, to pornography.

Men make up the majority of gang members.

Men are the majority of the homeless.

Men make up the majority of suicides.

Men make up the majority of people who are
murdered.

Men make up the majority of the prison
population.

Men are the majority of the unemployed.

Men are the majority that die at work.

Men are the majority that die in wars.

Men are the majority that lose custody of their children in a divorce.

As we can see, most of these awful statistics are down to
either education, work or economics. These are all ripe for
organised campaigns, suggesting change.

Educationally, for instance, we've already seen how
making boys learn to write before they're physically capable
has dozens of knock-on effects. There are numerous studies
and books, setting out how and why modern education is
much harder for boys than girls – the biggest meta-data
study, in 2014, from the American Psychological Associ-
ation, included over a million different students, from over
30 countries, and suggested the two main reasons. The
first, that female students simply feared failure more, and so
studied harder; and the second, that the modern shift to

long-term coursework, rather than last-minute exams, making up a high proportion of the final marking, favoured the ways girls perform. Of most interest to me was the less-emphasised factor that girls' cerebellums reach physical maturity at 11, while for boys, it's 15. As yet there is no attempt to take into account *this* physical difference between girls and boys – even as feminist campaigns acknowledge female biology, and demand free sanitary towels in every girls' toilet.

Failing at school is massively implicated in many of the other problems boys, and men, face: disruptive behaviour, exclusion, joining a gang, becoming an addict, going to jail.

And, of course, your academic results then inform what kind of job you get – the lower your results, the more likely you are to take up a 'physical' job, such as mining, labouring or factory work, which are both more dangerous, and – with the changing economy, and globalisation – more at risk of becoming obsolete. And so to unemployment, and homelessness.

Additionally, these are the jobs which – even if you a) keep them and b) aren't killed by them – are less likely to have flexible working hours and paternity leave: meaning that, in the case of divorce, it's your wife who will be deemed to have been the primary carer. So now you only see your kids every other weekend, as well.

As we can see, there would be plenty for any putative new Men's Movement, or feminism for men, to get stuck into. Aside from the difference in girls' and boys' mental biology, many commentators have suggested that some of boys' early struggles with education are because teaching, for younger children, is dominated by female teachers – and that boys respond better to being taught by men. So we might also need to look at why teaching younger children is seen as a 'woman's job', and how to encourage men to go full *Dead Poets Society* with a bunch of six-year-olds. Maybe it's because they need better pay. Or maybe it's because men are worried about being seen as 'paedos'. Either way – both of these are proper, chunky, economic and cultural topics which need a productive day at the coalface of the Men's Movement.

But while these are all real and observable problems, which would require political and legislative change to tackle, from what I have noticed about why, and when, things change, the main thing that's missing at the moment is: energy. Excitement. Positivity. Hope. Invention. Novelty. *Fun*.

In the twenty-first century, as things stand right now, it doesn't seem exciting, or fun, to be a man, or a boy. If there is a Battle of the Sexes, then, PR-wise, women and girls are nailing it. All the energy, and joy, is with the women right now. Beyoncé will sing 'Who run the world? (Girls)' and quote Chimamanda Ngozi Adichie on her albums; the *Broad City* girls write a masterclass on female friendship, and hide weed in their pussies; the prime minister of Finland gets drunk and twerks; Michelle Obama sells out stadiums; Rihanna is a billionaire; the Kardashians run a matriarchal empire.

Every week, newspapers, magazines and websites are full of features like 'Five Women Who Are Changing the World Right Now', or 'Top Ten Most Inspiring Women'. On the news, if you see a woman, it's because she's become a First: the first woman to win 23 Grand Slams; the first woman to be picked to go to the Moon; the first woman to become a self-made billionaire. There is now a continuing narrative of noticing and celebrating women.

By way of contrast, when you see a man on the news, it tends to be because he's a) murdered a woman; b) shot up a school; or c) invaded another country. There are *no* lists of 'Ten Most Exciting Young Men in the World'. That would be seen as . . . problematic.

We just aren't excited about men, and boys, in the way we are about women, right now.

And so the boys, and men, who complain, 'It's all about women, and girls, right now,' are *right*. No one *does* know when International Men's Day is. There *is* no Minister for Men. There *are* no books called *101 Inspiring Boys from History*. Feminism has created this constant, self-affirming loop – telling women, and girls, quite rightly, how amazing they are. We presume that, as time goes on, there will be even more of them. We keep saying 'the future is female'. Because women are empathatic, and emotionally literate, and can multitask, and are excellent at networking with other women, and can sing about being powerful feminist women while looking great in fishnet tights and a basque.

But: what's amazing about boys, and men? What *are* the good things about masculinity? What should we be celebrating – being excited about – that men and boys do uniquely well? If anyone ever *did* do something on International Men's Day, what *is* the inspiring message we would be pumping to our boys – in the same way we pump it to our girls?

I had spent so long tackling the dark side and problems of men – the things that make them unhappy about themselves – that when I asked myself this question, initially, I struggled. I had to go outside for a ciggie, to clear my head, and have a think. What *is* good about masculinity? I couldn't remember, in my lifetime, seeing such a list. I felt like I was starting from scratch.

When I came back, I compiled the following:

Non-judgemental – there's no backstabbing, or bitchy comments; they just accept you, however you are.

Protective – they will do everything to keep the people they love safe, even if it puts them in danger.

Up for anything – if you want to spend a day seeing if your gaffer-tape-mended inflatable boat is now seaworthy, three men will jump on board with you; no need to ask twice.

Brave – they're the first ones down the stairs if there's a weird noise in the night.

Joyous – if you want an uncomplicated day of fun, no deep or morose stuff, it's men you call. They will make you laugh until you cry.

Hard-working – they will work, uncomplainingly, at even the hardest and dirtiest jobs.

Incredibly loyal – when they love you, they love you
for ever, no matter what.

Then I realised I was basically describing dogs.

So I went on both Twitter and Facebook, and asked:
'Men, and women – we hear so much about what is toxic
about masculinity. To the point where we all seem to think
everything about masculinity is toxic. But: what is *good*
about it? What should we be celebrating?'

The replies went on for three days. I was saddened by
how many thought they needed to put a caveat – 'It's all
subjective!' 'There is no human trait which isn't shared by
both men and women!' 'All the positive traits about masculinity can tip over into toxicity!' – but the general consensus
chimed, primarily, with mine:

Non-Judgemental

'I've worked in tech for 30 years, mostly with men. One of
the many things I appreciate is their ability to quickly forgive and forget differences in opinions. They rarely seem to
hold a grudge. I appreciate this about them.'

'Saying things as they see it. Can be harsh – but at least
you know! As opposed to behind-your-back whining . . .'

Protective

'How instinctively protective they can be.'

'An instinctive protective nature to those they love, regardless of gender. Not because they think they're "weaker" or they "have to", but out of pure love.'

'Their absolute *need* to protect and nurture those they love.'

Up for Anything

'The ability to do things just for fun, e.g. sports, gaming, trainspotting, whatever the hell they want to do. Us women have been conned into thinking everything has to be self-improvement.'

'How men will go on any errand so long as you present it as a "quest".'

'Playing into adulthood – sports, video/board games etc., which is healthy and vital to enjoyment in life.'

Loyal

'Straightforward answers to any dilemmas. "Yes your bum does look big in that – but it's a lovely bum" – that kind of thing.'

'They love their mums.'

'They will do *anything* for those they love. Even pick up a stranded teenager from a train station halfway through a Cup Final.'

Brave

'I've seen young men intervene to stop physically weaker people – old people, women, gays – from being harassed and intimidated. That's one of the most beautiful things ever.'

'I've seen men run across the street to break up fights between complete strangers.'

Hard-working

'We have three sons in the trades. Hard work. Out in the cold and rain all winter. Heavy lifting. Never complaining. They do it gladly because it's "men's work" and they love it.'

'My father, and now my husband, work incredibly long hours in incredibly tough jobs – they're both fire-fighters – and they never even really mention it. It's just who they are, what they do.'

Joyous

'I love men. The humour, the banter, the relationship dynamic. A night out with the lads has a completely different vibe to a night out with the girls. Simpler in many ways.'

'Zest for life and insatiable sense of humour and fun. I love this in my sons.'

'I don't really believe in traits being inherently gendered, but I do love how all men and boys will dig a hole on the beach.'

'We tell stories with sound effects. This is underrated.'

There were also a few I hadn't considered:

A Huge Urge to Be Helpful

'The "rush to help". My mates might not always be able to help – but by God we can all stand around and rub our chins together. And that is the best bit.'

'I'm a dad, and my approach is always some sort of Gordian knot thing. Like – what's the simplest way to resolve absolutely everything? SMASH PROBLEM. My parenting superpower is to be aware of intricacies, but not let them paralyse decision-making.'

Dandyism

'Dandyism, of course. Especially when it's subtle – the exact angle of the buttonhole or fold on the turn-up of the Japanese denim, or whatever. It's neither a gay nor a straight quality, and it's different from flamboyance or strutting confidence, but something special of its own.'

Tinkering

'Tinkerers. Makers. Hobbyists. Enthusiasts. The whole "sanctuary of the shed" thing. Doesn't matter if it's Geoff from Wiltshire who looks like a *Time Team* reject, used to roadie for Jethro Tull, is part-made of Swarfega, and spends 95 per cent of his time at the bottom of the garden – or the old Bengali guy with a hole-in-the-wall stall in the market, who can bring a 30-year-old TV back to life, or whatever. There's something about that ageing male desire to fix things up *in their own space* that is hopeful, and slightly subversive in its absolute rejection of the pace of life, and mad consumer culture.'

Relationship with Nature

'A certain special melancholic relationship with the elements and the land, epitomised in fishing, Monty Don, and the poems of Ted Hughes.'

And Just a General Sense of Mucking In

'The downside of Never Talking About Anything Important is really obvious – but the speed of bonding it offers with strangers is incredible. It builds workplaces and platoons and gangs with ease. Agree on one thing – a sports team or a favourite film – and that's all you need to be friends for life. You will pull fallen masonry off a man who ten minutes ago seemed to like *Blake's Seven* as much as you, and that's the only connection needed to accept them as part of your tribe.'

While it was a properly heartwarming exercise – the men's sense of surprise at being asked to talk about what was *good* about them was palpable – it was also very striking that no fewer than seven people observed, 'I realise I am basically describing a dog,' 'This is also what dogs are like,' 'Can't remember if we're talking about men, or dogs, now,' and, from four men: 'Men are basically dogs.'

If men *are* like dogs, in some ways, then it's no wonder that all the recent conversations about 'masculinity being toxic' has resulted in *either* a sense of depression and resignation in men; or else snapping, snarling misogyny and Manosphere nihilism. After all, if a dog starts being treated with suspicion – if it can tell people are frightened of it; if all it hears is people angrily calling it a 'bad dog'; if *all* conversations about dogs are about how bad they are – it will either slink away, under the table, crushed; or else start barking and believing it *is* a bad dog.

As someone obsessed with the programme *Dogs Behaving (Very) Badly* – in which expert dog-behavourialist Graeme Hall spends every week patiently explaining that there is no such thing as a 'bad dog', only bad owners who have inadvertently fostered bad behaviour in their pets – I started to think: the way we talk about men, and particularly young men, and boys, is exactly like this. We overreact to natural behaviour – boisterousness, barking. We make them do things that are unnatural – sit down in school all day; *learn*, rather than *do*. The saturation in pornography means they don't see any examples of how to correctly behave around women, and girls – and so, of course, they go bananas, and distress everyone, when they come across them in real life.

But, most importantly of all, we don't *enjoy* them. When do we love a dog most? When it's doing what it loves. Running, playing, working, protecting, figuring out how to round up some sheep, playing with other dogs – or else exhaustedly putting its head on our lap, to be stroked, and told what a good old dog it is. Loved.

As one woman on Twitter said, 'I teach high school pupils. Teenage boys are brilliant. They're lunatics who seem to love fun, and the majority are really sensitive – but society doesn't encourage that in them. We habitually talk about them as if they're just always a problem.'

When was the last time we properly celebrated, and enjoyed, watching boys and men doing what they love?

Looking at all the love for men, and boys, on Twitter and Facebook, frequently made me feel quite tearful. People said things so *tentatively*! At first, a few asked, 'Is this a feminist trap?'

Oh, so the opposite! The absolute opposite! For, by the end of it, I was so filled with love and appreciation for all the men I know that I started going through my life, and listing all the pivotal, crucial men I have known, and how much I enjoyed them being very, very male. The *good* side of masculinity.

My father – who never let any problem get the better of him, and always exuded an air of being able to fix anything. Broken washing machine, dodgy clutch, unpayable bill – he would just nod, slightly tetchily, and then go into the garden and roll a fag. He would sit, for five minutes – inhaling deeply, staring at the sky – and then chuck the fag to one side, and come back into the house with a plan. Every time, he fixed it. However huge, or insurmountable.

The boys at school who, when I was rejected by the girls, silently folded me into the football team, even though I was shit. And, I've just remembered now, protested to the teachers when one said, 'Girls can't play football.' 'Moran's on the team!' they said. God, I'd forgotten. Instant loyalty.

The first male friend I had, as a teenager – Matty – who just frankly said, to my face, 'You're being a knob,' when I was being a knob: but with no bitchiness, or judgement. Just a very solid and correct piece of advice that I absolutely took on board.

All the male colleagues, when I first started being a music journalist, at the age of 16, who totally accepted a weird child in a hat – so long as I could make them laugh. There was no interim period. Straight in. Part of the team.

The male friend who, when my husband was abroad, took me to the hospital when I needed an abortion. 'I can drive. And take you for a fabulous fucking lunch afterwards. I presume that's how we deal with abortions?'

The male friend who, during the worst spell of my life,

sent a bottle of champagne, with a note that read: 'The best revenge is a life well lived.' I still have the note on my fridge.

The male writing partner who, on hearing that, during an otherwise successful business meeting, a man had asked me if I would sleep with him, as part of the deal, simply got up from the table, and went outside to punch him. When I stopped him – saying, nobly, 'It *is* a good deal! For us! I don't mind!' – he insisted we cancel the deal. 'I can't work with men like that. Never.' It lost us, potentially, a lot of money. He didn't give a fuck.

The male friends who, when I was in the middle of a Twitterstorm, all waded in to post with simple, loyal defences – even when it made their own lives shit.

The laughing – just the endless laughing – when I'm with my male friends. Pure, no-strings ridiculousness. Sometimes, the medicine you need *isn't* deep conversations – but the gift of untrammelled silliness.

All the teenage boys, friends of my daughters, who stream in and out of the house – climbing out of windows, rigging up extension leads to watch the TV in the garden 'when it's too hot in the house', confidently 'busking' the cooking, rebooting the Wi-Fi system, restringing guitars, and flying drones over neighbours' gardens to locate lost footballs. Sitting at the kitchen table and patiently inputting the email addresses of my daughters' enemies, so they subsequently get spammed by the Scientology mailing list. Walking the girls back home, every night, without ever mentioning it.

And then, of course, the men I *don't* know, but who've impacted my life: listening to 'Life on Mars?' on repeat;

crying at a Rothko in New York; reading *Moby-Dick* and feeling like I *know* Melville, and he's now a friend . . .

Every man and woman can run a montage like this, in their heads: the energy, fun, creativity, risk-taking, loyalty, practicality and *joy* of what men, and boys, bring us.

It was this irresistible sense of female excellence that has fuelled the last decade or so of feminism – women craved to see female heroes doing well, and being celebrated, because, as Civil Rights activist Marian Wright Edelman said, 'You can't be what you can't see.' Once you are surrounded by women being acclaimed, and applauded, it becomes easier to see how *you* might do well, and be applauded.

This is the rocket fuel that brings about change: a giddy sense of both the possibilities and the rewards. Although, as most of this book shows, there *is* a huge amount for boys, and men, to gain from questioning masculinity – seeing things from a female perspective, and learning things from women – when we ask the question, 'What about men?', the *best* starting point would be: what is *good* about them? What is it that the world gains every time a boy is born? What is positive about masculinity? What do we love about it? What do we want to see more of? What would we miss if it were gone? How can we enjoy it at its very best? *Who* is doing it best? And how can we bring that about for *every* boy and man?

There should be *no* shame in being a man. Being made to feel shame for how you are born is something every other progressive movement is trying to remove. Trying to impose it on the one group that *didn't*, until recently, feel shame – straight white men – benefits no one. There's no point in shouting at a baby for something some other man did a hundred years ago. No one gains anything in that situation. You're just shouting at a baby. Systems remain absolutely unchanged. All you do is bring about useless, febrile, incurable guilt, instead. Guilt that can lead to terrible things.

Masculinity is *not* a bad thing – just as femininity is *not* a bad thing. If feminism can celebrate and adore a woman who drives around in a pink car with giant plastic eyelashes on the headlights, spends her time baking cupcakes and sings songs to her cats, then it should also celebrate and adore a massively ripped, bearded man who lives in a log cabin, roasts pigs with a blowtorch and builds tractors from scratch.

To be a man is an excellent thing.

But to be a man should also be *all* the things. All the things he wants, or needs.

I wish for any man, or boy, everything I have wished for my daughters: that they can be proud of who they were born as; that this will never be a burden to them; that they can appear as they like; that they understand both their own pain, and that of others; that they can love out loud, with their whole hearts, because they understand that love is a verb – a *doing* word; and that they never belittle or destroy what they envy, but recognise it for what it is: almost certainly, a future you wish for yourself.

Because, ultimately, the idea that men and women are at war with each other – battling for supremacy – is a madness: like siblings fighting in the back seat, when we're all in the same car, going to the same place. When I started writing that sentence, I was thinking of Cornwall – but, of course, in reality, our destination is the grave. And so soon! We cannot waste time! We are together, no matter what!

And as I write the last page of my book about men, I looked at the last page of the first book I wrote about women, *How to Be a Woman* – and realised that everything I had said about women, back then, was everything I feel about men, too. That this book is all just the same thing, but with more testicles. In 12 years, my fundamental beliefs about gender haven't changed at all:

So, in the end, I suppose the title of the book is a bit of a misnomer. All through those stumbling, mortifying, amazing years, I thought what I wanted to be was a woman. A princess. A goddess. A muse.

But, as the years went on, I realised that what I really want to be, all told, is a human. Just a productive, honest, courteously treated human. I am neither pro-woman, nor anti-men – just, 'Thumbs up for the seven billion.' I just want to be one of The Guys.

We're *all* just one of The Guys.

And it is time, now – after decades of beautiful, exciting, *necessary* love and attention being given to women, and girls – to both start asking, and *answering*, the question, 'What about men?'

Epilogue

Of course, I realise that my noble, inspiring ending *does* leave some questions still unanswered. Some more specific, prosaic, possibly petty claims that, feminism aside, there *are* still ways, in the twenty-first century, it's easier to be a woman than a man. In the spirit of completeness, I accede to these queries, and have, here, compiled the final, exhaustive list – so that no one can accuse me of leaving my examination of the genders incomplete. Here are, finally:

All the Ways It *Is* Easier to Be a Woman Than a Man

ONE: We don't get erections. You know that whole gender stereotype – that women are more subtle; more mysterious; more secret; more delicate; more unknowable? Ninety per cent of that is down to the simple, physical fact *we don't get erections.*

Women can totally conceal their sexual arousal – and this is, undoubtedly, a useful thing.

Whatever thoughts and feeling we are having, they are – unless we've had six shots of Schnapps, and suddenly feel, like Elaine in *Seinfeld*, 'chatty' – totally hidden in our pants. Our sexuality is *private*. Our genitals are inside us, which keeps our sexy thoughts totally hidden. We retain, at all times, control. For us, the revelation of our feelings is *entirely optional.*

Men, on the other hand – men do not have this considerable social luxury. You can't hide a boner. You are a hostage to your genitals. Particularly if you're wearing the Incredibly Tight Jeans of Modern Men, as discussed before. There are *no* secrets in those trousers. If you're wearing them, and you get horny, then you're basically having to cope with Dick Tourette's – at any moment, your penis could do the equivalent of shouting 'I WANT TO BANG YOU!' and everyone will know.

That is, undoubtedly, a disadvantage. I can't imagine how alarming it would be to have a pivotal body part that has a very different social agenda to you, and could 'make a scene' at any moment.

I would imagine it's very like being married to Kanye West. A lot of the time, it's amazing hanging out with a powerful force of nature – but every so often, it goes 'off road' and causes headaches for everyone.

Kanye, then, *is*, in a very real sense, a dick.

So that's definitely one way it's easier to be a woman than a man.

TWO: 'Huh – *men.*' In the course of the average conversation, women appear to be able to dismiss 48 per cent of the world's population – men – simply by going 'Huh – *men*', whenever they like.

Men cannot do this about women. Not since – and this is a rough estimate – the last broadcast episode of *Men Behaving Badly*, in 1998; the last time playful sexism was allowed on mainstream terrestrial TV.

This seems unfair. Mean, almost. I mean – it's sexist, isn't it? To dismiss *an entire gender*, so regularly, and flippantly. Aren't women being sexist at men, with their 'Huh – *men*'? It seems like it.

True confession time – I say 'Huh – *men*' a lot. Off the top of my head, the last two times I said it were:

1) On hearing a story of a male author who decided his 'self-care' for that day was to light a cigarette on a plane, 'because I wanted one', and who was so insistent he finish it that the departure of the plane was *held up so he could finish it on the tarmac, before reboarding.* That got a big 'Huh – *men*'.

2) The dude riding a very loud motorbike down my street at 2am, *revving* outside the house, enjoying the noise. My friend! Have you considered – a bicycle? The form of transport that does *not* involve everyone within a three-mile radius knowing you are 'on the move'?

I'd like to make one thing very clear here – and forgive me if you have already heard this a thousand times – but when women go, 'Huh – *men*,' *we don't mean you*. Unless you're an asshole. But then, we tend not to say it in front of the assholes.

Indeed, if we're saying it in front of you, it's almost certainly because we *don't* think you're an asshole – and we are inviting you to join us in boggling over *the bad men*. The men you are *not* like. The old-fashioned kind of men. The problematic kind of men. When men on the internet reply to women Tweeting 'Huh – *men*' with 'NOT ALL MEN' – WE KNOW. *That is already implied.*

What 'Huh – *men*' is addressing is . . . Toxic Masculinity. I promise this is the last time I'll mention it, as the book is nearly over, but, one last time: half of all conversations about Toxic Masculinity are about how it's screwing *men* over. Indeed, this is so fundamental to its usage that I'd like to boil it down to Moran's Rule Number Two: 'The patriarchy is bumming men just as hard as it's bumming women.' In other words, 10 per cent of the men are ruining it for the other 90 per cent.

This isn't based in any fact. I haven't researched it in the slightest. But . . . that's what it *feels* like? In all my conversations with women, and men, during this book, this was a theme that came up over and over: that 90 per cent of men are just nice guys, trying to get through the day – but there is a wearisome 10 per cent who are the ones whom *everyone* fears. Often, men more than women.

This 10 per cent are the jerks in the office who make jokes about 'retards' and 'soy-boys'; these are the men you're worried are going to start a fight with you; hit you; stab you; chase you down the street.

These are the men who will shout 'GAY-BOY!' at you if you wear an almost-pink tank top, or order a soft drink instead of a Pint of Death.

These are the men who roam around in intimidating gangs after football matches; the ones who make your daughters and wives scared; the ones you fear will bang on your front door if you ask them to move their wheelie-bin out of *your* wheelie-bin area.

These are the men who have out-of-control dogs that bit your Schnauzer; and start wars; and who made you call The Fight Pub 'The Fight Pub'.

The 10 per cent are the ones who take coke and short the pound; or make girls wear hijab *when they don't want to*; or join Fathers 4 Justice, or spend all days on Incel sites praising mass shooters.

These are the guys who make violent pornography in which women's heads are pushed down toilets; or program algorithms to push people towards extremism; or run sex-trafficking gangs from their Romanian bolthole; or, yes, take you on a 'journey through sound' through their experimental DJing, when everyone was happily dancing to ABBA.

Because of this undeniably awful, small minority of men, women can say, 'Huh – *men*.'

But men cannot say 'Huh – *women*', when talking about narcissist lunatics, or sighing martyrs, or fun-crushers, or stalkers, or the emotionally manipulative, or terrible Lady Bosses, or ex-girlfriends who go around telling everyone you've got a really tiny knob – because you get accused of being 'sexist'.

And, so, yes. That *is* unfair. But not quite as unfair as you think it is. We're kind of doing it to . . . help you? To show you're we're on *your side*? Which is why we're going to carry on doing it. Soz.

THREE: Drag queens. Drag queens are like superhero versions of girls. All over the world, there are now multiple clubs, TV shows and YouTube channels where men are pretending to be women, which is very flattering for us ladies. At the very least, it has made many, many people aware of what a specialised skill 'wearing heels' is.

By way of contrast, very few women are pretending to be men. There is no *RuPaul's Drag Race* of drag kings. Ant and Dec might have dragged up on *Saturday Night Take-away*, but Claudia and Tess have not popped up on *Strictly* in jeans and beards. No one seems interested in pretending to be a man – that's not a game, culturally, anyone seems to want to play – and that's sad.

I can only presume it's because men are too *boring* for anyone to pretend to be them. That there's no fun to be had in being a man. Why would women dress up in much *duller* clothes and hair, for 'fun'? Women dressing as men is a make-*under*; a glow-*down*; the sudden removal of 'enjoy-ment' from the table.

I feel that diss on your clothes, shoes, hair and manner-isms quite strongly.

FOUR: We've got all the best songs. As mentioned before, the last few decades have seen a boom-time in empowering

Lady Anthems, with amazing women singing amazing songs about how amazing women are. There are thousands and thousands of playlists, dedicated to this genre. The PR on being a chick is *on point*.

By way of contrast, I cannot really think of what I would put on a playlist called 'Inspiring Anthems for Boys and Men' – once you've removed all the songs about 'bitches', and 'popping bottles in the club', which are themes I feel have been . . . adequately addressed, now.

There's nothing joyful you could use as inspiration while doing a spin class, that actually details being a nice, funny, relaxed, hard-working and pleasant man, or boy. There are no joyful and silly songs about e.g. having a willy, in the same way women now have 'WAP' ('Bring a bucket and a mop for this wet-ass pussy').

If I worked for the British Arts Council, I'd put some funding into creating the genre of 'Modern Uplifting Pop Songs About How Awesome It Is to Be a Boy, But Without Being Seen Through the Prism of Either Financial Clout, or "Pussy-Slaying" ', as a matter of cultural emergency.

FIVE: We can go on and on about how great we are. Women can – and do – spend all evening cheerfully talking about all the ways women are just better than men. Although there are no formal stats on this, by my reckoning, there has been a 3,000 per cent rise in this kind of chat in the last 20 years, and most 'Girls Nights Out' will contain *at least* one (1) half-hour communal debate on this issue.

Most men, however, would feel very uncomfortable celebrating what they are good at.

SIX: You know the old joke, 'Why do women wear make-up and perfume?' 'Because they're ugly, and they smell'? Well, *yes*. Women can, as the Scots say, 'cover pooey with hooey' – we can basically bullshit our way into looking far more attractive, and smelling far more luxurious, with the judicious use of make-up, curling tongs, wigs, bras, corsets, shapewear tights, high heels, judiciously picked dresses, false eyelashes, tit-tape, Botox, perfume, arse-lifts and tit-jobs.

But for a man who believes himself to be plain, ugly, fat or just 'generally unspectacular', there are very few zhuzh-options available to him. He can . . . get a haircut, and put on a nice shirt? If he's feeling *really* bold, he could use concealer on his spots. But that's about it.

All the other tricks in a woman's repertoire are unavailable to him, lest he be accused of being too feminine, too fussy, too fake, too gay.

I sometimes wonder if the recent trend for beard-growing is an attempt by modern men to slightly expand their box of 'physical transformation' tricks: allowing, as it does, for radical alteration on the prime real-estate of the face. In the hands of a talented beard-wrangler, a man can choose to topiary the bottom half of his face into pretty much any shape he wants.

But that's about the only major-league alteration a man has available to him. And given that this means gaining extra 'sexual capital' can only be done by either a) hitting the gym and getting ripped, or b) gaining the actual *capital* capital – money – no wonder one of the recurrent worries of so many men is that they aren't muscular, or rich, enough, to be seen as successful, 'proper', alpha men.

A very poor woman who eschews the gym can still be seen as 'feminine' in a nice dress, with her hair done.

A very poor man who eschews the gym . . . well, that's a lot harder. And that's unfair. As Andrew Tate said, 'Women are the gatekeepers of the sexual marketplace.' In this, he was correct. But it's only because men are too scared to wear Spanx, wigs, glowing highlighter, mascara, Lip Venom plumping serum, and heels. Or to dress up like a dandy highwayman, or pirate. But I think we covered the rest of this in the chapter about clothes.

SEVEN: At no point in our teenage years do women have to attempt a) parkour or b) freestyle rapping – two things which seem to be a necessary, and often very humiliating, part of being a young man. I've lost count of the gangly youths I've seen basically run over and kick a wall in a car park, shouting 'PARKOUR!', while their mates laugh at them.

EIGHT: Women can totally lie about their physical needs, at your expense. 'I'm macrobiotic/vegan/on a cleanse/ Keto,' women will say, piously, as they order something incredibly dull and virtuous in a restaurant; implying, at the same time, you're a total hog for ordering your Actually Nice Man Food.

Ten minutes later, of course, they'll be begging for your

genuinely delicious chips/pie/steak with the pass-agg words 'I just want a *bite*!' – or, indeed, just scooping the whole lot off your plate, and straight into their mouths ('I'm making today my Cheat Day').

While this is a trait that has long been noticed by generations of irate, chip-depleted men, it has further iterations I'm surprised you're not equally angry about. Women refusing to wear a coat – 'It won't go with this outfit' – and then shivering in the rain until you give them *your* coat; women wearing stupid shoes – '*All* the girls are wearing heels!' – and then hobbling down the street until you give them a piggyback; women announcing 'I'm packing minimally!' and then ramming *your* suitcase with books, toiletries, three more stupid pairs of shoes and some mad hair device that looks like Satan's BBQ tongs.

Women like to pretend they're some floating intergalactic entity – like e.g. a hologrammatic pillar of light – without physical function; and then totally monopolise *your* resources when it turns out that, yes, they *do* have physical needs, after all. And, if you're a 'gentleman', there's nothing you can do about it. You just have to carry that woman/suitcase/order more chips. As we get carried around, wearing your coat and eating your chips, we are thinking, 'Yes. Today, it is easier to be a woman than a man. This pretty much makes up for FGM, to be honest.'

NINE: We can make actual human beings inside us. We are the ones who continue the human race. Our tits turn into dinner. We produce a whole new organ – the placenta; and a whole extra pint of blood – like superheroes. But the good ones. And then, after we've done it, we can – as I have explained, many times previously – go on about it *for ever*.

It allows us to bond with any woman in the world; it gives us something to boast about if we're feeling otherwise lacklustre, and, if we ever need anything doing – whether by a partner *or* a child – we can just start talking about how long we were in labour, and how many stitches we had, and bingo! Someone else is putting that flat-pack wardrobe together. It is an extraordinary, lifelong, life-*creating* power.

And yet, I have never heard a man say he wishes *he* could do it – and that seems weird to me. After all, it's the biggest baller move ever – being the one in charge of the continuation of the human race! – and yet, I have never, in all my life, in any conversation, however drunk/high/frank/ intimate, heard a man say he wonders what it would be like to be pregnant, and give birth. It seems like such a likely jealousy – but one that is never mentioned.

Men, do you never even think of it? Have you *never* wished you could make a whole, new, tiny person inside you? Don't you wonder if you could cope with the ultimate challenge – the pain of birth – like a warrior; turn yourself inside out, over and over, to give someone their *life*? I boggle that you never mention it – I really do.

By the way, if it turns out that literally *no* man reading this *has* ever wished he could be pregnant, or give birth – that you are perfectly satisfied with the way things are; and, indeed, are actually really squicked-out and grateful you don't have to – don't tell us. Act as if you envy us. Pretend we are as gods. Women do still need to feel that they *are* superior in their ability to give birth – or else the whole 'having your fanny ripped to pieces in the process' thing does start to look like a *slightly* worse deal.

And finally:

TEN: Periods. Periods might be painful, messy, embarrassing, and only slightly less expensive than stuffing your knickers with tenners every month, then flushing them down the toilet – but they are also one other thing: an absolutely failsafe excuse.

Have you been a complete bitch? Done something absolutely dum-dum? Been as clumsy as a clown in gloves? Forgotten a birthday? Eaten a whole chocolate Swiss roll with your bare hands, in under two minutes, hunched over the steering wheel of a Ford Ka in the car park of John Lewis? Why, you have the ultimate excuse at your disposal – you can blame it all on your jam-rags!

For the 15 days before, it's down to PMT. For the five days during – self-explanatory. And then for 15 days afterwards, we're anaemic! It was the lack of *iron* that made us call your mother 'Hagrid'! You cannot blame us for our *biology*. Periods are the ultimate Bagsy No Returns.

But do men have any such excuse? No. Everything *you* do that is wrong/stupid/evil is simply down to *you* being wrong/stupid/evil. You could *never* blame fucking up an interdepartmental meeting on your balls, in the way we can airily cite our menopause. There is *no* outsourcing of culpability to 'nature'. And I am sorry – I truly am. It is another terrible unfairness that biology has given you no such equal

'Get Out of Jail Free' card. For you, much like your anus, your onus is a one-way street.

On the other hand, you *are* free to wear cream-coloured trousers on holiday without ever worrying that, when you stand up, it looks like you have a tin of Heinz Spaghetti Hoops leaking out of your pants, so – swings and roundabouts.

Acknowledgements

Every time you write a book, it's different. Sometimes it's fast, sometimes, it's slow. Sometimes the whole thing is in your head – other times, you just have a vague idea of where you're going, but you only find out what you think when you actually get into the pages. This book went through two drafts – the first long, slow and thoughtful, and then the second one was an 80% rewrite in two weeks flat, whilst listening to The Tamperer ft. Maya's *Feel It* on repeat. Basically, in the middle of every paragraph, imagine me screaming 'WHAT'S SHE GONNA LOOK LIKE WITH A CHIMNEY ON HER?' over and over. And then stop imagining it, because it's so distressing.

For the first draft, I want to thank Team Tits: Nadia Shireen, Sali Hughes and Lauren Laverne, who endured endless conversations where I pretended to listen to what they were saying, and then replied, 'The thing about *men* is, right,' and then bored them with whatever research I'd done that week.

For the second draft, I want to thank Team Testicles: Hugo Rifkind, Dorian Lynskey, John Niven, Sathnam Sanghera, and David Baddiel, who were astonishingly generous with their time when I started bombarding them with questions, emails, texts and demands to 'Pub? NOW?'

Bob Mortimer: your text made me cry. If I write a book

you, the man behind the Chris Rea Egg In a Bath Story, like, I can die happy.

Extra special thanks to 'Sam', for talking so honestly about porn – your chapter resonates so hard, although 'resonates so hard' sounds really rude. You are a remarkable young man. Although that sounds quite dodgy as well. Argh! You're just awesome! Thank you!

Team Ebury: thank you for your constant faith, hard work, genius input, pertinent questions, ability to spot potentially problematic issues, and tolerance of meetings where I end up drawing a cock and balls on a whiteboard, shouting, 'This is the marketing campaign, right?' Robyn Drury, Andrew Goodfellow, Claire Scott and Natalia Goncalves – you are excellent.

Georgia Garrett: as has now become customary, I will just repeat: if you stop agenting me, I will die.

And finally, Pete. I know I'm a fabulous wife, mate and pal, but you have just tolerated a solid year of me womansplaining men to you, a man. And then given me hour-long foot rubs. Aside from the dog, obviously, I love you more than anything in the world.